The Amgen Story

25 Years of Visionary Science and Powerful Medicine

The Amgen Story

25 Years of Visionary Science and Powerful Medicine

David Ewing Duncan
Foreword by Dr. Leroy Hood

TEHABI BOOKS

1980–2005

The Amgen Story

My introduction to Amgen began with a phone call in 1980 from Bob Schimke, a Stanford University geneticist. Bob was helping to start a new genetic engineering company and asked if I would be interested in joining the effort as part of Amgen's Scientific Advisory Board (SAB). I had just helped to found Applied Biosystems with Bill Bowes, and I was

game for a new adventure. I particularly liked the idea of working with Bob, who was a first-rate geneticist. (Ironically, he dropped out of the effort early on and was replaced by Winston Salser, a molecular biologist from the University of California, Los Angeles, who became head of the SAB.)

During these early days of biotechnology, several companies had already been started—such as Cetus, Genentech, and Biogen—and there was a sense in the air that anything was possible. This opportunity was particularly exciting because all of us, scientists and funders alike, were trying to figure out what it would take to create a genetic engineering company. It was a fascinating evolutionary process, and it took time to discover what science to do and how to do it. In this regard, the SAB played a critical role in charting Amgen's path.

We assembled a marvelous SAB for the new effort—perhaps the best I have ever been associated with. The board included Arno Motulsky, one of the fathers of human genetics; Norman Davidson, a pioneer in molecular biology; John Carbon, one of the first to see the power of yeast as a model system; Marv Caruthers, the inventor of the DNA synthesis chemistry that revolutionized biology; and Irv Weissman, one of the founders of stem cell biology.

Of course, another key player during these early days was Amgen's first CEO, George Rathmann. Perhaps the best biotech CEO I have ever known, George was aggressive, smart, knowledgeable about science, inspirational, superb at raising money, and willing to take gambles. He brought a focus, intensity, and excitement to Amgen that pulled all of us—staff and advisors alike—into the Amgen adventure. Together, George and the SAB pushed the idea that proteins could be therapeutics—a key part of Amgen's subsequent highly successful strategy. Meeting every few months, we conceived projects that were all over the map, from chicken growth hormone to clever oil-eating bacteria.

EPOGEN® (Epoetin alfa) became the first billion-dollar-a-year biotech drug, and from it, Amgen was given the resources to eventually develop into a billion-dollar company. But EPOGEN® brought a lot more than monetary gain—as we soon learned, it was changing lives. I discovered this firsthand in 1989, when I traveled with my family to New Zealand for Christmas vacation. While there, I stopped to visit an acquaintance. The woman had chronic kidney disease and had recently been given EPOGEN®. She told me, "I went from a person barely surviving from one dialysis treatment to the next to a real person who once again could lead a normal life. I had almost forgotten what it was like to live." That moment, I saw what years of biotech research on EPOGEN® had ultimately achieved.

Amgen has taught me much about science, business, and people. It has also brought me friends in the science community, many of whom I've continued to be close with over the last twenty-something years of my career. Looking ahead toward the next ten to twenty years, I believe that medicine will move from being reactive—where patients wait until they are sick to be cured—to being predictive, preventive, and personalized. This revolution will pose enormous challenges for the health care and pharmaceutical industries. All of the rules of the biotech game will change dramatically, but for those who can adapt, there will be marvelous opportunities. I look forward to seeing how Amgen approaches this new frontier: As a company with an incredible history of anticipating the needs of patients, Amgen will undoubtedly rise to the occasion.

Dr. Leroy Hood
President, Institute for Systems Biology
Member of Amgen's Scientific Advisory Board, 1980–1989

⇐ *Opposite:* George Rathmann, playing bridge with his grandson, George, in Palo Alto in 2004. Rathmann oversaw Amgen during its discovery and development of EPOGEN® and other products. Today he benefits from EPOGEN®, which he receives during kidney dialysis treatments.

pre-1980

The Rise of Biotechnology and Amgen

"Biotechnology is just beginning—how it will impact our lives twenty-five years from now is hard to imagine. The whole biological revolution is still in its infancy."

— **Kirby Alton, development, hired in 1981**

During the fall of 1980, biochemist Tim Osslund heard about a new biotech company in the Newbury Park area of Thousand Oaks, California, tucked among the scrub oaks and shale-edged creeks in a small industrial park just off U.S. Highway 101. A recent graduate in protein biochemistry from the University of California, Davis, twenty-two-year-old Osslund was returning home to Ventura County to look for a job in the mountain-rimmed valley north of Los Angeles, which at that time was shifting from soybean farms and cattle ranches to curving streets of ranch-style homes. Most people in the valley had never heard of DNA, let alone biomolecules. ⚲ Trolling up and down DeHavilland Drive, then a main artery in the small industrial complex, the newly married Osslund drove into a parking lot situated beside a squat, prefabricated concrete building, half of it taken up by the Continental Ministries evangelical choir, located down the street from a Rolls-Royce warehouse. "I saw a discarded ultra-centrifuge box outside," Osslund remembers. "Ultra-centrifuges are used in biotechnology, so I knew I was in the right place." Inside the small space he saw a solitary man sitting behind a desk in the roasting heat. Barrel-chested, with a thick, slightly graying black beard, this was George Rathmann, the new company's CEO and one of three full-time staff members. "There was no lobby or secretary, there was just George at his

Opposite: These are among Amgen's longest-tenured staff members—those who joined the company during its first twelve months and remain at Amgen today. From left: Vernon Mar, Dennis Fenton, Jody Simon, Ralph Smalling, Sylvia Hu, Carie Sindt, Avantika Patel, and Sid Suggs. Not pictured: Chi-Hwei Lin, Mike Mann, Tim Osslund, Tom Boone, and Frank Martin. Behind them, Building 1 displays the original Amgen logo.

desk," says Osslund, "and that was Amgen." Or, rather, "AMGen"—Applied Molecular Genetics, as it was then called.

Some twenty-five years later, the tangled oaks on the mountains and in the creek beds are still there, but virtually everything else has changed. Osslund's beard has turned pepper-gray, and Rathmann's completely white. The company that started out so improbably in what was dubbed Building 1—the staff knew more buildings would follow—has become the eighth-largest drug-producing company in the world in terms of revenues. Now called "Amgen," this successful start-up has projected annual revenues in the $10 billion range at the end of 2004, employing fourteen thousand people in twenty-seven countries and the Commonwealth of Puerto Rico. With a stock market capitalization that has exceeded $80 billion, Amgen is the most successful biotech company in history. The company provides medicines to millions of patients each year, with seven drugs on the market—and more in the pipeline.

Today Osslund, at age forty-seven, is a veteran Amgen researcher best known for helping to resolve the atomic three dimensional structure of the company's blockbuster drug, the protein G-CSF (granulocyte-colony stimulating factor), later branded as NEUPOGEN® (Filgrastim). Osslund designs new proteins for possible drugs in a small office in Building 2, not far from where he first approached Rathmann in 1980, applying to be a protein purifier. Osslund didn't get hired right away. "George told me he was looking for cloners," recalls Osslund, "not purifiers. But he kept my résumé." Six months later Osslund was hired—working first as a protein purifier, then as a cloner. He was staff member number twenty-two.

Bill Bowes's "Half-Baked Idea"

Amgen began as one of those wild ideas concocted by entrepreneurs when a new technology or discovery is moving from the research stage to the real world of products and business. For Amgen, the visionary who put forth these ideas was venture capitalist William K. (Bill) Bowes, with an assist from another, younger venture capitalist, Sam Wohlstadter. Bowes, who is soft-spoken and gentlemanly, was then a fifty-three-year-old investor with a keen eye toward finding the next wave of technologies. A year after starting Amgen, he cofounded U.S. Venture Partners. Through this organization, Bowes has been a key player

February 28, 1953
James Watson and Francis Crick discover the double helix.

1955
Fred Sanger determines the amino acid sequence of insulin.

1961
Francis Crick and Sydney Brenner theorize the "Central Dogma" of molecular biology.

1971
The first biotechnology company, Cetus Corporation, is founded in Emeryville, California. Chiron Corporation acquires Cetus in 1991.

1972–1973
Paul Berg, Herb Boyer, and Stanley Cohen discover recombinant DNA.

1975–1978
University of California, Santa Barbara Professor John Carbon (Amgen Scientific Advisory Board member) and coworker Louise Clarke construct the first genomic DNA libraries and isolate purified single genes from various organisms.

1975–1985
Geneticist Lee Hood (Amgen Scientific Advisory Board member) and colleagues pioneer the DNA gene sequencer and synthesizer and the protein sequencer and synthesizer that comprise the technological foundation for contemporary molecular biology. The DNA

sequencer revolutionizes genomics by allowing the rapid automated sequencing of DNA and makes the human genome project possible.

in founding such major companies as Sun Microsystems, Applied Biosystems, and Advanced Cardiovascular Systems.

Bowes became a venture capitalist after working for twenty-five years for the investment bank BLYTH & CO. Inc. in San Francisco (which later merged with Paine Webber and brought Genentech public). He plunged into the venture world as it began to take off in the late 1970s, watching it grow into a powerhouse that has exceeded $80 billion in market capitalization.

At BLYTH, Bowes had been involved in what was arguably the first biotechnology company, Cetus. He joined its board in 1972, but left in 1978 because he thought Cetus lacked direction. Around that time he witnessed the founding of Genentech, which was built on a wave of enthusiasm after the discovery of recombinant DNA and other technological leaps that allowed the industrialization of genetics to produce drugs.

Genentech was founded on April 7, 1976, by another venture capitalist, Robert Swanson, who had read about the discovery of recombinant DNA by Stanford University's Paul Berg and Stanley Cohen, and University of California, San Francisco's Herbert Boyer. Swanson realized this new science could be used to start a company, and he enticed Boyer to be his cofounder. They scored a quick success by cloning the gene for human insulin in 1978 and the gene for human growth hormone in 1979. This propelled Genentech into a supercharged initial public offering (IPO) in October 1980, when the stock price rose from $35 to more than $80 in less

Right: An October 1980 article from *Nature Journal* announces the initial public offering of Genentech, a South San Francisco biotechnology company.

Below: Standing in the Building 1 lab during Amgen's first year of operation, researcher Tim Osslund (left) shows a purification column to research head Dan Vapnek.

Genentech makes splash on Wall Street

Washington

"One of the most spectacular market debuts in recent history." That was how the *Wall Street Journal* described the first day of public trading in shares in Genentech, the San Francisco company which has been among the leaders of those aggressively pursuing the commercial exploitation of recombinant DNA technology.

Initially the company has proposed to offer one million shares at between $20 and $30 each. But demand was so great that an initial price of $35 was fixed for members of an under writing syndicate through which the shares were made public last week. An extra 100,000 shares were made available, providing the company with an investment — once brokerage commissions had been deducted — of $36 million.

During the day of frantic over-the-counter trading, in which more than half of the shares were resold by their original purchasers, the price rose at one point to $89 a share, eventually dropping back to $71. As the company has 7.5 million shares, this gives it a value of more than

$500 million.

On paper, the Wall Street dealings have made multimillionaires of Genentech's two founders, Mr Robert Swanson, its president and chief executive, and Dr Herbert Boyer, vice-president and professor of biochemistry at the University of California, San Francisco.

Both own just under a million shares in the company. The principal shareholder is Lubrizol Incorporated of Cleveland, which previously bought 1.5 million shares in the company at $10 each. Kleiner and Perkins, an east coast venture capital firm, hold almost a million shares. The remainder are divided between directors and employees of the company.

Some employees have benefited from originally being paid in shares rather than cash. Robert Scheller, for example, a graduate research student at the California Institute of Technology, was given 15,000 for helping with research on human growth hormone four years ago. The stock is now worth more than $1 million.

The prices reached by the shares during the first day of public trading were con-

Nature Vol. 287   23 October 1980

Below: Then known as Applied Molecular Genetics, Amgen opened Building 1 in 1981.

1977
Stanford University geneticist Bob Schimke (Amgen Scientific Advisory Board member) discovers a method for amplifying genes so proteins can be made in greater quantity.

1979
First meeting of Amgen venture capitalists

1980
University of California, Los Angeles geneticist Winston Salser begins forming Amgen's Scientific Advisory Board.

AMGen

April 8, 1980
Venture capitalists establish AMGen (Applied Molecular Genetics Inc.) as a California corporation.

1980
CEO George B. Rathmann is hired.

1980
Company headquarters are chosen in Newbury Park, California. (Rathmann prefers to use "Thousand Oaks" on the company's letterhead.)

Early 1980s
UCLA microbiology professor Arnie Berk (Amgen Scientific

Advisory Board member) and Amgen's Jeff Browne construct expression vectors based on viral promoters for expression of cloned genes in animal cells. This is later applied to the expression of human erythropoietin in Chinese hamster ovary cells.

than an hour, settling at $71.25 at the end of the day. (It later plummeted, then rose again on a market roller-coaster ride that is a trademark of this volatile industry.)

For Bowes, the Genentech hit suggested a model for starting a company. With the new start-up, he could learn from the mistakes at Cetus and the successes at Genentech, and build a company that would put science first. This meant seeking out top scientists and management. So Bowes started brainstorming with Sam Wohlstadter in the late 1970s, and the two began looking for a scientist even before they had thought of a product.

Eventually, they signed up Winston Salser, a professor of molecular genetics at the University of California, Los Angeles, known for developing the first in-vitro biosynthesis of a complete active enzyme in 1967 and for other work in cloning and recombinant DNA. Bowes remembers him as "very promotional, very energetic, all those things. Lots of chutzpah, which is what it takes."

The Biotech Gold Rush

The biotech industry originated with some remarkable discoveries in the early 1970s, when geneticists Paul Berg, Stanley Cohen, and Herbert Boyer discovered recombinant DNA—a method for splicing genes from one organism into another.

Opposite: A molecular model of DNA

Discovering Recombinant DNA: The Core Science Behind Biotech

Biotechnology was born in 1972 at Stanford University, when Paul Berg created the first recombinant DNA molecule by combining the cancer-causing monkey virus SV40 with a virus that attacks bacteria, called a lambda bacterial virus. He used a technique that directs a "restriction" enzyme to splice out a specific strand of DNA. This enzyme can then be inserted into another organism, which begins producing proteins for that gene.

Worried about the potential dangers of his experiments, Berg stopped short of the next phase, inserting the monkey gene into the bacterium E. coli. This common lab bug would quickly reproduce and create billions of E. coli containing the new monkey gene. So he wrote the famous "Berg Letter," proposing a moratorium on this research until its safety could be assured.

That same year, Stanley Cohen and Herbert Boyer produced the first recombinant DNA organism, based on Boyer's discovery of restriction enzymes in E. coli that sliced sequences of DNA in a way that their ends could be reattached. These discoveries and techniques are the basis for many biotechnology products.

Top: Stanley Cohen, a pioneer in recombinant DNA, at Stanford University in November 1980 *Above:* Microbiologist Herb Boyer at the University of California Medical Center in San Francisco, circa 1973. He is framed by a projection of DNA.

Bill Bowes: Innovator

Bill Bowes has a gentle smile for a venture capitalist—
although anyone would be smiling after launching
what he once called a "half-baked idea" for a biotech
company and watching it grow into a company with a
stock market capitalization that has exceeded $80 billion.

He got the idea after sitting on the board of
Cetus, a biotech start-up in the San Francisco Bay
Area, founded in 1971. At the time, he was working in
investment banking, where he had been riding the Bay
Area's early high-tech wave, helping to take public
Hewlett-Packard, Ampex, and Memorex.

Right: On October
21, 2002, Amgen
CEO Kevin Sharer
dedicated a bronze
statue of founder
Bill Bowes in front
of Amgen's new
William K. Bowes Jr.
Building.

The son of an investment banker father and a physician
mother, Bowes was born in 1926 at the old Stanford University hospital in San Francisco. He stayed in the area, attending Stanford,
but his education was interrupted by service in World War II and
just after—first in the Philippines, and later as part of the occupying force in Japan in 1945. He graduated from Stanford University
with an economics degree in 1950 and from Harvard Business
School in 1952.

Above: Bill Bowes
and his wife, Ute,
at the dedication
of the William
K. Bowes Jr.
Building—Amgen's
new corporate
headquarters

A few months later, Bowes started at the investment bank
BLYTH & CO. Inc. and soon showed an aptitude for picking
fledgling high-tech companies. "I started to prowl around down
here [in Silicon Valley]," he recalls, "looking for business for the
firm, and also observing the scene."

Bowes left BLYTH and made a few investments with
friends—including in Amgen and two other successful "applied"
companies in 1980: Applied Microcircuits and Applied Biosystems.

As we celebrate Amgen's 25th anniversary, please accept a copy of *The Amgen Story: 25 Years of Visionary Science and Powerful Medicine* with my compliments and thanks for all that you have done to make our company a success.

This book tells the story of Amgen's birth and growth and our impact on the burgeoning industry of biotechnology. Ultimately, it's a compelling story of how the Amgen spirit shaped and changed the practice of medicine.

The stories told in these pages capture many qualities that set us apart: our energy and optimism, our shared values, our high-performance culture, our visionary science—and most importantly, our dedication to dramatically improving people's lives.

I'm proud of all that we've done for patients, and I'm proud of your contributions. Going forward, we are setting our sights even higher. Our silver anniversary is a time to celebrate our achievements, while looking forward. I hope that reading this book will remind you of what your hard work has made possible and inspire you to even greater achievements in the future.

Sincerely,

Kevin Sharer
Chairman and CEO

Above: Bowes retired from the Amgen board in 2002. He remains active in his firm, U.S. Venture Partners, and in a wide range of philanthropic activities.

Above: Financing was key in the early days. In an early photo, founders (from left) Bill Bowes and Sam Wohlstadter discuss venture capital-raising strategies with CEO George Rathmann.

He then started U.S. Venture Partners in 1981. Since its founding, USVP has raised $2.5 billion and invested in 271 companies, including Sun Microsystems, New Focus, Check Point Software Technologies, and others now worth $313 billion in market capitalization, with $26 billion in revenues and eighty-three thousand staff.

"I thought early on that biotechnology would go in many different directions," Bowes reflects, "and that at least one of those directions was going to be medical therapeutics. That's what appealed to me—using biotechnology to relieve human suffering. My mother was a doctor, and I was always close to the medical world."

Bowes retired from the Amgen board in 2002, but is still active at USVP. He is rightfully proud of Amgen. "It's creating something out of nothing. It's a thrill to look at a company and say, 'By God, if I hadn't been around, they wouldn't be around.'"

In some circumstances, these inserted genes could then be incorporated into the new organism's cell machinery to produce specific proteins that might be used as drugs or as studies for drug targets. When inserted into quickly reproducing organisms such as the bacterium E. coli, recombinant DNA sequences are able to make large quantities of a target protein. This breakthrough was a starting point for the biotech industry and created the basic science that allowed biotech companies to develop future products.

After this discovery, scientists and entrepreneurs alike realized that virtually any protein from any organism could be produced in large quantities. This set off a gold-rush fervor in biotech—an industry now worth hundreds of billions of dollars in market capitalization, with tens of billions of dollars in revenue.

Other scientists made discoveries in the 1970s and 1980s that catalyzed the industrialization of biotech. They included Kary Mullis, who by 1985 had won the Nobel Prize in Chemistry for his Polymerase Chain Reaction (PCR) method for mass copying of DNA, and early Amgen Scientific Advisory Board member Lee Hood, who helped invent machines that rapidly sequence genes and proteins. These scientific developments were exciting, but nevertheless the question

Above: Lee Hood, a key member of the Scientific Advisory Board, is a leading scientist in molecular biotechnology and genomics. He and his Caltech lab colleagues pioneered the DNA gene sequencer and synthesizer and the protein sequencer and synthesizer, the technological foundation for contemporary molecular biology. The DNA sequencer has also revolutionized genomics by allowing the rapid, automated sequencing of DNA.

remained: Would any of these industry breakthroughs lead to commercial products?

A Revolution in Business and Technology

The potential for products crackled like electricity, especially in the Silicon Valley hotbed around Stanford University and the University of California, San Francisco, where Bill Bowes hatched his idea to launch a biotech that would rival Genentech.

The United States sorely needed the success generated by the biotech industry. In the late 1970s the country was in a recession, with old technologies and the steel and automobile manufacturing industries facing hard times. Inflation and unemployment raged, and America seemed to be stumbling. In 1979 former president Jimmy Carter even famously spoke of a national malaise. These jitters were keenly felt in California, where old-line industries such as defense and shipping were in sharp decline. Yet even as the rest of the nation reeled, scientists nurtured California's gold-rush mentality and willingness to try new ideas. Here, the country was producing the first flashes of fire in a revolution that would eventually help transform America—and the world— as high tech cranked up in Silicon Valley, building on the foundation laid by Hewlett-Packard.

Biotech was at that time an infant industry, with only a handful of companies, including Cetus and Genentech in the Bay Area and Biogen in Cambridge, Massachusetts. As Bowes assembled Amgen, he and other biotech pioneers

Above: A sign of the times during the 1970s oil shortage

HISTORICAL AMGEMS

Q: What was the name of the street currently known as Amgen Center Drive?

A: Camino Dos Rios. The Thousand Oaks city council voted to rename it Amgen Center Drive on November 25, 1998.

faced the need to create a new science-based business paradigm. Most pressing was Amgen's need to raise sufficient cash to discover, develop, and manufacture recombinant products—overall, a process that would take many years. Money wasn't the only factor; as George Rathmann later pointed out, it wasn't even clear that the U.S. Food and Drug Administration (FDA) would approve bioengineered products.

Another crucial issue was whether scientists could patent living organisms made through recombinant DNA and biological molecules taken from living organisms—an uncertainty mostly resolved in a landmark 1980 decision by the U.S. Supreme Court that allowed bioengineered organisms to be patented. This case broke loose the legal foundation for the biotech industry, and was one reason that the 1980 Genentech IPO was received with such fervor by investors.

"We didn't know where the technology was going to lead us," says Bowes. "But we wanted to take that leap."

Below: Caltech chemical biologist Norman Davidson chats with a colleague in 1982. A member of Amgen's Scientific Advisory Board, the late Davidson was well known for his groundbreaking work in molecular biology. He pioneered new methods in physical chemistry and electron microscopy, the latter proving especially useful for genetic mapping and exploring the information properties of DNA and RNA.

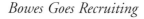

Bowes Goes Recruiting

Bowes, like most successful venture capitalists, knew that success depended on getting the right people. So he sent Salser off to find the best scientists while he began assembling a team of business advisors, investors, and managers. Salser contacted Norm Davidson, the late legendary molecular biologist, at the California Institute of Technology (Caltech). Davidson agreed to partic-

ipate, and Salser eventually rounded up a cast of superstars in molecular biology and genetics (listed as shown in Amgen's first annual report):

Daniel Vapnek, Ph.D.
Chairman of the Scientific Advisory Board,
Director of research, Amgen

Arnold J. Berk, M.D.
Associate Professor of Microbiology,
University of California, Los Angeles

John A. Carbon, Ph.D.
Professor of Biochemistry,
University of California, Santa Barbara

Marvin H. Caruthers, Ph.D.
Vice President, Amgen development
Professor of Chemistry,
University of Colorado, Boulder

Norman R. Davidson, Ph.D.*
Norman Chandler Professor of Chemical Biology,
California Institute of Technology

Above: Standing in front of an audioradiogram of a DNA gel in 1984, Dan Vapnek, head of research, discusses the results of an experiment to analyze the structure of one of Amgen's synthetic genes with Kirby Alton, head of development.

David T. Gibson, Ph.D.
Professor of Microbiology and Director of the Center for Applied Microbiology, University of Texas, Austin

Leroy E. Hood, M.D., Ph.D.*
Bowles Professor of Biology and Chairman of the Division of Biology, California Institute of Technology

Arno G. Motulsky, M.D.*
Professor of Medicine and Genetics, University of Washington

Robert T. Schimke, M.D.*
American Cancer Society Research Professor of Biology, Stanford University

Richard O. Williams, Ph.D.
Senior Scientist, International Laboratory for Research on Animal Diseases, Nairobi, Kenya

Ralph S. Wolfe, Ph.D.*
Professor of Microbiology University of Illinois

Major Consultants:

Eugene Goldwasser, Ph.D.
Professor of Biochemistry, University of Chicago

Irving L. Weissman, M.D.
Professor of Pathology, Stanford University

(* indicates membership at the time in the National Academy of Sciences)

Meanwhile, Bowes rounded up an investment and management team, starting with venture capitalist Franklin "Pitch" Johnson, an old friend of Bowes's from Harvard University. After a post-Harvard stint working the floor of a steel mill, Johnson had cofounded the venture firm Draper and Johnson Investment Company with Bill Draper in 1962. He had completed some graduate work in molecular biology in 1965 at Stanford University and loved it, and he had spent years tracking the business and science of biology. When Bowes approached him about Amgen, Johnson was ready.

Another catch was Raymond Baddour. "I thought Ray would lend academic weight to the enterprise because he was a heavy at the School of Chemical Engineering at MIT," says Bowes. Then the Lammot Du Pont Professor of Chemical Engineering and past chairman of the Department of Chemical Engineering, Baddour was officially recruited as an Amgen advisor and board member by Tosco, an oil shale recovery company and early Amgen investor.

The team also needed a good lawyer, and they found one in Ed Huddleson Jr. of Cooley Godward. Huddleson then brought in Alan Mendelson, at that time a junior partner. Bowes rounded out the investment team with Moshe Alafi, cofounder of Biogen and Cetus, and Donald R. Longman of Schering-Plough. He also brought on board Joseph Rubinfeld, a Bristol-Myers executive who briefly became Amgen's vice president.

Below: Venture capitalist Franklin "Pitch" Johnson in June 2004. An early Amgen investor, Johnson worked closely with Bill Bowes to recruit George Rathmann and launch the company.

Opposite: The April 27, 1980, minutes from Amgen's board of directors meeting list just two members at the time—Bill Bowes and Winston Salser.

MINUTES OF THE ORGANIZATIONAL MEETING

OF THE BOARD OF DIRECTORS OF

AMGEN

The organizational meeting of the Board of Directors of AMGen (the "Company"), a California corporation, was held at the offices of Cooley, Godward, Castro, Huddleson & Tatum, One Maritime Plaza, San Francisco, California 94111 on the 27th day of April, 1980, at 2:30 p.m.

Edwin E. Huddleson, Jr., the sole incorporator named in the Articles of Incorporation, Winston Salser and William K. Bowes, Jr. were present at the meeting.

The incorporator chose as directors of the Company the following persons:

Winston Salser
William K. Bowes, Jr.

Mr. Salser was designated Chairman of the meeting and Mr. Bowes acted as Secretary of the meeting.

The Chairman announced that all of the directors were present and that the meeting, having been duly convened, was ready to proceed with its business.

Articles of Incorporation

The Chairman announced that the Articles of Incorporation of the Company had been filed with the Secretary of State of the State of California on April 8, 1980. He

1.

Scientific Advisory Board Sets the Stage

While it may be difficult to imagine a group of the world's most famous scientists sitting in folding chairs around a picnic table, these brainstorming sessions were typical of Amgen's early Scientific Advisory Board (SAB) meetings. Winston Salser, the board's founding scientist, brought together some of the best biotech-worthy brains of that era.

It was a time when companies like Genentech were taking off, and university scientists were eager to see their research parlayed into commercial ventures. "Every member had a specialty or important discovery that turned out to be critical in the successful development of the company," says the University of California, Santa Barbara's John Carbon, whose expertise involved inserting foreign genes into yeast and using the yeast as a host to make foreign proteins.

Through their various discoveries, research, and brain power, each member brought important insight and helpful criticism. "We had a lot of ideas on how to get things expressed and cloned, and what targets we wanted to pursue," says SAB member Arnie Berk, associate professor of microbiology at the University of California, Los Angeles. "After our meetings, we'd do our own research, then report back on what projects seemed to make the most sense for the company."

The group met and talked by phone frequently in the early days, recruiting and interviewing young scientists and recommending to CEO George Rathmann who would be best

Above: John Carbon was an important member of the Scientific Advisory Board. An early biotech pioneer, Carbon and his coworkers studied biochemistry and the genetics of transfer RNA from 1963 to 1973. Their work led to the introduction of recombinant DNA techniques to construct genomic libraries, the development of yeast as a system for DNA cloning, and the first isolation and characterization of functional centromere DNA.

"Once Amgen started hiring experts in certain areas, they often knew more than the SAB members did. But meeting was helpful because it forced Amgen to get organized and think about what they were doing. It was a tremendous, fantastic, and stimulating period. It's been very gratifying to see Amgen's success."

— **Arnie Berk, Scientific Advisory Board member, University of California, Los Angeles**

suited for the promising start-up. In fact, many scientists like Frank Martin joined Amgen primarily to work with the SAB.

"I was working in Marv Caruthers's lab in Colorado," says Martin, "trying to learn some of his DNA synthesizing methods, and he said, 'You might want to check out this company.' Amgen was just getting started, but initially, I wasn't interested in living in Southern California. I ended up joining Amgen for two reasons: First, I couldn't help but be impressed with George Rathmann. But second, with the SAB in place, I knew that the scientific advice was going to be really good. They were clearly positioned for success, and I wanted to be part of that."

"The SAB helped us identify the projects they thought had the best chances of technical success," agrees Raymond Baddour, formerly a longtime Amgen board member. "Once that happened, we were able to put our own people to work to pursue those prospects. The SAB played a very significant role in positioning Amgen for success." △

Above: (From left) Al Banks, Marv Caruthers, and David Gibson at an early meeting of the Amgen Scientific Advisory Board at the Holiday Inn in Thousand Oaks. Caruthers also led the Amgen development group in Boulder. He and his University of Colorado, Boulder colleagues developed techniques currently used for chemically synthesizing DNA.

Below: This agenda for the April 14, 1980, organizational meeting—which took place just days after Amgen's incorporation—helped identify the company's direction.

AMGen
APPLIED MOLECULAR GENETICS, INC.

1138 Hartzell Street
Pacific Palisades
California 90272

Suite 4300
555 California Street
San Francisco, CA 94104

AGENDA --- April 14th meeting, California Institute of Technology

Lee Hood   Winston Salser
Norman Davidson   Bill Bowes
Arnold Berk   Sam Wohlstadter
Bruce Wallace   Pitch Johnson
        Ed Huddleson

Stanford
Schimke
Carbon
Caruthers
Yanofsky

Wolfe
Gibson
Motulsky
Messenzue

I   Opening remarks.
    A. Scientific orientation of the Company. (Winston).
    B. Financial and business orientation. (Bill).
    C. Introduction and background of the financial advisors. (Bill).
    D. Funding goals. (Bill).
    E. Structure of the company. (Winston).

II Focussed goals for the meeting.
    A. Invitation for Lee Hood to join the Scientific Advisory Board.
    B. Discussion of AMGen access to microsequenator technology: Could involve AMGen contracting for work to be carried out at Cal Tech or elsewhere or obtaining help in setting up a microsequenator in-house.

    C. Discussion of oligonucleotide sequence synthesis: licensing agreements which would be fair to Cal tech and U. Colorado Staff, to AMGen and to the larger scientific community.

III General goals for the meeting will include preliminary discussions of the following topics:

    A. Staffing.
        1. General staffing of the Corporate laboratories.
            a. President.
            b. Recruiting and salary levels for postdoctoral researchers.
            c. Recruiting and salary levels for technicians.

        2. Specific technical needs which will influence staffing.

            a. synthesis of primers and perhaps large gene segments.
            b. amino acid sequencing.
            c. immunological screening.
            d. development of efficient expression vectors.
            e. hybridomas.
            f. expression in yeast, and possibly other organisms.

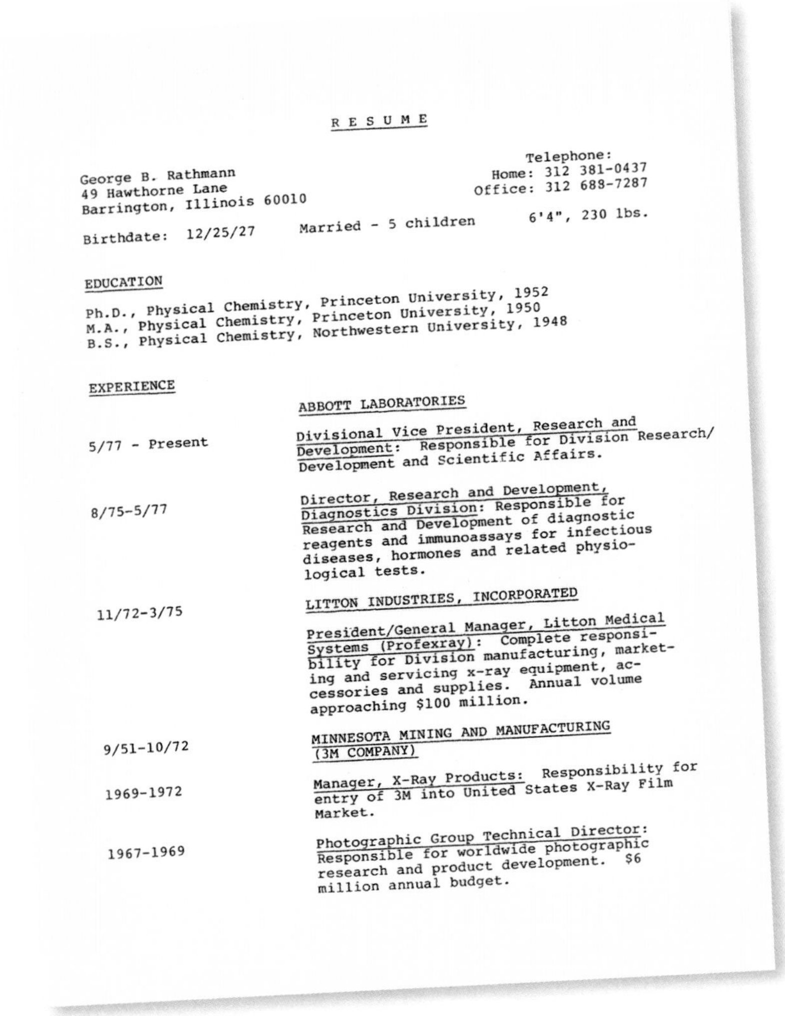

George B. Rathmann
49 Hawthorne Lane
Barrington, Illinois 60010

Telephone:
Home: 312 381-0437
Office: 312 688-7287

Birthdate: 12/25/27   Married - 5 children   6'4", 230 lbs.

EDUCATION

Ph.D., Physical Chemistry, Princeton University, 1952
M.A., Physical Chemistry, Princeton University, 1950
B.S., Physical Chemistry, Northwestern University, 1948

EXPERIENCE

ABBOTT LABORATORIES

5/77 - Present
Divisional Vice President, Research and Development: Responsible for Division Research/Development and Scientific Affairs.

8/75-5/77
Director, Research and Development, Diagnostics Division: Responsible for Research and Development of diagnostic reagents and immunoassays for infectious diseases, hormones and related physiological tests.

LITTON INDUSTRIES, INCORPORATED

11/72-3/75
President/General Manager, Litton Medical Systems (Profexray): Complete responsibility for Division manufacturing, marketing and servicing x-ray equipment, accessories and supplies. Annual volume approaching $100 million.

MINNESOTA MINING AND MANUFACTURING (3M COMPANY)

9/51-10/72

1969-1972
Manager, X-Ray Products: Responsibility for entry of 3M into United States X-Ray Film Market.

1967-1969
Photographic Group Technical Director: Responsible for worldwide photographic research and product development. $6 million annual budget.

Above: Despite the investors' eagerness to hire Rathmann, he still submitted his résumé.

Opposite: (From left) Bill Bowes, Pitch Johnson, and George Rathmann relive a seminal scene from Amgen's history almost twenty-five years later: the 1980 meeting in Johnson's Palo Alto backyard, where Rathmann agreed to become Amgen's CEO.

Each of these men provided early seed money for the company—about $81,000—plus a loan of $75,667, which Amgen later repaid.

"We had some fairly good discussions about naming the company," recalls Bowes. "My idea was Applied Molecular Biology. That was dinged by everybody, but what we came up with was Applied Molecular Genetics. The 'genetics' came from Winston Salser."

Finally, Bowes needed an excellent CEO, which he found in a charismatic, fifty-two-year-old division vice president at Abbott Laboratories, who was interested in a brief sabbatical in Salser's lab in late 1979. George Rathmann was a rising star at Abbott, where he had built up a successful medical diagnostics unit. Previously, Rathmann had worked at 3M, thriving in the loose managerial structure that allowed small groups to behave entrepreneurially by developing new products. "He could build visions inside companies, which meant he could build a company," says Bowes.

Rathmann, who had received his Ph.D. in physical chemistry from Princeton University, wanted to spend time in Salser's lab after hearing Phil Whitcome, one of his product managers, talk about recombinant DNA. Whitcome had been one of Salser's post-doctoral students. "As soon as I heard more details about recombinant DNA, I was just enthralled," says Rathmann. "To me, it was just the most wonderful thing in the world." He returned to Abbott and tried to convince the company's management to develop a Genentech-style unit within the company but was told this would be too costly.

In early 1980, Salser suggested that Bowes contact Rathmann. Bowes and the other investors immediately liked him, but there was one problem: Rathmann and his wife, Joy, did not want to leave their stable life on the north shore of Chicago for the wilds of California.

The venture capitalists insisted that Rathmann and his wife at least come out and take a look. They showed the Rathmanns the

"George infused the company with an enthusiasm for success. There is no scientist at Amgen that wouldn't have given his right arm for George. He was an energy source, and people fed off his enthusiasm and hard work."

— Phil Whitcome, strategic planning, hired in 1981

Above: Amgen has had three logos in its twenty-five year history. At top is the first logo, and its second incarnation is shown above.

beaches, the razor-edged mountains, the clear skies, and, of course, the sunshine. After this trip softened the couple up, the venture capitalists began some old-fashioned arm twisting, eventually convincing Rathmann to say yes in October 1980—with Joy's reluctant blessing.

Rathmann was an excellent scientist and businessman as well as a shrewd judge of talent, and he was able to attract gifted young people to come work in the sleepy town of Thousand Oaks. Now regarded as one of the founding fathers of biotech, Rathmann understood both the complexities and potential of this young industry, and his vision for Amgen was far-reaching. "We worked very hard on recruiting George," says Bowes, "and he may have been the most incredible start-up chief executive the world has ever seen."

Rathmann started work that fall, eventually moving into a house near the beach in Ventura and into Amgen's tiny new office and lab. The site was suggested by Bruce Wallace, then a thirty-two-year-old post-doctoral candidate in Salser's lab, because it was equidistant from several universities, the housing was inexpensive, and the air smog-free.

This landed Rathmann behind a lonely desk in that hot, muggy room, far from the bustle of Abbott and the green wetness of Chicago, when a long-haired Tim Osslund showed up asking for a job.

Above: George Rathmann and his wife, Joy, relax at a 1983 company picnic.

Left: Farmers herd sheep near the Ventura Highway in this 1967 archival image. The Security Bank building was demolished in the 1990s to make way for Building 29.

Thousand Oaks: Then and Now

The city of Thousand Oaks was just sixteen years old in 1980 when Applied Molecular Genetics—a start-up that was little more than a gleam in its founders' eyes—came to town. Right away, the company unveiled its ambitious plan for growth. Amgen's goal was to recruit world-class scientists to an area offering an ideal climate and an exceptional quality of life. It was a plan that would attract and sustain clean industry, an educated workforce, and an involved citizenry.

For Thousand Oaks—a city that prided itself on its bucolic atmosphere with parks and open spaces, with controlled growth and a balanced mix of residential areas, modern shopping centers, schools, business, and industrial centers—Amgen's plan "fit that model perfectly," says city council member Dennis Gillette, at the time the city's police chief. Gillette recalls, "When Amgen presented its master plan to the city, the chamber was packed with people testifying in favor."

Larry Horner was on the city council in 1980 and served as mayor four times in subsequent years. One of Amgen's leading local advocates, Horner explains, "Being from Indianapolis, where Eli Lilly is headquartered, I knew personally the contributions to quality of life a science-based company like Amgen could make to Thousand Oaks. I was jumping up and down at the idea of a company with that kind of potential coming here." Horner credits Amgen for helping mold Thousand Oaks into the city it is today. "Whether through individual volunteers or through financial contributions, Amgen participates on virtually all levels of society," he says.

Top: Thousand Oaks in 1970—after incorporation, before Amgen

Above: Thousand Oaks and Amgen, 1987

Above: Before Thousand Oaks incorporated in 1964, the rural countryside's main attraction was Jungleland, a popular park that featured performing jungle animals. This little girl holding a pygmy goat visited in 1962.

Indeed, with Amgen as its neighbor, Thousand Oaks has grown from a population of seventy-seven thousand in 1980 to more than 125,000 today. Yet the city has stayed true to its master plan, boasting a balance of development and open space. Today it has fifteen thousand acres of open space, or one-third of the city's total area, not including parks and golf courses. Built on land allocated for a typical industrial park, Amgen has sustained this theme of openness as it has expanded. Modeled after a sprawling college campus, the grounds feature a seven-acre, pedestrian-friendly open area, much to the appreciation of the local populace.

Amgen's success has brought international recognition to a city that could have been a struggling suburban community, says Horner. Thousand Oaks residents pay no local property taxes, he explains, a perk that would have been difficult to sustain through economic downturns without Amgen's formidable tax base. Amgen scholarships, teaching awards, and staff involvement help keep local schools among the academic top ten in California, and the city's active arts scene is peppered with substantial Amgen sponsorships.

"You just couldn't ask for a better corporate neighbor than Amgen," says Horner. Having witnessed the changes to the town over the last twenty-five years, both Horner and Gillette agree: Amgen has helped Thousand Oaks become the city it aspired to be. △

Above: The Sherwood Country Club golf course, shown here, and Thousand Oaks recreational parks offer green escapes even beyond the fifteen thousand acres the city has designated as open space.

Top: Judy Thompson, a longtime Amgen development staffer, walks her dog along a ridge overlooking Amgen in July 2004.

Above: Thousand Oaks and Amgen, 1998

Twenty-Five Years of Amgen

Amgen's story officially begins a few months earlier, however, with the company's incorporation on April 8, 1980—a three-page document signed by Cooley Godward's Ed Huddleson Jr., Amgen's first outside legal counsel, and listing Bill Bowes as the "initial agent for service of process." This launched the first phase of the company, from 1980 to 1988 (see Chapter 1: Amgen Takes the Plunge), a period in which Amgen's rapidly growing team took the latest in recombinant DNA and other technologies and tried it on virtually everything. Under George Rathmann, Amgen raised $19 million in 1981—enough to fund a team of brilliant scientists who went to work on a number of projects. In the first three years, they attempted, among other things, to develop organisms that would extract oil from shale, grow chickens faster, develop specialty chemicals, and create potential drugs. These years saw the company struggling to develop and market viable products—and, as the money ran out, to avoid almost certain financial collapse.

In 1982, Amgen hired Gordon Binder as CFO. The next year, at a time when the company was running out of cash, Binder managed Amgen's IPO during a rare window in the stock market when biotech was golden. The offering of 2.35

HISTORICAL AMGEMS

Q: What Thousand Oaks restaurant was once the site of Amgen's all-staff meetings?

A: Reubens

Left: (From left) John Fieschko, Ramon Seva, and Dennis Fenton in an early image with some fermentation equipment in the Building 3 clinical manufacturing facility

Below: A copy of Amgen's original incorporation documents

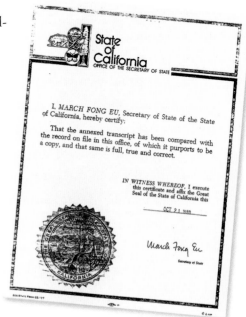

million shares at $18 a share raised $40 million. Soon thereafter, Amgen's most significant moment occurred in October 1983 when researcher Fu-Kuen Lin successfully cloned the erythropoietin gene, which led to the development of EPOGEN®—a recombinant protein that stimulates the bone marrow to increase production of oxygen-carrying red blood cells.

On June 1, 1989, the FDA approved EPOGEN® for the treatment of anemia associated with chronic renal failure patients on dialysis. As Amgen's first marketed drug, EPOGEN® has had a phenomenal run— in 2003 alone, its U.S. sales were $2.4 billion. In early 1986, Larry Souza led a team of scientists to clone the granulocyte-colony stimulating factor (G-CSF) gene, which led to development of NEUPOGEN®, Amgen's second blockbuster drug. Approved by the FDA on February 21, 1991, NEUPOGEN® decreases the incidence of infection associated with chemotherapy-induced neutropenia in cancer patients with non-myeloid malignancies who are undergoing myelosuppressive chemotherapy. By the time EPOGEN® and NEUPOGEN® appeared on the market, Amgen had become a full-fledged human therapeutics company.

In 1988 Rathmann retired as CEO (though he stayed on as chairman of the board until 1990), and Amgen's second CEO, Gordon Binder, took over. During the early 1990s

Below: Rubik's cubes were all the rage in the early 1980s. Phil Whitcome of strategic planning was so taken with them that he had several made with the early Amgen logo and gave them to visitors.

THE SOLUTION IS ...

(see Chapter 2: Breakout: Profits and Worldwide Expansion), sales of Amgen's two hit drugs soared. Then on March 5, 1991, another landmark victory came when the U.S. Court of Appeals for the Federal Circuit ruled that Amgen's patent regarding recombinant erythropoietin was valid, enforceable, and infringed by Genetics Institute—a legal tangle that had been hanging in the air for four years. Also during this time, Amgen engaged in arbitration against its partner and licensee Johnson & Johnson regarding the parties' respective rights to Amgen's erythropoietin product.

From 1990 to 1994 Amgen also expanded its reach, building its Fill and Finish facility in Puerto Rico and its Distribution Center in Louisville, starting the nonprofit Amgen Foundation, and receiving FDA approval for expanded uses of NEUPOGEN®. In 1994 Amgen acquired Synergen, a Boulder-based biotech company that had an exciting product candidate.

The company continued to expand at a breathless pace in the late 1990s (see Chapter 3: Growth and Struggles). But after the spectacular unleashing of EPOGEN® and NEUPOGEN®, Amgen struggled to find a third act—another blockbuster drug. The Synergen acquisition failed to be the hit Amgen wanted. And several additional attempts to generate success proved disappointing, including the company's third drug, Infergen™ (Interferon alfacon-1) approved by the FDA for treating patients with chronic hepatitis C virus.

Above: A stress reliever toy created by Amgen's marketing team touts the benefits of EPOGEN®.

Opposite: Manufacturing staffers oversee a filling machine to dispense final, formulated product into vials ready for distribution.

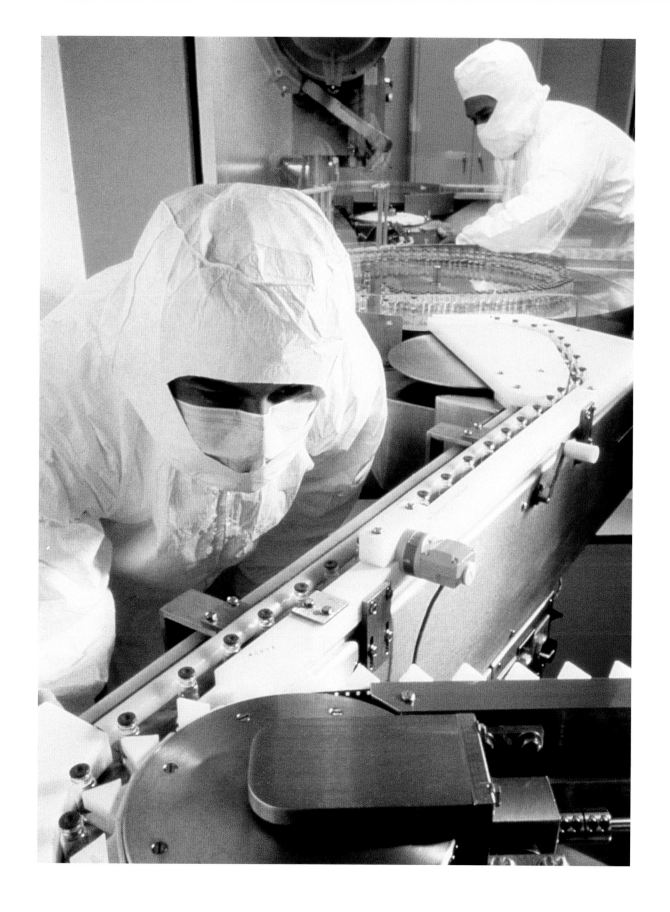

Above: A 1997 portrait of CEO Gordon Binder (left) and president and COO Kevin Sharer

Opposite: Dorothea Miller (left) and Julia Swayne worked in Amgen's international clinical safety group in the late 1990s. They helped monitor the safety profile of Amgen products during development and post-launch.

boom of the late 1990s. The number of staff hit 6,355 by the end of 1999, with annual product sales of $3 billion.

In 2000, Gordon Binder retired and Kevin Sharer took over as CEO. Having served as the company's president and COO for seven years, Sharer was able to bring to Amgen his experience working in large companies such as General Electric and MCI. The former naval engineer and expert on nuclear submarines shook things up, going outside the company to bring in talented lieutenants to retrofit Amgen from a fast-growing start-up into a competitive global giant. (See Chapter 4: A Worldwide Leader.)

One strategy was to go shopping. Sharer did just that, stunning the biotech and pharmaceutical world by purchasing Immunex—a deal worth $17.8 billion. Immunex provided the blockbuster Enbrel® (etanercept) and other key research that enhanced the company's capabilities in inflammation research. Enbrel® is approved for use in the treatment of five inflammation-related diseases: rheumatoid arthritis, psoriatic arthritis, polyarticular-course juvenile rheumatoid arthritis, ankylosing spondylitis, and (for the treatment of patients eighteen years or older who are candidates for systemic therapy or phototherapy) chronic moderate-to-severe plaque psoriasis.

Five new drugs were added to Amgen's shelf during Sharer's first

Drugs for obesity and a new platelet growth factor also seemed destined for success, only to fail in clinical trials.

The surprising success story, however, was Aranesp® (darbepoetin alfa). An improved erythropoietic product, Aranesp®—developed by a team led by researcher Steve Elliott in the early 1990s—requires less-frequent dosing to increase the production of red blood cells for patients with anemia. When Amgen and Johnson & Johnson had a dispute over the rights to Aranesp® under an agreement forged in the mid-1980s, Amgen won a huge victory in 1998 after arbitration, confirming that this new drug was not part of the agreement and that Johnson & Johnson had no rights to the product.

Amgen's stock soared, riding in the heady upper tier of biotech stocks during the

HISTORICAL AMGEMS

Q: What legal situation was BusinessWeek referring to in its March 27, 1989, article: "It's a bit like being sued for divorce just as you're entering the delivery room"?

A: A lawsuit filed by Amgen's corporate partner, Johnson & Johnson's Ortho Pharmaceutical, which asked for an injunction to stop Amgen from marketing EPOGEN®

Below: An Aranesp® Volkswagen "bug," given out by Amgen's marketing team at trade shows

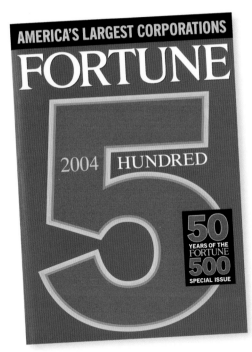

Above: In 2004, Amgen was ranked No. 246 on the FORTUNE 500 list—a jump from 305 in 2003 and 403 in 2002.

few years at the helm: Aranesp® and the less successful Kineret® (anakinra), an anti-inflammatory for the treatment of rheumatoid arthritis, in 2001; Enbrel® in 2002; Neulasta® (pegfilgrastim), which decreases infections associated with chemotherapy-induced neutropenia in patients with non-myeloid cancers receiving chemotherapy, in 2002; and Sensipar® (cinacalcet HCl), which treats secondary hyperparathyroidism in chronic kidney disease patients on dialysis and elevated calcium levels in patients with parathyroid carcinoma, in 2004.

Amgen continued to fill the pipeline with therapeutic candidates by the end of 2004, with increased expenditures in R&D, several drug candidates in human trials, and projected sales of $10 billion—bumping the company up to number 246 on the FORTUNE 500 list by 2004.

Today, Sharer sees challenges on the horizon, both with keeping the drug pipeline full and in staying committed to the spirit of the company. The Amgen spirit, with its focus on both science and patients, was established by George Rathmann back when Amgen hoped to simply be ranked among the top ten biotechs. Just two decades later, the company had become the world's largest biotech. Sharer, however, is quick to say that success has not come so easily. "If this were

easy, there would be dozens and dozens and dozens of Amgens," he says.

Goggles and Genes

Today, just steps from Building 1, Tim Osslund—one of Amgen's longest-tenured staff members—works in a cozy, dimly lit office that enables him to better read the images he is about to pull up on his computer. Still boyish, with long hair and a "wow, look at this!" enthusiasm, Osslund dons a pair of oversized goggles, preparing to read the 3-D images on the monitor. He calls up on screen the image of the protein G-CSF. In 1992, Osslund collaborated with University of California, Los Angeles scientists to untangle its structure—a major breakthrough for the basic scientific understanding of this protein, which had gone on the market a year earlier. It looks like a typical protein, with long, pearl-like strands of amino acids wadded up in a ball like spaghetti, its shape providing clues as to how it interacts with other proteins in biochemical reactions.

"I still really get excited about this stuff," Osslund says gleefully. He sounds as eager as he did twenty-five years ago, on the day he peeked into a humid room where a single, perspiring man plotted the launch of a tiny biotech.

"Hindsight is 20/20 in terms of R&D choices, and Amgen's success depends greatly on the company's pipeline. We'll be very interested to see how the pipeline comes together in the next few years and how the company handles macro issues such as Medicare reimbursement."

— **May-Kin Ho, analyst, Goldman Sachs & Co.**

Below and opposite: Elizabeth Dole (left, seated), former president of the Red Cross, CEO Gordon Binder, and researcher Tim Osslund (right, seated) use special goggles to see proteins in 3-D. During Dole's visit in June 1996, Osslund gave her a tour of Amgen's X-ray crystallography lab.

In Memorium: Bruce Wallace

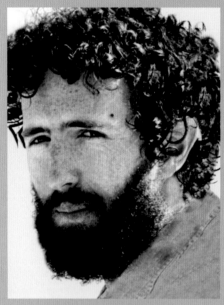

Bruce Wallace, one of Amgen's first staff members, tragically died in a paragliding accident on September 20, 2002, in the Sierra Nevada Mountains, just eight months after retiring from Amgen. With sparkling eyes and inexhaustible energy, Bruce is remembered for his wit, passion, and loyalty to his friends and colleagues, and his love for his wife and four children.

In 1980, Bruce Wallace was a thirty-two-year-old post-doctoral student in Winston Salser's lab at the University of California, Los Angeles. Salser, Amgen's founding scientist, asked Wallace to find space for a new start-up called Applied Molecular Genetics.

It was important to be close to the University of California campuses at Los Angeles and Santa Barbara as well as the California Institute of Technology for interchange. Yet Bruce thought outside the box and considered Newbury Park. While it wasn't near any university, the homes were affordable.

Wallace also wanted a location away from the smog, with a low cost of living, excellent schools, and room for expansion. That spring, he took out a lease for three thousand square feet of office space in what is now Building 1 on the Amgen campus. There was no furniture when he and the architect began designing the interiors, so they sat on the floor and mapped out offices, a dish room, a cold room, and several lab spaces.

For twenty-two years Wallace worked as Amgen's jack-of-all-trades, in the beginning helping with nuts-and-bolts operations such as recruiting, human resources, facilities, and purchasing. Just before

Above: As one of Amgen's first staff members, Bruce Wallace located the space for what would become Building 1 in Thousand Oaks. Recognizing the need for more in-depth molecular biology and biotechnology training, he helped found The Amgen–Bruce Wallace Biotechnology Lab Program at Pierce College in Woodland Hills, California. The workshops have provided hands-on activities and theory exploration for more than six hundred teachers and one hundred thousand students since it began in 1990.

Above: A 1980 employment agreement with Bruce Wallace

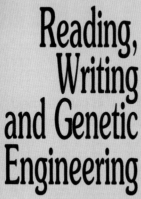

By LINDA COOPER, News Chronicle

Reading, Writing and Genetic Engineering

Biotechnology headed for Conejo area high school classrooms under Amgen program

NEWBURY PARK — "Biology is no longer the science of cutting up frogs and worms and looking at mice," said Bruce Wallace, a facilities planning and safety manager at Amgen.

That is especially true for science students in the Conejo Valley, Las Virgenes, Oak Park and Moorpark school districts, who will get a chance to work with DNA and gene cloning, thanks to Amgen.

A grant from Amgen to the Conejo Valley Unified School District is enabling Newbury Park High School biology teacher Hugh Nelson to spend this school year working with Wallace and developing a genetic engineering program. Nelson will then help teachers present the program to their students.

"That's a pretty nice cooperative program," Conejo Valley Unified School District Superintendent William Seaver said.

The genetic engineering program is part of a three-part project for Amgen, which also includes the teacher intern program and a lecture series. Amgen put together a lab for the classroom projects, at a cost of about $10,000, Wallace said.

The lab is simple enough that it can be done without complications and if there are problems, Amgen researchers will be just a phone call away, Nelson said.

The lab does not involve human genes or germs. It parallels what genetic engineering labs are doing across the country, Nelson said.

In the plasmid fusion lab students will take plasmid, which is a piece of DNA, from bacteria and use enzymes to cut the DNA, then put it back together in different pieces so they get a new organism, he said.

"I am extremely excited. It's a chance of a lifetime for me," said an enthusiastic Nelson.

'We're a company that's built on education and as individuals we value education because of it. We are where we are through education. Educated people make better choices.'
— Bruce Wallace

Nelson was chosen after he participated in a teacher intern program at Amgen in 1989. He was selected because he helped develop ways to move the experiments into the classroom, Wallace said.

"He was in the right place at the right time and showed a lot of interest in the development," he said.

Nelson has been teaching for 20 years, 18 of those at Newbury Park High School. He holds a master's degree in biology from Harvard University and a bachelor's degree in botany from the University of Michigan.

"This is really quite rare," Wallace said of the school project. Only a small portion of schools in the nation, about one in 1,000, have genetic engineering programs, he estimated.

In California, the local school districts will be the only ones south of Santa Cruz to have such a program, Nelson said.

The teachers are all very excited about the program, he said.

"I think they're enthused that someone is making an effort to make their job easier as well as more up to date," Nelson said.

He is worried, though, that apathetic students might not appreciate it.

"They are not very excited by school so it is hard to generate enough enthusiasm to show them that this is new and different, he said.

Still, "the bright kids know that they're being treated to something real special," Nelson noted.

They are aware of DNA, but after they participate in the lab they'll be able to say "I touched it and I held it in my hand," he said.

Amgen is working with the schools because most of its staff members are highly educated and some are former educators, Wallace said.

"We're a company that's built on education and as individuals we value education because of it," he said, adding that about a quarter of the staff have doctorates.

"We are where we are through education," Wallace said.

"Educated people make better choices. They make greater contributions and this country needs that," he said.

Newbury Park High School biology teacher Hugh Nelson will spend this year working with Amgen to develop a genetic engineering program which he will help other teachers present to their students. HOLLY McFARLAND/News Chronicle

his retirement, he headed up Amgen's office of environmental health and safety. He also initiated a local high school education series now named "The Amgen–Bruce Wallace Biotechnology Lab Program."

"He cared about people, community, education, and learning, and had a profound passion for life," remembers Scott Trousdale, senior manager of environmental health and safety and a colleague and friend of Wallace's. "But more than anything else, his wife and family were his prized possessions. All in all, Bruce was just the most wonderful, fun, interesting, and unpretentious person I've ever been around."

Above left: An October 1990 *Thousand Oaks News Chronicle* article on the program started by Wallace *Top:* Teachers Hugh Nelson and Marty Ikkanda help administer the Biotech Lab. *Middle:* Wallace and Gordon Binder at a company function in 2000

Above: Amgen's environmental health & safety group gathers 'round the Christmas tree in 1992. Clockwise from bottom left: Marcia Brandt, Scott Trousdale, Ted Quiroz, Bruce Wallace, Ken Backer, Susan Baros, Sommer Dean, Regina Pacheco, and Shirley O'Donnell

1980–1988

Amgen Takes the Plunge

"Amgen filed five INDs with the FDA in 1985—a feat Big Pharma couldn't achieve. And the only reason we could is because very few of us had filed before, so we didn't know how hard it would be."

— Mike Narachi, research, hired in 1984

n early October 1983, light rains from a freak hurricane fell on the Conejo Valley, adding to the several inches of water already drenching the area in the wake of El Niño storms. At Amgen, CEO George Rathmann had just called a monthly staff meeting at the Holiday Inn in Thousand Oaks (today's Palm Garden Hotel). About 120 staff members gathered to hear the usual announcements, jokes, and encouragement from their leader. Standing 6′4″ at the podium, with his beard and slightly impish smile, Rathmann was about to deliver some astonishing news to the scientists and staffers—news that would change the future of biotechnology. ⚑ The news had come at a critical juncture in Amgen's history. Just four months earlier, Rathmann and CFO Gordon Binder had rescued the company when they convinced Binder's friend Bob Hotz of Smith Barney to lead an IPO, despite Amgen's lack of commercial products and a bank account approaching zero. The stock had plunged since the IPO on June 17, 1983, from $18 to less than $6. But Amgen had raised more than $40 million from the offering, enough to keep the company alive for a few more years. ⚑ Obviously emotional, Rathmann cleared his throat. "Will Fu-Kuen Lin stand up?" he said. "We'd like to recognize you for a new discovery." Lin, a young researcher from Taiwan, had successfully cloned the erythropoietin gene,

Opposite: Chi-Hwei Lin (left) and Fu-Kuen Lin, key members of the research team that cloned erythropoietin in 1983, return to the Building 1 lab in July 2004.

which is responsible for a protein that stimulates bone marrow to make new oxygen-carrying red blood cells. He had been working on the project day and night for more than two years, using some brilliant strategies to capture a sample of the gene that would enable the creation of one of the most successful drugs in biotech history.

"But Fu-Kuen wasn't at the meeting," remembers Rathmann, "so somebody went to get him. And fifteen minutes later he came, but we'd already announced the fact that he had isolated the erythropoietin gene. When he walked in, the whole organization cheered and gave a standing ovation. It was a beautiful moment. He was dumbfounded."

Years later, during a lawsuit Amgen brought against Genetics Institute for infringing Amgen's erythropoietin patent, Lin was asked if he had ever received any recognition at Amgen for his work. As he began to share the story of that company meeting, Lin, in an extremely out-of-character display of emotion, became so choked up that the judge called a five-minute recess.

"I'm sorry. I was emotional," Lin told the judge when everyone settled back in. "I remember in one of the company meetings shortly after we cloned the erythropoietin gene

that I had a cold and could not even talk. But when I walked in, everybody stood up and applauded. I was very touched. Even now."

Rathmann's Magic

The road to Lin's discovery starts with Amgen's incorporation in the spring of 1980. But the story really takes off that October, when George Rathmann arrived as the new president and CEO. Fresh from Abbott, Rathmann moved into Amgen's tiny digs and made his office in the front corner of Building 1. The next year he moved into a trailer in a Rolls-Royce warehouse down the street to free

Above: George Rathmann in one of the Building 2 laboratory bays in 1982

Below: One of the first keys to Building 1

April 8, 1980
AMGen incorporates.

1980
George B. Rathmann is elected president and chief executive officer.

1980
Number of staff: 3

1981
First Fermentation Seminar

1981
Amgen opens its first off-site location in Boulder, Colorado.

1981
The company changes its name to Applied Molecular Genetics Inc.

June 17, 1983
IPO

October 1983
Fu-Kuen Lin isolates the gene for human erythropoietin.

1983
The company changes its name to Amgen.

1985
Number of staff: 196

1985
Larry Souza's team clones granulocyte-colony stimulating factor (G-CSF), later named NEUPOGEN®.

December 3, 1985
Amgen initiates the first human clinical trials of EPOGEN®. Trials are conducted at the University of Washington and the Northwest Kidney Center in Seattle.

up space for more scientists in Building 1.

"I had pneumonia twice because it was freezing in the back of that warehouse," recalls Susanne Hersh, one of Amgen's first five staff members. Hersh joined as Rathmann's assistant, and in the beginning, he paid her by personal check. She was quickly promoted to manager of compensation and benefits.

Rathmann, dubbed "Mr. Biotech" by *Red Herring* magazine in 2000, has been called one of the great geniuses of high-tech entrepreneurialism. "George was a scientist and a businessman," says Bill Bowes. "He was the whole package. I think he was one of the great founding CEOs of any company in any industry. George is the kind of guy that people want to follow. He got top people to follow him out from Abbott, to break with their comfortable existence and go to Thousand Oaks, and he recruited young kids out of great universities."

"George Rathmann was called 'Golden Throat,'" agrees Jeanne Fitzgerald, another early Rathmann assistant and now Amgen's senior director of marketing operations. "He went out and raised money, convincing investors to invest in biotech when it was a very risky and uncertain field."

Rathmann was eager for Amgen to be as successful as Pfizer. But his immediate goal was to catch up to the other biotech

Above: An original T-shirt for Amgen's first softball team in 1982. "We had to buy our own shirts," Dennis Fenton recalls. "The guys from all the warehousing companies around here used to clobber us."

1985
Amgen licenses recombinant human erythropoietin to Johnson & Johnson for all indications in the U.S. except for the treatment of anemia associated with chronic renal failure in dialysis patients. Johnson & Johnson also receives rights to all indications outside the U.S., except China, which Amgen retains, and Japan, which Amgen licenses to Kirin.

October 27, 1987
Amgen receives its first patent on DNA used in producing EPOGEN®.

1987
Amgen Biologicals achieves $1 million in sales.

October 1987
Amgen brings action against Genetics Institute for infringement upon the production of recombinant erythropoietin.

1987
Number of staff: 344

1988
Gordon M. Binder is elected CEO after George Rathmann retires.

July 6, 1988
Amgen ships its first lot of EPOGEN® bulk product to Parke-Davis for fill and finish.

September 28, 1988
Amgen and F. Hoffmann-LaRoche announce an agreement that sales forces of both companies will market NEUPOGEN® in Europe upon FDA approval. Amgen retains full marketing rights to NEUPOGEN® in the United States.

to develop new technologies and processes. Medical projects included creating T-cell interferon to shrink tumors and fend off viral diseases, creating a trypanosomiasis vaccine to prevent sleeping sickness in cattle, and identifying a process for producing large quantities of erythropoietin for anemia. Industrial projects consisted of using recombinant DNA to produce ethanol and other chemicals from waste cellulose to turn out large quantities of acetone, butanol, acetic acid, and other chemicals; and to create bioengineered microbes that would remove sulfur from crude oil and oil shales.

To pay for these grand experiments in technology, Rathmann aimed to raise roughly $15 million to cover four years of work. This, he said, was the absolute minimum required to even begin to rival Genentech.

His timing could not have been better. In 1980, the Supreme Court had ruled that living organisms made through recombinant DNA and biological molecules taken from living organisms could be patented. Genentech successfully cloned gamma interferon after cloning human insulin in 1978 and human growth

start-ups—especially Genentech. Admirably, Genentech founder and CEO Robert Swanson had joined forces with recombinant DNA pioneer Herb Boyer and other top scientists, building his company with only $11 million in initial financing. With Genentech as his model, Rathmann was passionate about the science Amgen could create. "The technology was so powerful," he says. "We knew that molecules in the human body could do amazing things."

But before Rathmann could delve into science, business beckoned. First on his to-do list: establish scientific goals. For this he turned to the Scientific Advisory Board. Already hashing out which projects to prioritize, Rathmann summarized their efforts in the October 23, 1980, offering memorandum. Their first priority? To capitalize on advances in recombinant DNA technology, genetic manipulation, and molecular biology.

The memo also cited fifteen major product "opportunities" and seven programs

hormone in 1979. For investors, Rathmann said, "it all became less scary." Indeed, in October 1980, Genentech's IPO had skyrocketed, and Cetus was close to issuing an IPO that would raise an astonishing $115 million—

Above: Amgen researchers (from left) Jeff Browne, Fu-Kuen Lin, Arlen Thomason, Larry Souza, and Nowell Stebbing meet with Scientific Advisory Board member Arno Motulsky. Motulsky is best known for his work in genetic resistance and susceptibility to disease.

unheard of in biotech. Rathmann prepared to jump into the middle of this first biotech bubble. Starting in familiar territory, he approached his old Abbott colleague, former president Kirk Raab, eventually garnering $5 million. Abbott's Robert Weist, who went on to become Amgen's senior vice president and general counsel, hand-delivered the $5 million check. "I remember making a photocopy of it for my kids to play with," he recalls. "Then I put the original in my briefcase, got on an airplane, and took it to California."

Rathmann then snagged another $3.5 million from Tosco—an oil and energy company that hoped Amgen could create microbes to increase oil supplies. "That $8.5 million was enough to whet the appetites of the venture capitalists that were left on the fence," says Rathmann. It turned out to be a wise investment. When Abbott sold its shares in 1991, it collected $230 million. Other major investors were Rothschild Inc. and Pitch Johnson's company, Asset Management Company. Together, they rounded out this initial effort, raising $19.4 million by January 23, 1981.

Amgen was in business, and now it needed to lure excellent people to the relatively remote Conejo Valley. Touting the strength of the Scientific Advisory Board and his own background in pharmaceuticals, Rathmann chose highly motivated scientists at the beginning of their careers, including Barry Ratzkin, Kirby Alton, Larry Souza, Frank Martin, Fu-Kuen Lin, Yitzhak Stabinsky, Tom Boone, Sid Suggs, Joan Egrie, Burt Ensley, Jeff Browne, Bruce Altrock, and Dennis Fenton. Phil Whitcome, the Abbott product manager who had first told Rathmann about recombinant DNA, left Abbott to join Bristol-Myers, and then came to Amgen as manager of strategic planning in 1981. Robert Weist joined Amgen in 1982.

Below: To find top scientists, Amgen initially placed job notices like this 1981 ad in publications such as *Science* magazine.

DENNIS M. FENTON, Ph.D.
Research Scientist

APPLIED MOLECULAR GENETICS, INC.
1892 OAK TERRACE LANE
NEWBURY PARK, CALIFORNIA 91320
(805) 499-3617

Above: CEO George Rathmann was no fan of business cards—he didn't want his staff members to get competitive about their job titles. Dennis Fenton, however, found it difficult to do business without them, so he had a copy shop print cards for him.

Right: Nowell Stebbing (left) and Dennis Fenton toast the opening of Building 3 with champagne. Fenton filled the new fermenters with red and white wine for the celebration.

Opposite: Each day chemist Ted Jones and his Boulder, Colorado, teammates created DNA hybridization probes and shipped them by Federal Express to Thousand Oaks to support Fu-Kuen Lin's erythropoietin work. Here, Jones synthesizes peptides at the Boulder facility.

Dennis Fenton remembers visiting Amgen in 1981. Then based in Connecticut, he was working as a researcher at Pfizer. Though he had an interest in biotechnology, he had never heard of Amgen. He interviewed mostly to get a free trip to California. "There was a window in Building 1 and all you could see was just brown California dirt," Fenton recalls. "George said, 'We're going to build a pharmaceutical company as big as Pfizer.' And I looked at him and thought, This guy is out of his mind.

"I flew back to my job in Groton," Fenton continues, "a very sleepy, boring town. Got off the plane, and I said to my wife, 'There's no way I'd ever work there.' But George called me back and he said, 'Listen, we want to hire you.' So we left the miserable weather in Groton and got out here for a second interview. It was 80 degrees, and my wife said, 'You're taking this job.' By now, the labs were under construction, there was energy, everybody was excited. And I got hooked."

Larry May, an accountant who became corporate controller and chief accounting officer in 1983, was also wary at first. Sent by a headhunter, he had never even heard of biotech. "I was literally one nanosecond from saying I'm not interested," he recalls, "but I thought, I need to brush up on my interview skills, and this would be a good place." He stayed for fifteen years.

Inevitably, as Rathmann fashioned his lineup, some of the original team disbanded, including Salser, who left Amgen in late February 1981.

Indigo and Fermentation Seminars

Now the real work began. The scientists started trying to clone all sorts of things, with some experiments resulting in bizarre outcomes. Researchers led by Burt Ensley cloned a unique cluster of genes (naphthalene dioxygenase) from Pseudomonas putida into E. coli, and all of a sudden the flask of E. coli turned from muddy brown to bright blue. They isolated the color and found out it was indigo.

During these early years the Amgen scientists often worked with Scientific Advisory Board members to achieve the board's goals. In addition to EPOGEN®, teams worked on oil shale microbes, diagnostics, and various

"When I first came, we were just in Building 1. And we had one bench. When a new person joined, we'd have to make room. So if each scientist had six feet of bench space, they would all lose a foot when we hired someone."

— Dan Vapnek,
research,
hired in 1981

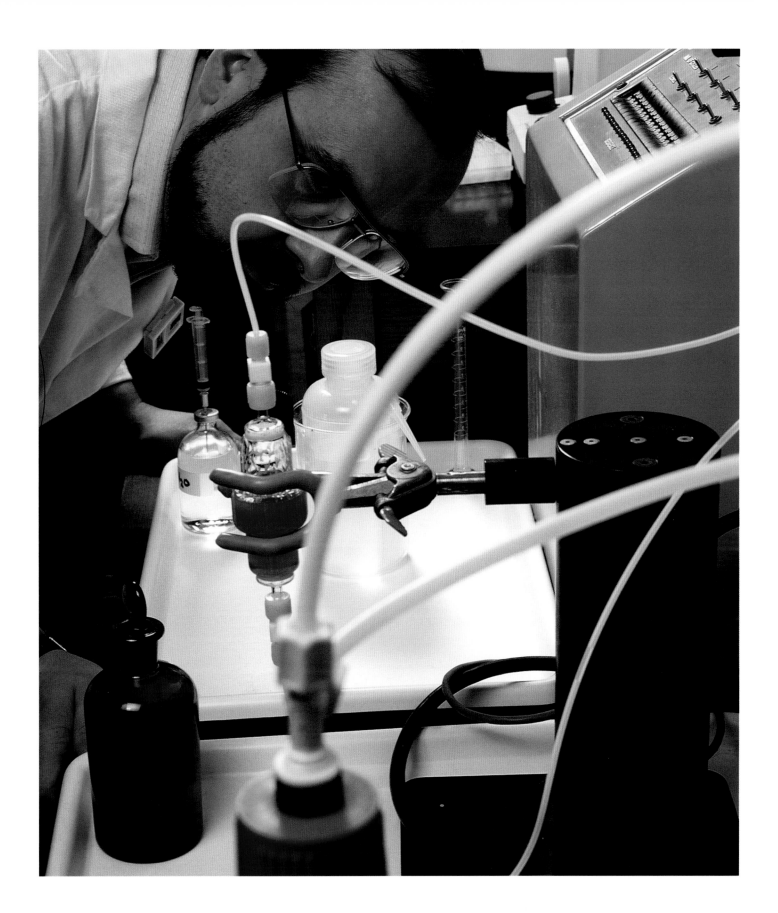

14 OCTOBER 1983 · VOL. 222 · NO. 4620 $2.50

SCIENCE

AMERICAN ASSOCIATION FOR THE ADVANCEMENT OF SCIENCE

Above: Amgen's research in cloning genes led to the company's production of indigo in E. coli in the early 1980s. The discovery and subsequent patent made the cover of *Science* magazine in 1983.

Opposite: Amgen scientists received this patent for their indigo-producing process in 1983.

vaccines. They also tried new projects such as cloning chicken, bovine, and porcine growth hormones to make animals grow faster. Staff member Mark Zukowski even engineered *Baccilus subtilus* to excrete a special enzyme that cuts up proteins, hoping to make a laundry detergent that removed stains.

From these endeavors, a great deal of original science emerged. For instance, from indigo, Amgen made multi-gene discoveries and a number of second-generation drug candidates such as alpha interferon 2, an improved bioengineered version of naturally occurring alpha inter-

feron. Researcher Larry Souza, who ultimately became Amgen's senior vice president of research, isolated and developed Amgen's chicken growth hormone, which was commissioned by Arbor Acres to create a genetic super chicken. His team did make larger chickens, but they didn't grow any faster, so the project eventually died. After that, Souza started work on the protein that would become Amgen's second blockbuster drug: G-CSF or NEUPOGEN®, as it was later named.

Meanwhile, Rathmann boosted morale, channeling the company's youthful energy and entrepreneurial spirit into activities that were fun and let off steam. To encourage his hardworking staff, he gave the nod to monthly beer and pizza parties that became known as Fermentation Seminars. One of the more famous parties was the Great PST Round-Up on September 18, 1987. There, in the Building 2 parking lot, the company served 450 center-cut pork chops from pigs that had received Amgen's porcine somatotropin (PST)—designed to reduce the amount of feed required for a pig to put on a pound of flesh—and lined them up against pork chops from control pigs. There was also square dancing and prizes, including a dinner for two at Porky's, a honey-baked ham, and a $25 gift certificate to the Newbury Park Meat Locker. For the great pork experiment, "staff voted on which tasted better," reported *Amgems,* the company's newsletter. The paper declared it a tie, but Tim Osslund remembers differently: "The PST chops were too lean. They tasted like leather. Everyone ate the control pigs."

"Some of the molecules in the human body can do amazing things. We could duplicate in the laboratory anything that's made in the human body. I remember thinking, If you just get yourself and the people in your organization thinking about patients, you're on the right track."

— George Rathmann, former CEO, hired in 1980

Below: Amgen's discovery of indigo, pictured in a vial with an early logo emblazoned on the label, was one of the company's first real breakthroughs.

A Royal Accident

When Burt Ensley, Barry Ratzkin, Jody Simon, and Tim Osslund accidentally cloned indigo in 1983, Amgen leaders briefly thought they had found a potentially profitable substitute for the dye used to color blue jeans. The experiment introduced other possibilities, too: one variation of this bioengineered indigo was a bright Tyrian purple. "We found out that Tyrian purple is the color used to dye the robes of ancient royalty," says Osslund. "It's from a mollusk and costs $1 million a gram. And we said, 'Oh, this is great!' But we found out you need a gram every thousand years. Apparently there's not a demand for dyeing royal robes."

The team made the discovery by adding genes from the bacteria Pseudomonas putida to E. coli. From there, the E. coli expressed indigo, turning everything, including the flask of E. coli and eventually even Amgen's fermenters, bright blue.

The outcome wasn't a commercial success, but the science used was novel enough to attract major media attention and landed the project on the October 14, 1983, cover of the prestigious *Science* magazine.

"That's the beauty of science when you're doing basic research," says Jody Simon, today one of Amgen's information systems managers. "Often you start on one path and then you're taken down another one. We wanted to just keep Amgen afloat so that eventually we'd get a real product licensed that would help people."

Left: Tim Osslund examines an agar plate that contains bacterium expressing indigo.

Scientists started a tradition of making special T-shirts for parties and events, and custom shirts with secret symbols for teams working on specific scientific projects. They also formed softball teams, and Tom Boone started Sunday afternoon Ultimate Frisbee games. "Most of us didn't have much money—many staffers were straight out of school," Boone remembers. "Some of us were just starting families. My kid was born three weeks after I started here. I thought [Ultimate Frisbee] would be great fun." Now, more than two decades later, the game is still going strong.

Saved by an IPO

In 1981 Rathmann had forecast that the $19.4 million raised in Amgen's financing would be spent over four years. Instead, he burned through it in about two and a half years, trying to catch up with Genentech and other competitors with substantial head starts. From 1981 to 1983, Rathmann struggled with the board, made up mostly of investors, over whether Amgen would be a pharma company or a boutique R&D. "For three years I was barred from making statements at the board meetings about how Amgen should become a pharmaceutical company, about using Genentech as a model for anything, about being science-driven," Rathmann says. Some of the board members wanted instead to be "market-driven" and pushed for Amgen to

Above: Amgen gave these T-shirts to new staff members.

THIS IS MY 1ST AMGEN. T-SHIRT!

focus on one product. Rathmann, however, wanted to diversify Amgen's research and keep the portfolio broad.

By 1983 he won the argument, and the company plowed ahead in four areas—human therapeutics, human diagnostics, animal health care, and specialty chemicals—using investors' money for the various projects. "Abbott paid for the diagnostics program," remembers Bill Bowes, "and specialty chemicals fell to Eastman Kodak and Texaco. Arbor Acres paid for the chicken growth hormone, while Upjohn funded the porcine growth hormone.

"THE GREAT PST ROUND-UP"

On Friday, September 18, people from every corner of Amgen gathered in the Building 2 parking lot for "The Great PST Round-Up". People were initially a bit curious about a pork chop from pigs that received porcine somatotropin (PST), but as the day wore into the night, curiosity faded into an awareness of a new and very promising animal drug.

Allan Miller, Amgen's manager for business development of animal drugs, said the 450 center cut pork chops obtained from the PST pigs and the control pigs seemed like a bit much for the Amgen Round-Up but with the enormous turn-out, most everything was eaten. The objective of the "Round-Up" was both to have fun and to increase Amgen's awareness of PST. The fun was provided by a few internationally fermented refreshments, square dancing and prizes. The prize winners were Craig Mead with dinner for two at Porky's, James Grant with a Honey Baked Ham, Jacob Matulich with a cuddly pig, and Mike McGinley with a $25 gift certificate to the Newbury Park Meat Locker. The increase in awareness was accomplished by our own taste test and some revealing photographs comparing the reduced fat and increased leanness of Amgen PST pork chops to control pork chops.

Amgen's taste test took into account juiciness, tenderness and meat flavor intensity. Even with the uncontrolled conditions under which the test took place, participants ranked all chops essentially the same. This result is very similar to the conclusions obtained by an official taste test at Cornell where, in a well-controlled study, meat from PST-treated and untreated pigs was compared. Tenderness was determined by obtaining shear values and sensory perceptions were evaluated in a blinded taste test that graded the pork samples in 9 different categories. Each sample was cooked to the same internal temperature and each "bite" tasted was the same size. The study concluded that pork from PST-treated pigs was of comparable quality to non-PST pork in all the parameters measured.

The subjective results are obviously favorable but what are some of the hard facts? PST is naturally produced in the pituitary gland of the pig and is synthesized recombinantly in E.Coli. The administration of additional PST to a pig enhances growth in several ways. Firstly, there is an enhancement in the feed efficiency, or more specifically the amount of feed required to put a pound on a pig is decreased by 20-30%. This large of an impact is dramatic and may even be revolutionary. Secondly, pigs gain weight faster and thus attain their market weight of approximately 230 pounds sooner. This means that without any changes in the facilities and without any additional hiring, a farmer can process more pigs per year. Finally, there is a distinct improvement in carcass quality. PST, being involved in growth and nutrient partitioning, channels more nutrients into protein synthesis and less into fat production. In light of the fact that our fat conscious society has made a move toward leaner meats such as chicken and fish, a leaner pork chop should be more marketable than what is currently being sold.

The primary objective of PST, therefore, is to create an economic benefit for the farmer. In a market where the meat packers will pay a premium for a leaner pig with more useable meat, PST will be a necessary element to each farmer. The farmer will be capable of raising a better pig at a lower expense. Allan Miller considers PST a major innovation that will have an impact worldwide. He anticipates the market for PST to be well in excess of $100 million.

Above: An article from the October 1987 *Amgems* about the "Great PST Round-Up"

Opposite: The indigo experiments had a colorful impact on the fermenters. "Every time they leaked, my hands—and then clothes—would turn blue," says Dennis Fenton.

Fermentation Seminars and Brew-B-Ques

Once a month, Amgen staffers descended on the parking lot between Buildings 1 and 2 (now a lawn) for beer and pizza. "There were only thirty or forty of us at the time, we were all young, and we liked a beer or two," recalls Kirby Alton, who retired from Amgen in 1999 as senior vice president of development. "George sometimes brought pizza, and we'd have a potluck. It was a great way for us to get to know each other."

But Rathmann felt these rowdy beer blasts were keeping staffers from their families. When Nowell Stebbing joined Amgen from Genentech, famous for its fun-loving Friday afternoon "Ho-Hos," he and his wife suggested making the gatherings more family friendly. Rathmann jumped on the idea, and the Fermentation Seminars—named after similar events held at Dennis Fenton's alma mater, Rutgers University—were born. From then on, staff members brought food and their spouses and kids. Sometimes the gatherings went well into the night. In those cases, Tim Osslund remembers, "Fermentation Seminars would sometimes adjourn to a house with a hot tub."

"We hosted Fermentation Seminars to get everyone together," remembers Ed Garnett, former vice president of human resources, "because there were a lot of transplants out here."

But the parties weren't just fun—often, the "seminar" part was real. "Many of the scientists were young and new to the area, so they didn't have the benefit of connections," says Osslund. "So we'd tie Fermentation Seminars with SAB meetings. The scientists would come and we'd tell them what research we were doing and they'd critique us." △

Top: R&R at a 1990 cookout *Above:* A few staffers play a friendly game of horseshoes at a 1997 company picnic.

"I'll never forget how on my very first day, people reached out and took me to the Fermentation Seminar and then to their homes for dinner. I knew nobody when I came out here—not a soul. Within six months, I had the greatest set of friends, who happened to be my co-workers. It was a great place to be. I fell in love with Amgen from day one."

— Bob Baltera, finance, hired in 1990

Amgen has a reputation for hard work and hard play. *Clockwise from top left:* Burt Ensley and his co-workers cut-up at a get-together; staffers enjoy a game of volleyball in 1990; Paul Hogan "Crocodile Dundee" holds a mock knife to a staffer's throat at a "Down Under Picnic" in 2000; the Rhode Island facility's first Fermentation Seminar in 2003; another Fermentation "first," in Puerto Rico in 2003, which started as a tennis match with (from left) Ronald Rivera, Greg Gerlovich, Carlos Berlingeri, and Luis Lopez, and ended up as a full-blown fiesta; a relay race at a 1997 picnic.

We also cloned the firefly light source, luciferase. The market, though, was small. Amgen discontinued it when it disbanded the specialty chemicals group."

At the time, the lead candidates for human therapeutics were interferons, immune system proteins. Amgen scientists worked feverishly to develop them, but their efforts never resulted in significant commercial products. (For example, Infergen™, marketed as a chronic hepatitis C treatment after its FDA approval in 1997, has had only modest sales.) Meanwhile, Fu-Kuen Lin was working on EPOGEN®, and Larry Souza on NEUPOGEN®. Neither project, however, was anywhere near a breakthrough.

In 1982, the industry had hit a low point. Despite making great scientific advances, biotech companies were shunned by investors. In August the *New York Times* reported: "Although more than one hundred new companies with names like Amgen and Genex have sprung up to explore the commercial possibilities of biotechnology, the

Below: Carlos Fisher and Avantika Patel in an early lab

only commercial product of gene-splicing to come to market so far has been a European vaccine against diarrhea in piglets."

In January 1983 controller Larry May came on board and learned what executives already knew: The company would run out of cash by that summer. "We had $5 million left, and we were going to run out pretty soon if we didn't get more money."

Rathmann approached Johnson & Johnson for money, but the prospect fell through with the Tylenol® tampering incidents that spring. He then went to the board to raise more money from the original investors. In late 1982 he presented his plan. "When I got to the end," Rathmann remembers, "it was very quiet. I never got a reaction from anybody in that room." The message was loud and clear: The board would not participate in another round.

Several weeks later, then-CFO Gordon Binder and legendary health-care investment banker Fred Frank of Lehman Brothers suggested that Amgen go public. Rathmann was wary. "We're not Genentech. We don't have a product," he argued. Frank replied, "You don't have to. Damon Biotech is going public, and they have less than you have."

Binder presented the IPO proposal to the board and, as expected, it was met with

Above: A May 1983 *Wall Street Journal* article announces Amgen's IPO.

skepticism by some board members. According to Rathmann, one of them said, "What have you guys been smoking? This is terribly unlikely." Phil Whitcome, who was at the meeting, remembers Rathmann's retort: "George said, 'Fred Frank thinks we can go public.' It was just like an E. F. Hutton commercial. When Fred Frank speaks, everybody listens. And they said, 'Fred Frank said that?' And Bill Bowes said, 'Okay.'"

Bowes made phone calls to Montgomery Securities and Dean Witter, and Binder lined up Bob Hotz of Smith Barney. "And all of a sudden," Whitcome recalls, "we had a lot of momentum. The board gave the green light in March 1983."

Even so, times were tense. Cash was running out, and the company had no marketable products—in fact, indigo, chicken growth hormone, and a group of interferons were featured as key science projects. Staff members

Above: Phil Whitcome of strategic planning in 1982

were getting nervous, many preparing their résumés. "I remember the time the cash reserve [was] very low," says Fu-Kuen Lin. "I later learned that one of our scientific supply companies did not want to give Amgen credit. That meant we couldn't have thirty days to pay."

But soon the IPO began to take shape and the markets began another upsurge in biotech interest. Computer technology and software in general had become market

Amgen's Lucky Star: Saved by an IPO

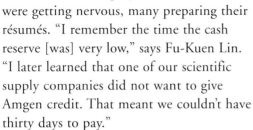

Alan Mendelson, the lawyer at Cooley Godward who filed for Amgen's 1983 IPO, recalls Amgen's first day as a publicly traded company: "Gordon Binder was on the Smith Barney trading floor in New York City. The stock was priced at $18 a share. The first trade came across at $16.75, and everybody gasped, because they knew that it was not going to be a good day. They quickly shooed Gordon out because clearly people were selling, dumping the stock right away. And the stock closed at $16.75…. It never traded at $18 until years later. It just kept going down from there.

"We barely made it with that IPO," continues Mendelson. "In fact, we were in the middle of a major dispute with Abbott, which we were able to resolve at the very last minute. If we had priced it a week later, we might not have been able to do it at all, and we probably would have raised anywhere from $12 to $15 million less," says Mendelson. "Amgen might have run out of cash." But the company raised $42 million—more than enough to keep the company afloat at the time.

"Amgen," George Rathmann says fondly, "does things under a lucky star." △

Above: This lucite cube contains a miniature version of Amgen's 1983 IPO prospectus.

Above: The original EPOGEN® team circa 1986. From left: Tom Strickland, Joan Egrie, Jeff Browne, Fu-Kuen Lin, and Mike Downing. The team was honored by *Nephrology News & Issues* in December 1990 with the magazine's first Quality of Life award.

million—substantially less than Genentech's cap of $655 million—Amgen seemed to be bearing it out. Yet this respite was not to last, leaving Amgen to simply hold on as the biotech sector continued its roller-coaster ride.

The Clone That Launched a Company

Meanwhile, Amgen scientists doggedly continued their efforts to create a product that would yield substantial profits. One particularly frustrating project was Fu-Kuen Lin's effort to clone the erythropoietin gene. For two years, Lin and his research associate Chi-Hwei Lin (no relation) had been trying—and failing—to clone the elusive gene. Once one of Amgen's most promising possibilities, the project had become a near-pariah in the entrepreneurial lab, where Rathmann left it to researchers to develop projects that would attract attention. "This was a measure of the project's success," says Rathmann, "if enough people were excited enough by it to sign on."

Above: Joan Egrie posts information on the EPOGEN® board.

Opposite: Fu-Kuen Lin examines X-ray film to identify gene coding for erythropoietin. The black areas show bacterial colonies containing the gene.

darlings, with Apple, Microsoft, and Compaq dominating the news. Knowing that the market window could close at any moment, Amgen's staff, investment bankers, and company lawyers worked intensely to complete preparations for the offering. One investment banker said the timeline was the shortest he'd ever seen. Amgen's IPO launched June 17, 1983. Just two weeks later, the IPO market took a terrible turn—Amgen had gotten in just under the wire.

By August, the markets dipped again when *Forbes* ran a critical article reporting on the phenomenon of biotech companies that were getting tens of millions of dollars in investment without a product even on the horizon. "Welcome to the wonderful world of biotechnology companies," the article stated. "Welcome to an investment fairyland where hopes and dreams count more than reality."

Amazingly, as a company with no commercial products and a market cap of $140

But the erythropoietin project no longer excited anyone but the tenacious Lin. "I could feel that at one time the project was [almost put] in the freezer," he recalls. "I could feel people getting less involved…. No one ever told me to give up this project. But it continued longer, and that was good for me, because at the time I was quietly on my way."

How Fu-Kuen Lin Did It

Above: Fu-Kuen Lin in his Building 1 lab *Opposite:* An electron microscropy image of the erythropoietin DNA taken by Sylvia Hu in December 1983. The "heteroduplex" shows erythropoietin cDNA from a monkey that has been hybridized to human erythropoietin DNA, revealing the identity and difference between the two molecules.

When Fu-Kuen Lin set out to clone the erythropoietin gene, he hoped to find it on a single fragment of DNA in a "library" of about 1.5 million fragments of the human genome.

Unfortunately, the information available for erythropoietin had too many possible coding sequences to be useful as a cloning strategy. Like all proteins, erythropoietin is comprised of a long strand of amino acids similar to pearls on a string. The order of amino acids is directed by the sequence of the nucleic acids in the DNA. Each amino acid is coded by the sequence of DNA bases—the A, T, C, and G strung along the double helix. Most amino acids are coded by more than one triplet of DNA bases. For instance, the amino acid alanine is coded by one of four possible base sequences: GCG, GCA, GCC, or GCT. The amino acid histidineis is coded by either CAC or CAT; and the amino acid leucine is coded by CTT, CTC, CTA, CTG, TTA, or TTG. So, even knowing some of the amino acid sequence of erythropoietin did not reveal any definitive DNA sequence present in the human genome.

Lin also tried to use complementary DNA (cDNA) cloning, but there was no cell line or tissue source that produced a sufficient amount of erythropoietin.

Despite these setbacks, he did not give up. Instead, Lin tried a new approach no one at the time thought would work: He obtained the internal erythropoietin amino acid sequence and then designed sets of hybridization probes—artificially made, short, single-stranded DNA fragments that latch on to their proper matching DNA sequences. The hybridization probes accounted for every

"When we cloned the gene for erythropoietin, we must have had 40 percent of the company working on sequencing. Anybody who knew how to sequence DNA was working in the lab trying to get the sequence of the gene. The day we knew we had the clone was the day that made Amgen a legitimate player in the industry. It was like getting our union card punched. We were admitted to the league of big science."

— Phil Whitcome, strategic planning, hired in 1981

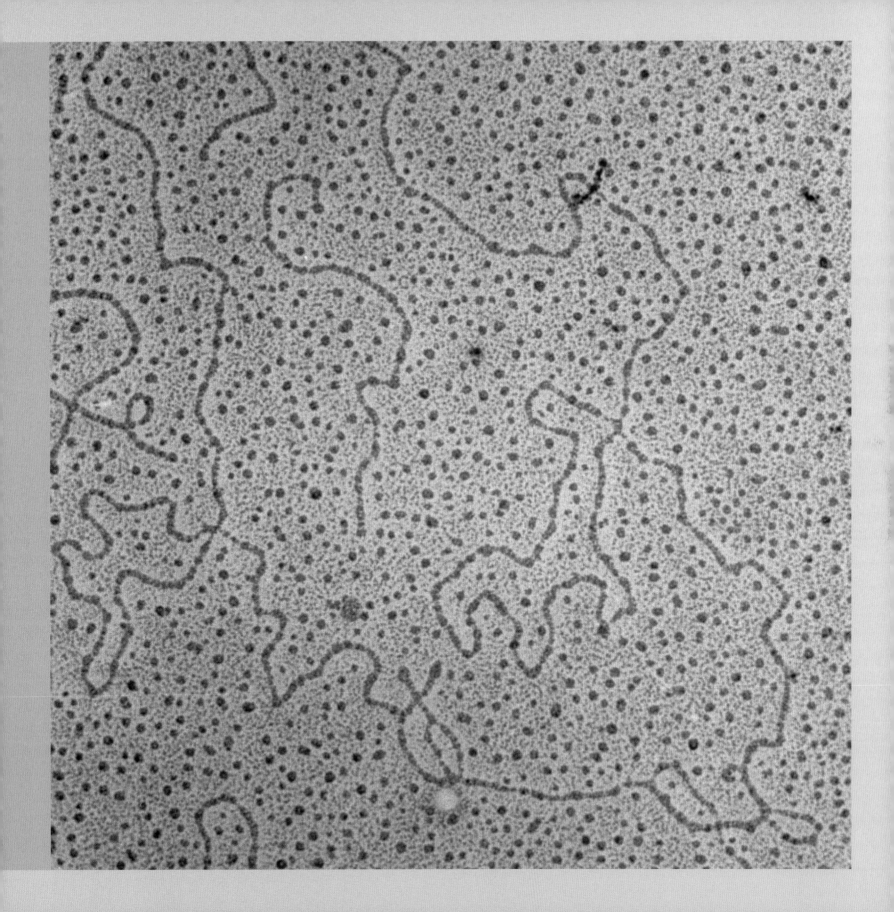

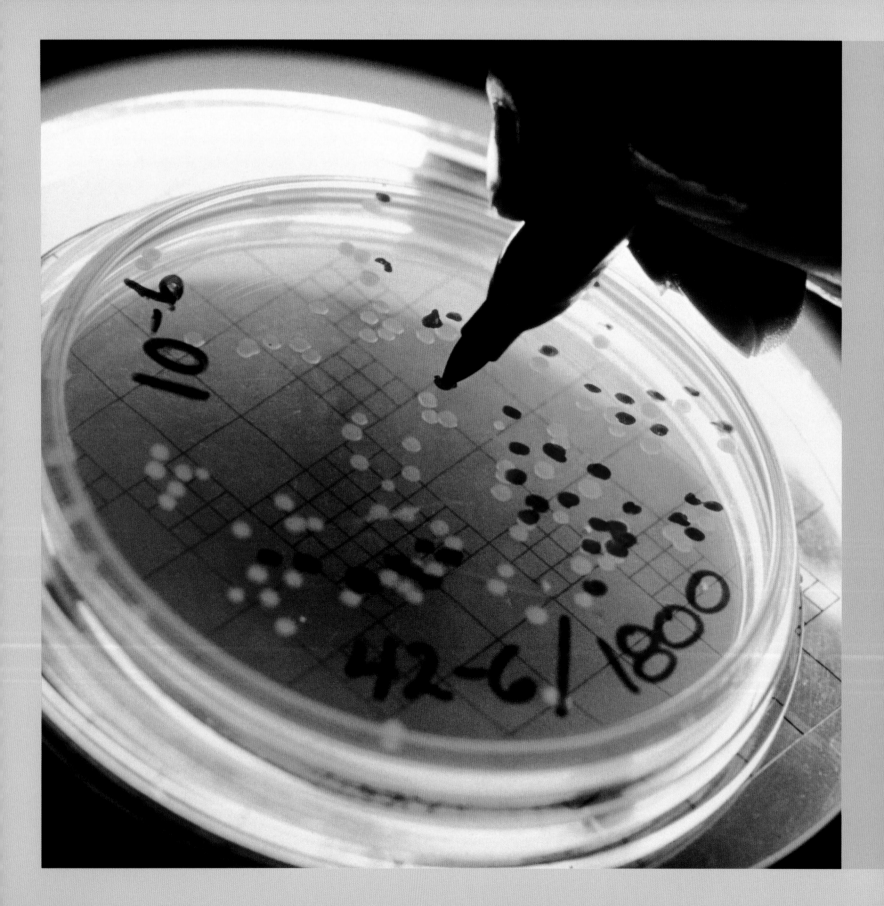

possible DNA coding for the amino acid sequence. Lin employed not just a handful of these probes, but hundreds of probes at a time to search for the correct DNA sequence.

The conventional thought was that the use of hundreds of mixed probes, each representing a different DNA sequence, would generate such a high level of false hits and background that scientists would not be able to discern the correct sequence. Lin's brilliant design and indefatigable determination, however, helped him overcome these potential problems. His work finally paid off in October 1983, when he isolated the human erythropoietin gene.

"We had to take an unconventional approach," explained Phil Whitcome in a December 1983 press release, "a combination of proprietary techniques developed at Amgen, ranging from protein microsequencing and gene synthesis to novel [nucleic acid] hybridization techniques. This helped us clone the erythropoietin gene."

"It turned out that's the approach that worked," Lin reflects now. He smiles. "Still, no matter how hard you work, you have to be lucky at the same time." It's a humble statement, but the truth remains: Lin succeeded where many others had failed. △

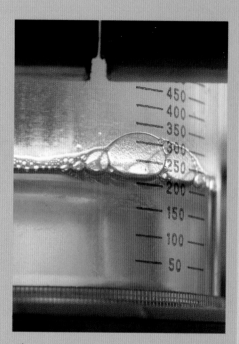

Above: EPOGEN® in a roller bottle *Opposite:* In this image from the original 1984 press packet for EPOGEN®, an Amgen scientist marks bacteria colonies on a nutrient agar plate to identify recombinant organisms that contain the gene for erythropoietin.

Above: George Rathmann and Fu-Kuen Lin at the tenth anniversary party for EPOGEN®.

Firm May Have Key to Treating Anemia

By ANDREW C. REVKIN, *Times Staff Writer*

A rare human hormone, produced in large amounts for the first time by a biotechnology firm in Thousand Oaks, has alleviated anemia in kidney patients and may be an effective treatment for millions of patients with other types of anemia, doctors said Wednesday.

In a report on preliminary human tests of the hormone, to be published today in the prestigious New England Journal of Medicine, doctors said the hormone, erythropoietin, reduced anemia in every test subject and eliminated it in most.

Moreover, the need for transfusions of blood to increase a patient's blood count was completely eliminated, said Dr. John Adamson, a hematologist at the University of Washington, Seattle, who led the study with Dr. Joseph Eschbach, a kidney specialist. Such transfusions are a frequent source of hepatitis and other infectious diseases in kidney patients and have been blamed for a small number of infections of the deadly AIDS virus.

The quality of life for the patients—which had been restricted by fatigue, depression and other symptoms of anemia—was also improved, Adamson said.

Hailing the study results, Stuart Keufer, executive director of the National Assn. of Patients on Hemodialysis and Transplantation, which represents patients with kidney disease, said bio-engineered erythropoietin has the potential to be the "most revolutionary" advance in treatment of kidney failure in 20 years.

The study, along with a British test that recently produced similar results, was financed by Amgen of Thousand Oaks, a small biotechnology company that has pinned many of its hopes for growth on erythropoietin.

Boon Predicted

Several financial analysts said Wednesday that the results of the preliminary trials will be a big boon to Amgen, which has more than five bio-engineered drugs in development and testing, but none on the market.

Peter F. Drake, a biotechnology analyst at the investment firm Kidder Peabody, said Amgen is two years ahead of Genetics Institute of Boston, which is the only other company well on the way to developing a version of the hormone. He said Amgen should have no problem getting its erythropoietin approved by the federal Food and Drug Administration by 1988.

As for the potential market, Drake said sales of the hormone for the treatment of dialysis patients alone could top $150 million by 1990.

If a new series of human trials, involving 300 kidney patients at nine medical centers around the country, produces similar results, erythropoietin "will clearly be a major breakthrough," said Dr. Allen Nissenson, who will be giving the hormone to kidney patients at UCLA. "That stuff is unbelievable in terms of how potent it is," Nissenson said.

Erythropoietin is normally produced in the kidneys and increases the blood's capacity to carry oxygen. It does this by stimulating cells in the bone marrow to divide, a process that produces the trillions of red blood cells that transport oxygen from the lungs to the tissues of the body.

But virtually all of the estimated 85,000 Americans with severe kidney disease lack the hormone, Adamson said, and thousands more with kidney deficiencies have abnormally low levels.

Please see HORMONE, Page 9

Researcher Dan Peplow holds a bottle in which bio-engineered cells are mixed with nutrients. Cells then regenerate and excrete the hormone.

Above: This January 1987 *Los Angeles Times* article reported on the groundbreaking potential of erythropoietin to help alleviate side effects of kidney disease. Pictured is Amgen researcher Dan Peplow, who manufactured erythropoietin for use in clinical testing.

Meanwhile, the bio-rumor mill was whispering that academic labs and other companies had already successfully cloned the erythropoietin gene, beating Amgen to the prize. One of Lin's biggest hurdles was to acquire sufficient amounts of urinary-derived erythropoietin. To find the gene in a human cell, first he needed to have good, reliable sequence information from the amino acids that comprised the protein chain. Unfortunately, that could not be obtained with the trace amounts of erythropoietin available to Amgen.

The major source of erythropoietin known at the time was from the urine of aplastic anemic patients. But there were few such patients in the United States. In addition, normal human urine contains very minute amounts of erythropoietin, so getting even a microgram of it required vats of urine. At one time, Dow Chemical had collected urine from the Italian army and done some purification in hopes of collaborating with Amgen, but the partially purified erythropoietin extract was found unsatisfactory.

In August 1983, Amgen consultant Eugene Goldwasser provided a small urinary erythropoietin sample from which some useful information was obtained to make DNA probes. By November, Lin had successfully "fished" out the erythropoietin gene from a human genomic library that matched the then-available amino sequences of the erythropoietin protein fragments he was working with. By now, he was getting all the help he needed from other scientists.

Lin's team matched the first segment of the gene sequence at night. The next morning, the young scientist called Rathmann. "I believe he was the first person I talked to," says Lin. "And he was so excited. Then he said, 'Well, next thing is to find the whole sequence. If you can find a piece of it, now you need to find the whole thing.'"

"It was a brilliant, brilliant piece of work," says Bill Bowes.

The discovery was publicly announced in December 1983, with a market of about two hundred thousand sufferers of chronic kidney disease in the United States alone. According

Below: A row of roller bottles in Building 6. These bottles are used to churn Chinese hamster ovary cells—just one step in the manufacturing of EPOGEN® and Aranesp®.

The Science of EPOGEN®

"If EPOGEN® therapy is administered early, patients may remain more physically active, involved in home and community activities, and are more likely to maintain general fitness and satisfaction with their personal and sexual lives. When administered as a regular part of dialysis treatment, EPOGEN® significantly improves the quality of life for dialysis patients."

— Dr. Allen R. Nissenson,
professor of medicine and
director of the dialysis
program,
UCLA School of Medicine

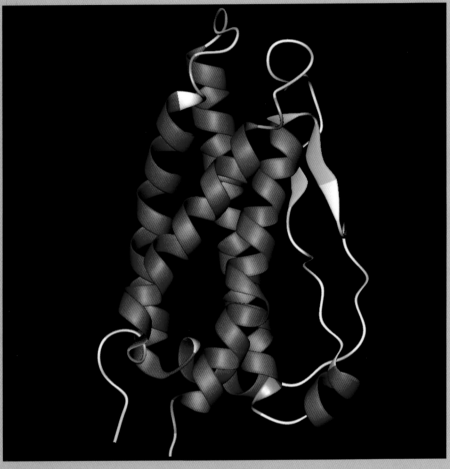

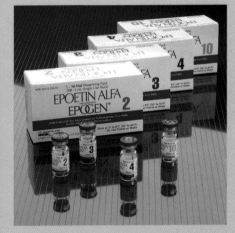

EPOGEN® (Epoetin alfa) is produced by genetically engineering Chinese hamster ovary cells and using recombinant DNA technology. The product is indicated for the treatment of anemia, a condition caused by low levels of red blood cells in dialysis patients with chronic kidney failure. Normally, when the body needs more red blood cells, the kidney produces the human protein erythropoietin, which then signals the bone marrow to produce more oxygen-carrying red blood cells. Kidneys that are not functioning normally, however, often do not produce enough erythropoietin, causing the red blood cell count to drop. EPOGEN®, the man-made version of naturally occurring erythropoietin, is used to stimulate cells in the bone marrow to multiply and form colonies. This increases the red blood cell count in about four to six weeks, and helps to correct anemia, often boosting the energy level of patients.

to an Amgen press release, sales were estimated to be "in excess of one hundred million dollars," a number that many considered optimistic at the time.

A Second Miracle

While Lin was toiling on erythropoietin, Larry Souza's team in Building 2 began working on G-CSF, the protein responsible for the synthesis of white blood cells known as neutrophilic granulocytes. These cells play an important role in the body's immune defense, but can be compromised during chemotherapy, which often destroys the fast-growing bone marrow precursors that produce white blood cells.

Above: Research head Larry Souza led the team in the creation of NEUPOGEN®, Amgen's second blockbuster drug.

Right: A microscopic view of a cluster of bloodborne, multi-lobed neutrophils that are generated when a patient is treated with NEUPOGEN®

Souza started working with a team of physicians at Memorial Sloan-Kettering Cancer Center (led by Karl Welte) that had isolated stem cells in the bone marrow that appeared to stimulate the production of granulocytes. "He'd gotten some partial protein sequence but not enough to do any cloning with it," remembers Tom Boone. "So it was decided that we would start working on it here. I was working for Larry at the time, and he asked me to do most of the hands-on bench-type stuff. So we got the cell line growing on a large scale. And then I began purifying the protein and handing it off to a person who did the protein sequencing."

Finally, they got enough protein sequence information to try cloning the gene.

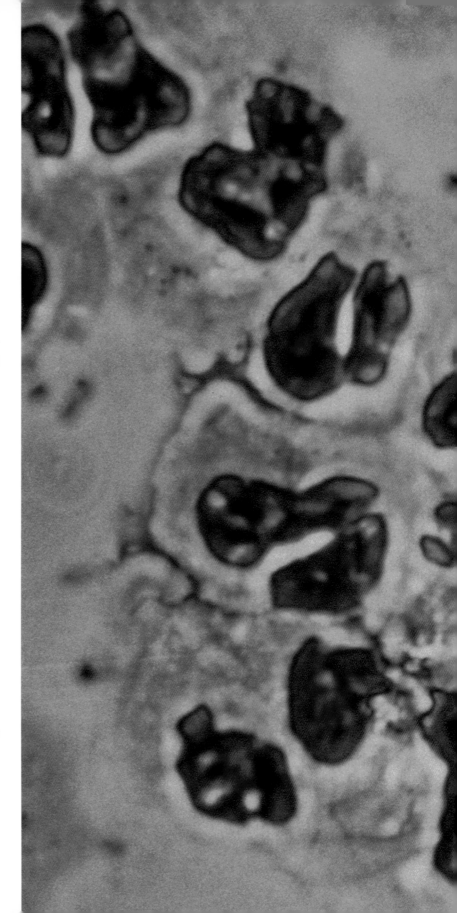

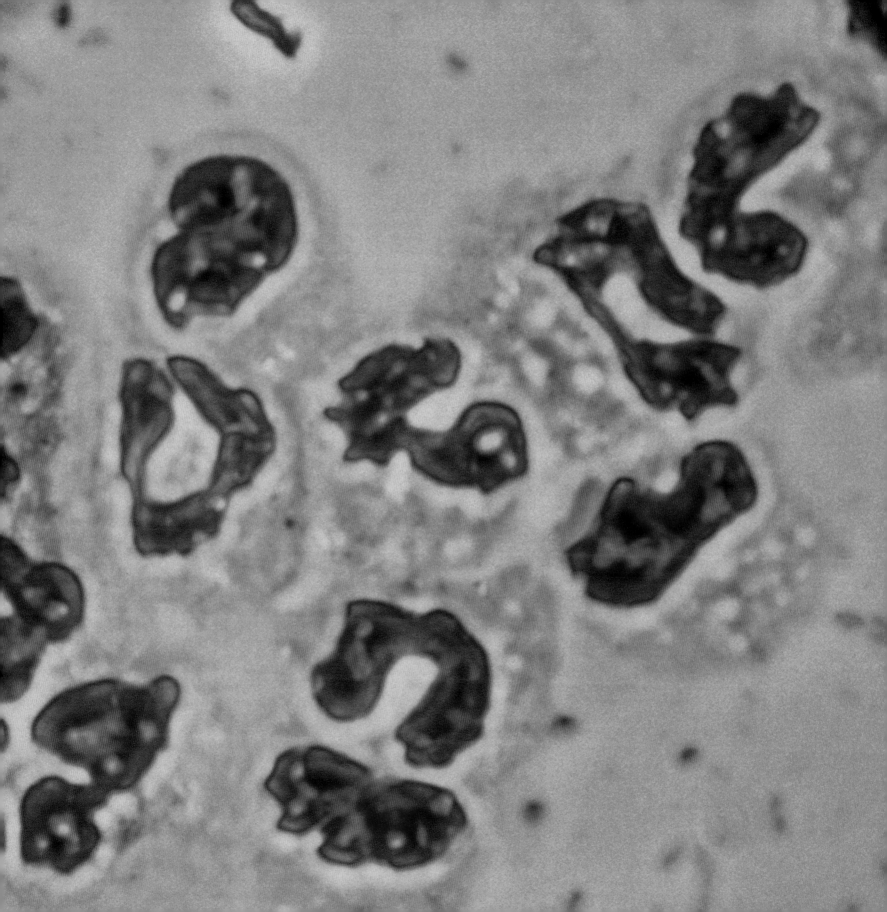

Says Boone, "We got lucky and ended up getting it the first time."

Then one day in 1985, team researcher and pharmacology expert Art Cohen—part of Larry Souza's research team—was running tests on lab animals to see if the G-CSF proteins were boosting white blood cell counts. Cohen had just run a standard test with a centrifuge to separate out blood cells that were stained with dye. He was looking at the results in a microscope when he made a discovery that would change the lives of those fighting cancer through chemotherapy.

Above: NEUPOGEN® researchers Tom Boone and Doug Murdock with Susanne Hersh of human resources in 1982

Opposite: Research associate Vicky Costigan evaluates the results of an agarose gel for the separation of DNA fragments.

Boone recalls, "He was sitting back in the corner looking at his microscope, saying, 'Wow, this is amazing' and 'Oh, I don't believe this.' It went on for a few minutes, and I said, 'Art, what's going on?'"

Cohen waved Boone over and said, "Look at this layer here…. Those are neutrophils." Neutrophils have, as their main function, the ability to fend off infections. But neutrophils, Boone puzzled, were not what they expected.

Cohen explained that this new protein could be used for chemotherapy patients. Within a few weeks, the Souza research team showed evidence that G-CSF accelerates the recovery of circulating neutrophils in laboratory animals treated with conventional chemotherapeutic drugs.

From Discovery to Drugs

By 1984 Amgen was beginning to resemble a real drug discovery company, with three buildings, 133 people, six computers, and several possibilities for products—including EPOGEN®, interferon, a hepatitis C vaccine, and a growth hormone for pigs. Now Rathmann needed to broaden the company's focus on research to include pre-clinical trials, human clinical trials, and manufacturing. This meant assembling staff to conduct the trials and oversee the regulatory testing and approval process.

He also needed to assemble a legal strategy—quickly. In 1983, one year before anyone else, Amgen had filed a patent application

Below: Amgen's first annual report debuted in 1984. It chronicled a groundbreaking year: EPOGEN® and NEUPOGEN® were in the works, and the company had achieved its public offering in June 1983.

Amgen 1984
Annual Report

Fiscal 1984 was a year of significant milestones at Amgen. Important commercial partnerships were established with Abbott Laboratories for infectious disease and cancer diagnostics and The Upjohn Company for bovine growth hormone. We announced five new product candidates: a unique consensus leukocyte interferon that has more antiviral potency than its natural counterparts; a gamma interferon for cancer therapy; erythropoietin (EPO) for controlling red blood cell production; Interleukin 2 for the stimulation of the immune system; and indigo dye, a product of proprietary gene cluster technology. The public offering in June netted the Company $39 million and provided the financial stability required to optimize downstream profits. We secured $10 million in financing for construction of a major production facility in Chicago and doubled fermentation capacity at Thousand Oaks.

regarding its erythropoietin work and immediately jumped into the competitive world of intellectual property. Strife had been brewing in the industry since 1980, when the U.S. Supreme Court ruled that recombinant DNA products and organisms could be patented. "The boom in biotechnology has not yet materialized," opined the *New York Times* in an August 1982 article. "But a boom of another sort is well under way in biotechnology patents." Amgen had already filed dozens of applications, including one for its development of recombinant erythropoietin, which eventually turned into seven different patents. (The last one was issued in 1999.) As the 1980s went on, the company shifted its focus to clinical studies to mine its early efforts to produce potential products.

Meanwhile, the latest biotech slump was deepening. In December 1984 Amgen's stock dropped to $3.75 a share, about an 80 percent drop from its opening IPO—its lowest point in the company's twenty-five-year history. Other stocks were down, too: Genentech's stock to $10.50, Chiron's to $4.75, and Biogen's to $8.00. Amgen's losses that year were almost $5 million. Rathmann still had enough cash to build an EPOGEN®-based facility in Thousand Oaks to begin animal trials, but he needed more funding if he was to keep up with Genentech and the other leading biotechs.

Above: An early EPOGEN® T-shirt

HUMAN RECOMBINANT INTERLEUKIN-2

Human interleukin-2 (IL-2), or T-cell growth factor (TCGF), is a 133 amino acid protein which supports the proliferation and long term growth of T-cells (1-3). In addition, IL-2 stimulates production of cytotoxic lymphocytes (4-6), natural killer (NK) cells (7,8) and lymphokine-activated killer (LAK) cells (9) in human and mouse systems. The native molecule, isolated from conditioned media of cultured lymphocytes, has now been cloned and produced as a recombinant-DNA protein. Pure recombinant IL-2 offers the researcher the advantage of a product free from contamination by other cellular mitogens, growth factors, and lymphokines, as well as lot-to-lot consistency. Such uniform product performance is essential for obtaining reproducible results.

Amgen Biologicals offers two human recombinant interleukin-2 molecules to the research market: an IL-2 natural sequence analog (IL-2 [ns]) and an IL-2 alanine-125 analog (IL-2 [ala-125]). The IL-2 natural sequence analog has the identical 133 amino acid sequence of native human IL-2 as reported in the literature (10) with the addition of a methionine residue at the amino terminus. IL-2 [ns] has been reformulated in a new detergent-free aqueous buffer solution which offers the added benefit of storage at 2°-4°C, the same as our IL-2 [ala-125]. The alanine-125 analog has a single internal amino acid substitution of alanine for cysteine at residue 125. This substitution confers upon the molecule a three- to five-fold higher specific biological activity than IL-2 [ns] and other commercially available IL-2 preparations. It is the only commercially available IL-2 with a specific activity comparable to the BRMP reference standard (14) provided by the National Cancer Institute. On a unit basis, IL-2 [ns] and IL-2 [ala-125] demonstrate equivalent biological effects compared to naturally produced IL-2 as determined by various cell culture assay systems (11).

In the summer of 1984, Rathmann cut a deal with the Kirin Brewery Company of Japan, garnering $12 million in cash to develop an erythropoietin product, with Kirin, in essence, receiving the rights in certain parts of Asia and Japan. Other product deals were also bringing in revenue. Amgen was still partnered with Abbott in a five-year, $19 million contract to research diagnostics for bacteria, viruses, and cancer. The company had also entered deals with Texaco in 1985 and with Kodak in 1986 to develop specialty chemicals. Additional outside-funded projects included developing interferon for cattle and growth hormones for trout, salmon, and catfish.

Above: A marketing brochure put out by Amgen Biologicals. While scientists searched for breakthrough drugs in the early 1980s, this division sold interleukins, immune response modifiers, antibodies, growth factors, hematopoietic factors, assay systems, DNA probes, and specialty chemicals, bringing in enough revenue to keep the company afloat.

Kirin and Amgen

Not long after Fu-Kuen Lin cloned the erythropoietin gene, Robert Weist, Amgen's first senior vice president and general counsel, received a call from Japan. "Sam Shimosaka of Kirin Brewery called to congratulate us and asked if we'd be interested in talking to them," remembers Weist. "They already had the majority of the domestic beer market, and the Japanese government had suggested that they diversify into something else. They were experts in fermenting and had a few senior scientists who were interested in biotechnology."

Above: A Kirin logo from the EPOGEN® press packet, 1984

Not long after, the Kirin contingent arrived on a Saturday—and Weist, George Rathmann, Gordon Binder, and Dan Vapnek were ready to strike a deal. "They brought a case of Kirin beer," recalls Vapnek. "In the end, we agreed in general that they would put in $12 million, we'd keep the rights to erythropoietin in the United States, and they could have the rights in certain parts of Asia and Japan. And that was that. Three months later we basically had a signed agreement."

In the summer of 1984, Amgen and Kirin formed a joint venture known as Kirin-Amgen for the worldwide commercialization of erythropoietin. Capitalized at $24 million, Kirin provided $12 million, while Amgen contributed $4 million in cash and intellectual property valued at $8 million. The arrangement provided Amgen much-needed capital while giving Kirin an avenue to biotechnology and access to a new product.

Kirin-Amgen represents Amgen's longest-lasting partnership. "The partnership is the model for an exceptional business relationship," says CEO Kevin Sharer. "It is durable and based on mutual trust and respect. It is a bridge between two companies and two cultures, with one common goal: to improve patients' lives." △

Top: When Kirin's head, Sam Shimosaka, came courting with cash in 1984, George Rathmann cut a deal for Kirin to license Amgen's erythropoietin product in certain parts of Asia. *Above:* George Rathmann and Chi-Hwei Lin celebrate the Kirin deal, which took place in June 1984.

"We discovered things that had nothing to do with what our money providers were after," says Bowes, "but they were awfully important for us in building the science."

The most important collaboration was with Johnson & Johnson in 1985. The deal was potentially worth tens of millions of dollars for the development and commercialization of the hepatitis C vaccine and Interleukin-2®. Johnson & Johnson conducted the clinical trials and secured exclusive rights in certain markets, and Amgen received milestone payments. According to Amgen's 1986 annual report, Johnson & Johnson had the rights to commercialize Amgen's erythropoietin product in areas outside of the United States and Japan and in non-dialysis U.S. markets.

This agreement would later be the source of a series of disputes that lasted for more than fourteen years between Amgen and Johnson & Johnson. Unfortunately, Amgen had no other recourse but to sign the agreement. According to Rathmann, the original deal simply came at a time when the company was poised to move into human trials but lacked the cash.

To determine whether any of the drugs would be commercially viable, Rathmann and others met with patient groups that might benefit from the new products if they passed muster at the FDA. "When I got there," he says, "I was overwhelmed. I saw people lying like zombies on their beds. And you realize

Above: A Thousand Oaks News Chronicle story announces Amgen's licensing deal with Johnson & Johnson in 1985.

Opposite: The 1986 plans for the EPOGEN® manufacturing plant create a backdrop for Bob Andren (left), the plant's first manager, and Mark Witcher, who succeeded him.

EPOGEN® Human Trials

Human trials began on EPOGEN® in December 1985. In a 1987 article in the *New England Journal of Medicine,* Amgen clinicians reported that gene-spliced EPOGEN® had corrected anemia and eliminated the need for blood transfusions in all twenty-five kidney-dialysis patients treated with it in Phase I trials. Over the years, Amgen has heard testimony from hundreds of patients whose lives have changed as a result of the  drug. The following letter came from a patient in Phase III trials in 1987, written to nursing staff at St. John's Medical Center in Oxnard, California:

"Thought I'd drop you a line and tell you what's happening with me and the EPOGEN® study here at UCLA. Within five weeks my blood count has risen over 16 percent, from 24 percent to over 40 percent. They had to drop me off the [medicine] for a few days because of too rapid an increase. I never could have thought it would have worked this [well] and so quickly. *No more transfusions!* Day by day, I feel a little better, with more color in my skin tone, a little more energy, and a little more able to concentrate on things. Most of all, my appetite has grown to the point that I have to really watch my diet." △

Above: Jose Perez, a dialysis patient and EPOGEN® user, tends to his fruit trees.

why they're zombies." The kidney disease had made them severely anemic, and Rathmann wanted to help.

Mary Kenney, Rathmann's former assistant and now Amgen's associate manager of law administration, remembers a woman who participated in the EPOGEN® trials visiting Rathmann one day. "After she left," Kenney recalls, "George came out to say how this woman had not had any quality of life.

Below: This platform in Building 6 contained the cell culture media tanks used in manufacturing Epoetin alfa in the early 1990s.

Just going into a grocery store drained her energy level. Her whole life changed because of EPOGEN®. George was very emotional."

Today, these stories are especially poignant for Rathmann, who suffers from kidney disease. In March 2003 he began dialysis—and EPOGEN® treatments. "Because of EPOGEN®," he says, "I'm no zombie. That sounds like an ad, but it's a very different day than it was back then."

Right: Without patents, the creation of new drugs would not be financially viable. These patents were issued for NEUPOGEN® (left) on March 7, 1989, and EPOGEN® on October 27, 1987. Both were patented about three years after their filing dates.

In 1985 the company began building a production facility in Thousand Oaks and commenced human trials for gamma interferon—then considered one of Amgen's best blockbuster prospects—that April. That same year Mike Downing joined Amgen to run clinical trials.

Downing recounts, "From January to September 1985, Amgen filed five investigational new drug (IND) applications. We also launched clinical trials for each of these products."

The Comm[...]
and [...]

Has received [...]
for a new an[...]
and descripti[...]
closed. The [...]
been compli[...]
termined tha[...]
shall be grar[...]

Therefore, t[...]

Unit[...]

Grants to t[...]
title to this [...]
others from [...]
invention th[...]
of America[...]
years from [...]
ject to the p[...]
as provide[...]

Commissione[...]

Attest Meli[...]

The United States of America

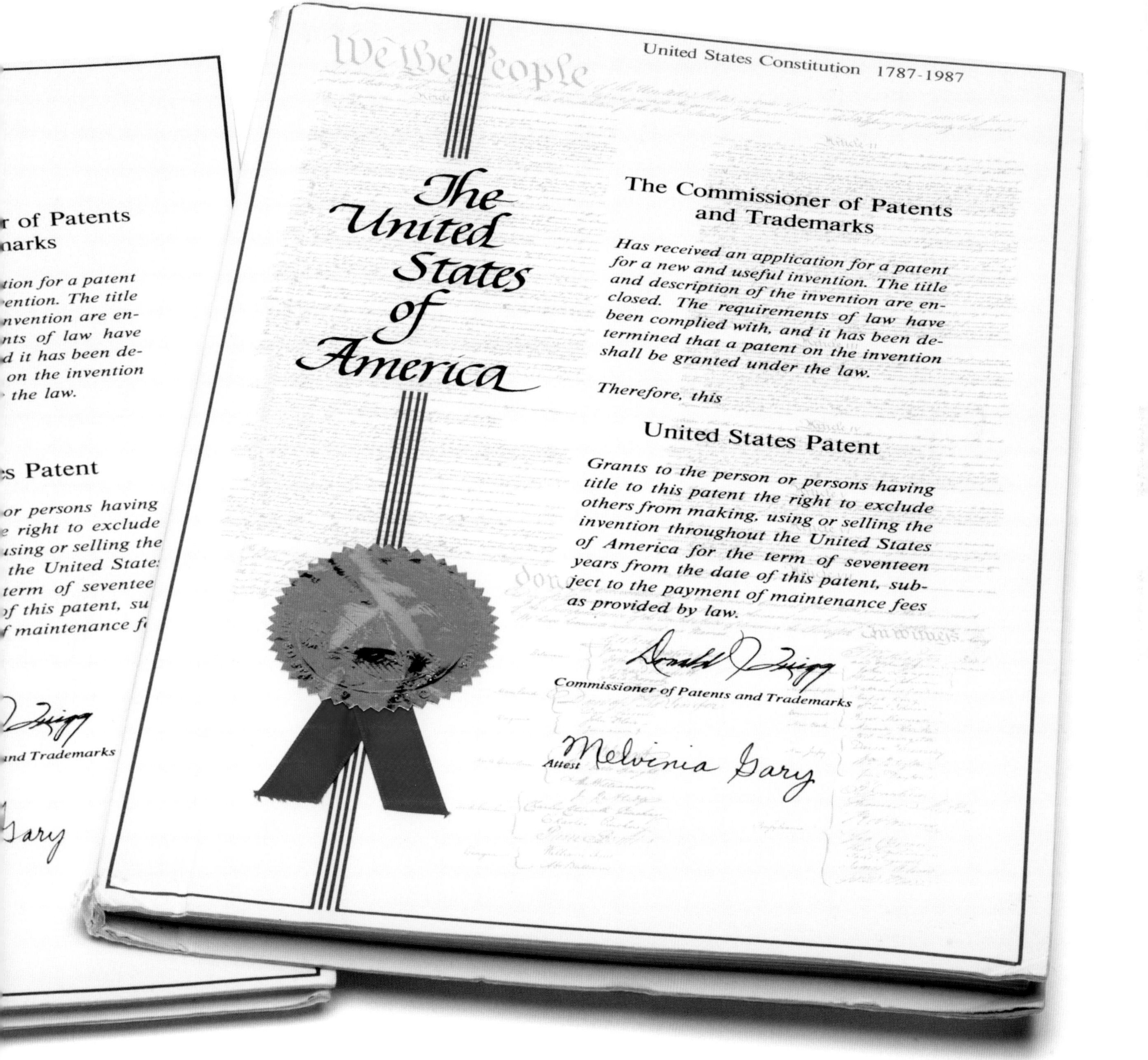

United States Constitution 1787-1987
We the People
The United States of America
The Commissioner of Patents and Trademarks
Has received an application for a patent for a new and useful invention. The title and description of the invention are enclosed. The requirements of law have been complied with, and it has been determined that a patent on the invention shall be granted under the law.
Therefore, this
United States Patent
Grants to the person or persons having title to this patent the right to exclude others from making, using or selling the invention throughout the United States of America for the term of seventeen years from the date of this patent, subject to the payment of maintenance fees as provided by law.
Commissioner of Patents and Trademarks
Attest Melvinia Gary

Simi Hostages

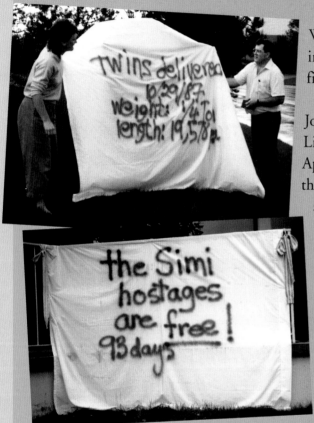

With Amgen staffers on the verge of turning EPOGEN® into their first marketable product, one giant step remained: filing reams and reams of FDA-required documentation.

In the fall of 1987, Amgen regulatory head Larry Johnson gathered up a team of twelve to prepare the Product License Application and the Establishment License Application, two forms that resulted in more than twenty thousand pages of paperwork. "We were already short on space at Amgen, so there was no room to spread everything out the way we needed to," recalls Ralph Smalling, then a regulatory affairs specialist and today Amgen's vice president of global R&D policy and analysis. "Although we were committed to the product, we faced many distractions in the office. It quickly became obvious that to take on this massive undertaking, we needed to get off campus."

So the staffers packed up their copy machines, paper, and pens—they did their work by longhand in those days—and headed for the Posada Royale Quality Inn in Simi Valley where a block of ten rooms became their new office space. The beds were replaced with tables, and regulatory administrative folks made numerous document runs each day, picking up raw materials for typing and returning with finished copies.

"We'd all work at Amgen for an hour or so in the morning, and then meet at the hotel around 9:00 a.m. to discuss what we needed to accomplish that day," Smalling explains. "Then we'd go to our rooms and work on addressing the FDA's

questions. Someone would knock on our doors around noon for lunch, then back we'd go. They'd knock again at 6:00 p.m. for dinner, and we'd work for a few more hours and go home to sleep. Then we'd start again the next day."

As members finished particular sections, they'd review them as a group and discuss areas for improvement. "We'd have fairly heated talks about what those documents needed to be," Smalling recalls. "You really had to check your ego at the door. But the wisdom of the group was always far better than the wisdom of one person."

The process went on for three long, grueling months. At the end, the team rented a truck to transport the binders—all copied in triplicate—to the airport to be shipped to the FDA.

When the team finally completed the file and shipped it out, clinical affairs director Mike Downing took his daughter's bed sheet and painted the words, "The Simi hostages are free! 93 days." The sheet hung over the entrance of Building 1 until George Rathmann asked that it be taken down because the company had not yet publicly announced the filing.

The original Simi Hostages set a precedent of willingness to do whatever it took to get the job done. In 1988, NEUPOGEN® product development team leader Mike Narachi and his team continued the sequestering spirit by renting a Westlake Village condo to prepare the NEUPOGEN® filings. These days, staffers adjourn to "war rooms" in the basement of Building 24.

"Looking back, sequestering ourselves was a perfect example of how we found creative ways to deal with huge challenges," Smalling says. "That type of spirit and thinking is what got us to where we are today." △

Above: Joan Egrie, who participated in the three-month filing, holds one of the infamous banners.

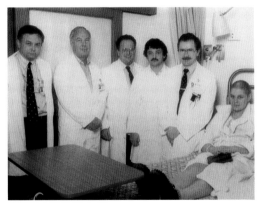

Above: The first bone marrow transplant patient receives G-CSF (later called NEUPOGEN®) from Amgen's clinical team in 1998 at the Royal Melbourne Hospital in Australia. From left: Richard Fox, Don Metcalf, George Morstyn, Nic Nicola, and Bill Sheridan.

Above: A G-CSF T-shirt

Opposite: A staffer manufactures G-CSF, which restores white blood cells after chemotherapy.

Of the five, only EPOGEN® was an unqualified success—ironic since Amgen had tried to partner with several of the Big Pharmas on the clinical trials, but none thought the market was big enough. The other four included Infergen™ for hepatitis C, gamma interferon, alpha interferon, and Interleukin-2® for cancer. All worked, but not very well. Other companies continued to pursue the drugs and put them on the market.

Amgen's second success story came in 1986, with successful human trials of G-CSF at Memorial Sloan-Kettering Cancer Center in New York City, and then later in Europe, Japan, and Australia. Larry Souza and Kirby Alton selected Australia as the site for G-CSF clinical trials because so much of the early science of colony stimulating factors had been developed there. George Morstyn was one of the principal investigators at Royal Melbourne. "We started in 1987, with Mike Downing carrying G-CSF to Australia in his luggage," he recalls. "I remember all the patients in our first study. They knew NEUPOGEN® might not help them, as some would need to start on low, almost ineffective doses to show the government the drug was safe. I was impressed with how committed they were to the study and to helping future patients, if not themselves."

Amgen Cowboys and Interferon

Convinced that alpha interferon could ward off disease, Amgen scientists went in search of an illness that would respond to it. They stumbled upon "shipping fever"— a condition that cattle acquire when moved by truck or railcar. "When you mix cattle, shipping them for twelve to twenty hours and then releasing them into a different climate, some of them lose weight and even die," explains Mike Narachi. "To see if interferon would prevent that, we planned a trial where we'd ship 750 cattle from Corvallis, New Mexico, to Boise, Idaho."

Trading their lab coats for cowboy hats and boots, the scientists got to work. The closest thing to a cow that East Coaster Dennis Fenton had seen was a dog. "I went to Corvallis and met my first cowboy," he recalls. "And he said, 'Okay, doc, the cow's going to come running down this chute. We're going to clamp its head, castrate it, and brand it. You just need to stick your needle in.' I was a vegetarian for weeks after that."

Meanwhile, Ralph Smalling filled the syringes with interferon and Narachi tagged the cattle's ears, keeping track of which cattle received the drug and which got the placebo. Kirby Alton was in charge of taking the temperatures—rectal temperatures—of the calves. "Instead of running out into the pens, a couple of them turned around and chased Kirby," Narachi chuckles.

The experiment was an interesting and worthwhile endeavor, but unfortunately, it didn't pan out. Amgen leaders decided to forego animal health therapeutics soon after. Ⓐ

Morstyn and his teams reported the many positive results to Amgen, which formed part of the data that led to the FDA approval of G-CSF—later named NEUPOGEN®. "After I joined Amgen in 1991, we obtained label extensions for the use of NEUPOGEN® in myeloid leukemia, severe chronic neutropenia, peripheral progenitor cell transplantation, and patients with AIDS in Europe," Morstyn recalls. "We were also able to apply what we learned to the development of Neulasta® and Aranesp®. Since then these drugs have helped millions of patients and have proven to be wonderful agents."

Now that EPOGEN® looked like a success, Rathmann began to focus on marketing—tougher for drug sales than for many other industries. On March 30, 1987, in anticipation of the FDA's approval of EPOGEN®, Paul Dawson was hired from G. D. Searle & Co. as the first vice president of sales and marketing. Dawson began hiring the first sales group in early 1988, with the goal of getting his people in their territories three to six months ahead of FDA approval. He was well prepared. FDA approval of EPOGEN® came in 1989.

Rathmann's Legacy

From the mid to the late 1980s, revenues continued to rise under Rathmann's leadership, hitting $10 million in 1985. The following year the company turned a small profit—$548,000 on $23.4 million in revenues, after $7.7 million dollars in losses the year before. That same year, in March

Below: Jill Heydock was no match in size to the 140 volumes of EPOGEN® FDA filing documentation, dated October 30, 1987. Today, such license filings can require up to four times that amount of electronic documentation.

1986, Amgen raised another $37 million in a public equity offering, and on February 17, 1987, the company reincorporated in Delaware as Amgen Inc. Meanwhile, the stock had rebounded from the pits of 1984 to $34.13.

On a roll, Amgen raised another $75 million in Amgen's third equity offering in 1987. By 1988 revenues had shot up to $44.3 million, with a profit of $1.7 million. Amgen had initiated clinical trials in fifteen countries and spent $39.2 million on R&D, three-and-a-half times more than in 1984.

Accolades—and media attention—began rolling in. In 1987 and 1988, Rathmann was awarded Biotechnology CEO of the Year and chaired the Industrial Biotechnology Association (later named the Biotechnology Industry Organization, or BIO) in Washington, D.C. He lobbied Congress against price controls, arguing that monetary regulation would stifle entrepreneurialism—emphasizing that most new drugs end up *saving* money in hospital costs. He also worked closely with former FDA commissioner David Kessler to speed up approvals of biotech drugs, with some success.

Meanwhile, Amgen's numbers kept getting better. By early 1987, the market cap was back above the bubble days in 1983, hitting $163.5 million. Amgen had also received approval of the first U.S. patent regarding recombinant erythropoietin, and manufacturing was preparing to produce five hundred thousand doses of recombinant DNA products, with a new $20 million,

HISTORICAL AMGEMS

Q: Prior to its approval, NEUPOGEN® was available under Emergency Drug Request, which had allowed Amgen to fill 150 requests. What country was this in?

A: Canada

Above: A staff member prepares for the NEUPOGEN® FDA filing in 1988.

Opposite: In 1994, the Thousand Oaks City Council voted to approve Amgen's Master Plan for the company's expansion over the next two decades. The plan was named Project of the Year by the Ventura and Santa Barbara County chapters of the National Society of Professional Engineers.

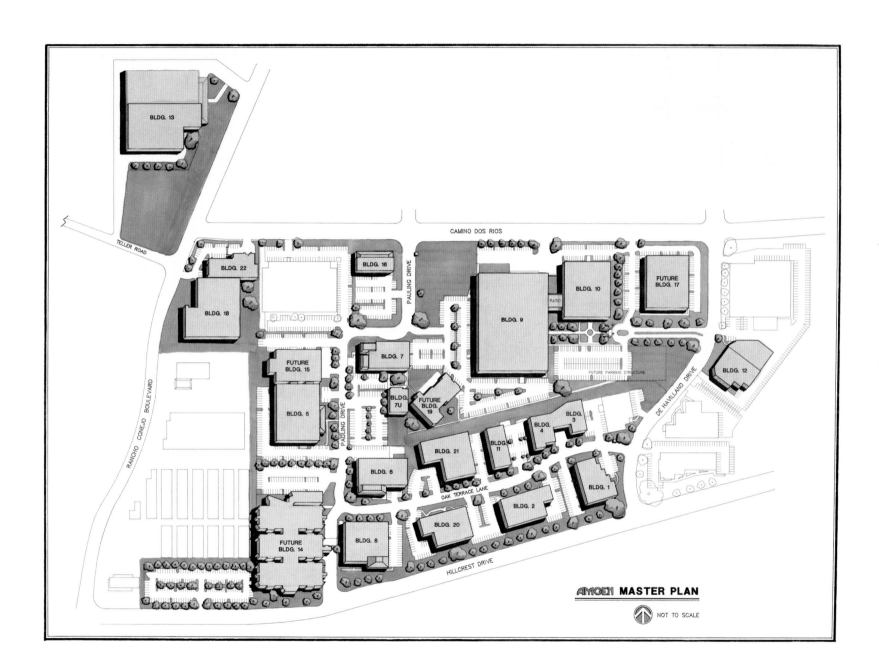

AMGEN **MASTER PLAN**

NOT TO SCALE

Above: George Rathmann's new job as CEO of ICOS made headlines at the *Los Angeles Times* in October 1991.

Opposite: This stainless steel tank in Building 6 is used to prepare nutrient media, which produces the crude EPOGEN® cell culture solution.

twenty-four-thousand-square-foot mammalian cell culture manufacturing facility for EPOGEN®, and a $13 million, fifty-nine-thousand-square-foot R&D building. Then, in October 1987, Amgen filed for FDA approval of EPOGEN®—more than twenty thousand pages of forms and data to use the product on chronic kidney disease patients on dialysis.

At the height of this surge, in October 1988, Rathmann walked into the board meeting and told the directors he planned to resign as president and CEO. Rathmann's reason was simple: He didn't want to run a company as big as Amgen was becoming. "I was worried that I was getting too old to really carry the burden of a company that size and magnitude," he recounts, "and there were people there that were capable of running the company. I figured that would be a great thing if they got a running start by launching EPOGEN® as the new management team."

Rathmann stayed active with the company as board chairman until 1990. He came in every day to an office in Building 10, and he was there when the FDA approved EPOGEN® on June 1, 1989. "We knew we needed to get on the market first," says Caroline Jewett, who began her Amgen career in the Building 6 manufacturing facility washing glassware and eventually went on to run the plant. "The day the approval came in, the champagne started flowing."

One month before Rathmann retired from the board in December 1990, Amgen's

850 staff members gathered to honor him and his wife, Joy. The couple was soon headed to Seattle, where Rathmann became CEO and chairman of ICOS Corporation. Mary Kenney, who joined Amgen in 1984, remembers the farewell ceremony: "Everybody got a George Rathmann mask with a T-shirt that imitated his tan jacket and tie. At some point in the script they made a comment about everyone beginning to look like George. And when he turned, everyone had on the masks. Then we gave George and Joy raincoats and umbrellas for their new home in Seattle."

Rathmann's successor, Gordon Binder, was promoted from CFO to CEO in 1988. He ushered in a new and promising era: EPOGEN® was awaiting approval by the FDA, NEUPOGEN® was not far behind, and once again the company was beginning to shift—this time to a biotech drug company with a blockbuster product.

Above and below: Required attire for George Rathmann's retirement party in December 1990: Rathmann masks, T-shirts designed to look like the tan jacket he often wore, and "I love Amgen" buttons.

The EPOGEN® Man: Fu-Kuen Lin

Today, the man whose erythropoietin clone launched a product that has treated millions of patients and earned tens of billions of dollars has retired to two loves: his garden, where he tends to more than one hundred avocado trees, and the study of traditional Chinese herbal medicine.

The interest in medicine was somewhat influenced by his father, a licensed traditional herbal doctor in Taiwan. One of eight children, Lin studied zoology and plant pathology at the National Taiwan University, then earned his Ph.D. at the University of Illinois, Urbana-Champaign in 1967. During post-doctorates in Indiana, Nebraska, Louisiana, and South Carolina, the peripatetic Lin picked up a broad knowledge of biology, biochemistry, genetics, and nucleic acid sequencing—and later recombinant DNA—before coming to Thousand Oaks to interview at Amgen.

"At the time," remembers Lin, "Amgen had the most advanced technology for sequencing amino acids in proteins. I was quite impressed when I talked with the scientists. I was so lucky because recombinant DNA work had just started at the time."

Lin, who had chosen to pursue erythropoietin, was one of seven scientists at Amgen. "When I joined," he recalls, "there was only Building 1. And there was one bench. Only two [people] could work at that bench at a time because the other part of the building that belonged to Amgen was still under construction." A few months later, he was given a longer, fifteen-foot bench.

For two years, Lin worked on the cloning problem. Though his fellow staff members admired his tenacity,

Above: Fu-Kuen Lin successfully cloned the erythropoietin gene in 1983—a key discovery that led to the development of Amgen's first blockbuster drug, EPOGEN®.

Above: Lin was featured on the cover of the December 1990 issue of *Nephrology News & Issues*, which honored Amgen's erythropoietin team with its Quality of Life Award. *Below:* An EPOGEN® napkin autographed by Lin for staff member Patty Biery. He wrote: "To Dear Patty, Long Live the EPOGEN®. Fu-Kuen."

Left: Fu-Kuen Lin in his organic garden at home near Thousand Oaks in 2004

Above: Researchers Linda Miller and Fu-Kuen Lin play volleyball at an early company picnic.

many thought he was wasting his time. "I really did not limit myself to work days from eight to five," he says. But he sets the record straight about one thing: "[Contrary to Amgen legend,] I did not have a cot in the lab. I lived only about twenty minutes from Amgen then, so it was convenient."

Lin explains his simple recipe for success: "Conventional thinking tells you everything is impossible," he says. "But then you have to think—you scratch your head, use your imagination, and you have to have an open mind. You try to override all the conventional wisdom and conventional thinking to make this impossible thing become possible." △

chapter two

← *Opposite:*
Wilhelmina Grant, a breast cancer survivor and NEUPOGEN® patient, says, "The only thing that helped me through chemotherapy was that I was able to continue working, attending karate classes, and enjoying normal activities because I never had a fever or an infection."

1989–1994

Breakout: Profits and Worldwide Expansion

"With EPOGEN® and NEUPOGEN® on the market and their tremendous sales, everybody and their brother wanted to be the next Amgen. Before then, there was a lot of hype around investing in biotech, but the stocks themselves hadn't performed well. By 1991 biotech was truly delivering on its promise to discover, develop, and commercialize drugs that were going to change medicine and create profits for shareholders. Amgen was delivering big time. For investors, this was the promise of what it was all about."

— **David Molowa, health-care analyst, UBS Securities LLC**

EPOGEN®
(Epoetin alfa)
Amgen clones erythro-poietin in 1983 and six years later, gains FDA approval for EPOGEN®.

NEUPOGEN®
(Filgrastim)
Approved in 1991, NEUPOGEN® is used to reduce infections in certain cancer patients receiving chemotherapy.

O n the morning of his thirty-second birthday, June 2, 1989, Steve Hale was at home in the San Fernando Valley. Watching CNN before heading in to work, he heard an announcement that he knew would radically change his day: The FDA had approved Amgen's first drug, EPOGEN®, the day before. ⚑ The approval marked the beginning of a tsunami of work—and a new era for the company. The six-foot-tall salesman raced out the door and drove to Amgen's Thousand Oaks campus, where the entire sales and marketing operation was housed in a trailer in the parking lot. There he met with Tommy Beard, vice president of sales. Beard told Hale to hurry to the distribution center to see what he could do to help. ⚑ Knowing that thousands of patients would benefit from the drug, Amgen staff had been working through the night to fill the first orders. At the warehouse, Hale filled his car with EPOGEN®—even placing product cartons under his seat and in his lap—and drove to UCLA Medical Center to distribute the first-ever commercial order. His first stop was the University of California, Los Angeles pharmacy. ⚑ "They had no idea what to do with me," he says. "So I went to the dialysis area, tracked down Dr. Nissenson, and told him I had a Jeep full of EPOGEN® for his dialysis patients." Dr. Allen R. Nissenson, professor of medicine and director of the dialysis program, headed with Hale to the dialysis center, where the

Opposite: Reviewing all franchise business plans, Jeanne Fitzgerald, senior director of marketing operations, and Ben Salazar, associate director, develop resource demand strategies that enable the team to successfully produce various marketing deliverables that the sales force uses to educate customers and patients.

FDA-approved EPOGEN® was administered to a chronic kidney disease patient—the first of several hundred thousand patients with this illness.

"It was just unbelievable," says Hale, who ended up with a double-parking ticket that day. "Thinking back, I probably had hundreds of thousands of dollars' worth of product in my Jeep."

Gordon Binder Jumps into a Maelstrom

George Rathmann's resignation as CEO in 1988 may have come as a surprise to many in the young company, but he had done a masterful job of preparing Amgen for the maelstrom about to be unleashed by the FDA's approval of EPOGEN®. Rathmann had not left the company; he continued working at the office each day as chairman of the board until he stepped down at the end of 1990. But despite all his preparations, the succession was rocky.

Rathmann had groomed two outstanding lieutenants in Gordon Binder, CFO, and Harry Hixson, senior vice president of business operations. Binder had been Amgen's CFO for six years after working at Litton Industries, Ford Motor Company, and System Development Corporation. In 1983 Binder had successfully executed Amgen's do-or-die IPO.

AMGEN

TURNOVER ORDER

1900 Oak Terrace Lane
Thousand Oaks, CA 91320
1-800 28 AMGEN

P. O. NUMBER	DATE	PHONE NUMBER	NAME
HB-272C06202	6/1/89	206-6555	R. Lewinsten

BILL TO	SHIP TO
Customer UCLA Medical Center	Customer UCLA MEDICAL CTR.
Address 10833 Le Conte	Address 630 Circle Dr. So.
City Los Angeles	City Los Angeles
State CA ZIP 90024-1709	State CA ZIP 90024
Attention C. Takazaki	Attention Pharmacy.

Primary Vendor 1) Bergen Brunswig #20622
Valencia, CA.

2) _____

NDC#	Prod#	Product Description	Quantity	Price/Box	Ext. Price
5551-3126-10		EPOGEN™ 2,000 u/ml 10 vials/bx			
5551-3148-10		EPOGEN™ 4,000 u/ml 10 vials/bx	10cs		
5551-3144-10		EPOGEN™ 10,000 u/ml 10 vials/bx	10c$		
				TOTAL	

Order Taken By: STEVE HALE Order Given By: Lewinsten

Territory # 80703 Title: _____

Signature: _____

white - Wholesaler   yellow - Hospital/Dialysis Center   pink - Representative   goldenrod - District Manager

---

March 7, 1989
Amgen receives its first U.S. patent for recombinant G-CSF (NEUPOGEN®).

1989
Immunex clones TNF receptor, later patented and named Enbrel®.

June 1, 1989
The FDA approves EPOGEN® for anemia management associated with end-stage renal disease.

1989
EPOGEN® is named "Product of the Year" by Fortune *magazine.*

1989
Amgen establishes European headquarters in Lucerne, Switzerland.

1990
George B. Rathmann retires from the board.

1990
Gordon M. Binder is elected chairman of the board.

February 21, 1991
The FDA approves NEUPOGEN® to decrease the incidence of infection associated with chemotherapy-induced neutropenia in patients with non-myeloid cancers receiving myelosuppressive chemotherapy.

March 5, 1991
The U.S. Court of Appeals for the Federal Circuit rules that Amgen's patent regarding recombinant erythropoietin is valid, enforceable, and infringed by Genetics Institute.

1991
Amgen breaks ground in Puerto Rico for its Fill and Finish facility and in Louisville for its Distribution Center.

Hixson, on the other hand, specialized in operations, marketing, and manufacturing. A former colleague of Rathmann's from Abbott, Hixson joined Amgen in the summer of 1985 as vice president of business development.

Both candidates were qualified but very different in personality, background, and leadership style. Rathmann and the board ultimately decided to name Binder as CEO and Hixson as president and COO in 1988.

Under this leadership arrangement, the Binder era began. Binder's style differed sharply from his predecessor's flamboyant but grandfatherly approach. "At fifty-three, Binder is thin, controlled, and more obviously stand-offish [than Rathmann]," wrote *California Business* in an October 1991 article about the Rathmann-Binder transition. "His skin is taut and tan, maintained by a regimen of tennis in the California sun."

The son of school-teachers, Binder won an ROTC scholarship to Purdue University in 1953

and joined the navy in 1957, serving as a junior officer on the aircraft carrier USS *Intrepid.* After his stint in the service, he went on to earn an MBA from Harvard University in 1962. "Gordon was a quiet, strong presence. But when he said something, it was usually pretty interesting," says Amgen board member Steve Lazarus of ARCH Venture Partners, who joined the board in 1987 and retired in 2004. "By the time Binder became CEO, we could no longer improvise in the way in which the company moved. We had to start systematizing it."

Mary Kenney, former administrative assistant to Rathmann and Binder, remembers Binder's silent strength in the face of enormous responsibility. "Gordon gave you the impression that everything was going to be fine," she says.

In reality, Binder faced a monumental challenge: sharing the leadership of the company with the more colorful and outgoing Hixson. "For two years, there was an uneasy peace," says Phil Whitcome. Rathmann recognized the unspoken conflict, too. "Probably there was some incompatibility," he agrees. "Though they did work together very well, when they had a gun at their heads. And I was the gun."

Above: An early EPOGEN® brochure

1991
Amgen establishes the Amgen Foundation for charitable giving.

1991
NEUPOGEN® is named "Product of the Year" by Fortune magazine.

1992
Kevin W. Sharer is elected president and chief operating officer.

1992
Number of staff: 2,335

1992
Amgen debuts at No. 427 on the FORTUNE 500 list.

1992
Amgen reaches sales of more than $1 billion.

March 9, 1993
The Puerto Rico Fill and Finish facility opens.

1994
Number of staff: 3,396

1994
The FDA approves NEUPOGEN® for patients undergoing bone marrow transplantation and for patients with severe chronic neutropenia.

1994
Amgen is ranked No. 326 on the FORTUNE 500 list.

1994
Amgen receives the U.S. Department of Commerce National Medal of Technology—the first biotech firm and one of only five corporations ever to receive this honor.

December 29, 1994
Amgen completes its acquisition of Synergen.

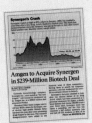

Below: In July 1990 the *New York Times* announces Amgen's appointment of Gordon Binder as chairman of the board.

New Amgen Chairman

Special to The New York Times

SAN FRANCISCO, July 24 — Amgen Inc., a biotechnology company based in Thousand Oaks, Calif., said today that Gordon M. Binder, its chief executive, had been named chairman. He succeeds George B. Rathmann, who was re-elected to the board and will serve as chairman emeritus. Dr. Rathmann said the move completed a management transition begun two years ago when Mr. Binder came on board as chief executive, along with Harry Hixson, Amgen's president and chief operating officer. Dr. Rathmann, who guided Amgen from its founding to the introduction of its first product a year ago, has recently been involved in the start-up of a new biotechnology company called Icos, which will develop drugs to treat inflammatory diseases like arthritis.

The matter intensified when Rathmann announced he was resigning from the board and moving to Seattle to join ICOS. By this point it was evident that "one person had to be in charge," says Rathmann. On February 7, 1991, Hixson left Amgen. From there he moved on to become chairman of the board of directors at BrainCells Inc. and Sequenom Inc. in San Diego.

Now firmly in control as chairman and CEO, Binder set about transforming Amgen into a full-fledged company. He continued the projects Rathmann started, building manufacturing, sales, and marketing capacity, while ramping up R&D and revenues. "He kept his foot on the gas pedal," says Tim Osslund.

Binder's strong financial background made him popular with Wall Street, but he also kept the scientists happy. "Even though Gordon came from the finance side, he understood it was research and development that got us here," says Dan Vapnek, former head of research. Bill Bowes agrees, saying, "Gordon knew how to build a company, and he loved the science. He grew in the job, and became an exceptional CEO." Binder explains that in those days, it was easier for someone without a science background to head up a biotech. "The science was embryonic," he says. "It would be harder today for someone knowing nothing but some math and chemistry."

Binder was not the chum that Rathmann liked to be with his managers and staff, but he became a shrewd judge of talent. Dennis Fenton says Binder's skill in assessing people and his willingness to take risks transformed Amgen and the life of its staff. With the unexpected death of Paul Dawson, Amgen's first head of sales and marketing, in February 1992, Binder needed to select a new leader— a difficult task given Dawson's huge popularity and successful track record.

Fenton recalls: "I remember the day Gordon called me in his office and he said, 'So, Dennis, have you ever thought about running sales and marketing?' And I looked at him and I thought, 'He's confused.' I said, 'Gordon, you have the wrong meeting. This is Dennis.' He said, 'No, I think you'd be really good at running sales and marketing.' I said, 'Gordon, I don't have an MBA. I don't even own a suit.' And he proceeded to say, 'You're exactly what Amgen needs.'"

The job—and Binder's faith in him— changed the course of Fenton's career. "I was an introverted scientist, didn't like to talk in public, hated to get behind a podium, and needed a lot of data to make decisions," says Fenton. "I said, 'Gordon, what if I fail?' He said, 'Look me in the eye—you'll be okay.' I trusted him and jumped."

Binder was also shrewd about details and the bottom line. Ed Garnett, former vice president of human resources, recalls one day in 1991, shortly after Binder had asked Garnett (then Amgen's logistics director) to ensure that the first NEUPOGEN® order would be shipped within a day of FDA approval. "All of a sudden," recalls Garnett, "there's Gordon Binder behind me, just standing there, very quiet.

Above: Gordon Binder was featured in a 1992 issue of *Fortune* magazine. *Forbes* magazine called him one of biotech's "most respected business minds." *BusinessWeek* called him "Amgen's Ace" and crowned him one of the top twenty-five managers in the world.

Opposite: Eric Bergeson (left), who went on to become Amgen's vice president of operations in Colorado, explains the erythropoietin purification process to Senator Dianne Feinstein at the EPOGEN® plant in Building 6.

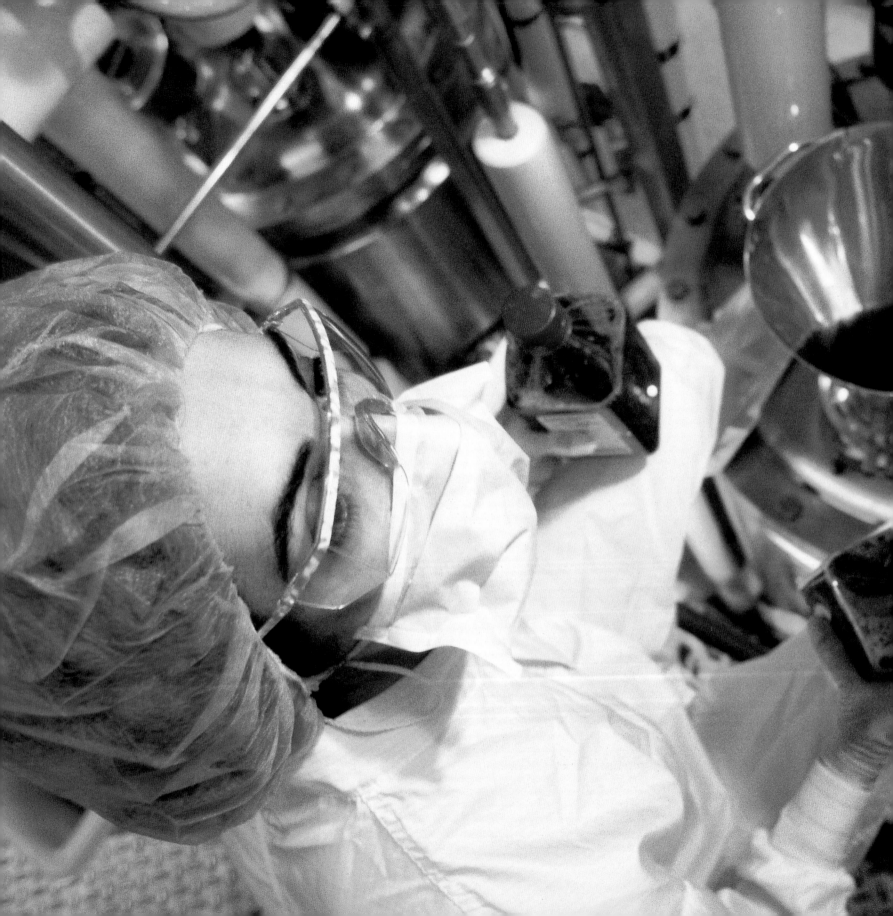

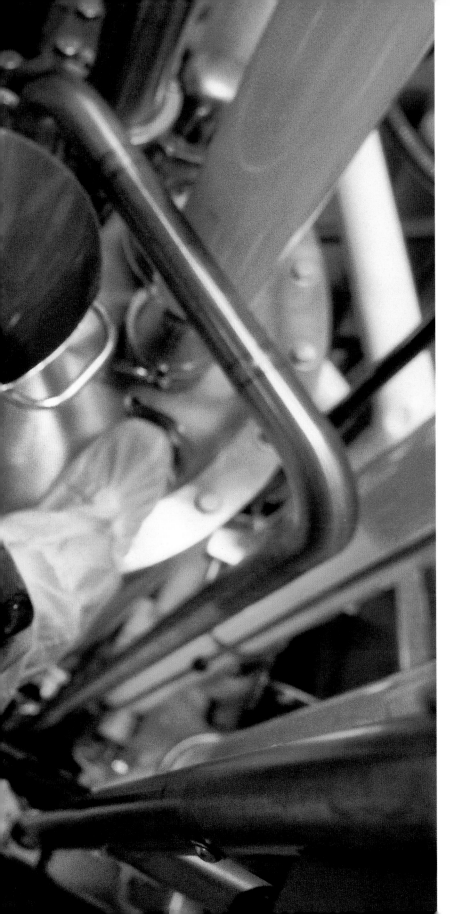

"He said, 'Ed, what the heck are these bills for—$85,000 for jet chartering?' I said, 'Well, those were the jets that brought the product out here.' And he asked, 'Well, don't you think you should have gotten approval?' I said, 'Don't you recall telling me you wanted to ship the very next day? We shipped $50 million worth of product thanks to those jets.' Binder said, 'Good investment.' And he walked out. He and I still laugh over that."

The Onslaught of EPOGEN®

In 1989, nine years after Amgen was incorporated, the company launched its first major product. Now employing 350 staff members, Amgen had spent more than $300 million to launch EPOGEN®, and expected to sell about $500 million in product a year—a goal that would vastly underestimate global sales. (As of March 31, 2004, cumulative sales of EPOGEN® had reached $18.2 billion.)

Cooley Godward lawyer Alan Mendelson remembers the electric energy on campus. "It was such an exciting place to be," says Mendelson. "We all felt we were on sort of a mission, both scientifically and otherwise."

Harry Hixson recalls gearing up the manufacturing facility in Building 6 for the expected rush of orders: "The EPOGEN® clinical trials had proceeded nicely, so we committed funds to build the EPOGEN® plant, which cost $20 million. When we committed to build the plant, we had $25 million in the bank; we were betting the house.

Above: Russell Edwards (left), regional director of Southeast Asia and Amgen Australia, and Ed Garnett, former vice president of human resources in 1999

Left: Manufacturing associate Lily Ansari handles bottles of fetal bovine serum used to batch growth media for EPOGEN®.

Manufacturing EPOGEN®

For fifteen years, Building 6 was one of Amgen's most energetic and profitable facilities. Construction began on the company's original EPOGEN® plant in 1986, and two years later, its doors opened. Inside the plant stood two large and two small stainless steel tanks, which methodically turned three thousand plastic roller bottles filled with red liquid once every minute. The room was always quiet, the only sounds being the low hum of machinery and the barely audible "swoosh" of churning fluids.

Building 6 was the world's only EPOGEN® facility until Amgen's Longmont, Colorado, plant opened in 1996. "This room is the premier model of America's prowess in biotechnology," wrote *California Business* in October 1991. It was also one of the most profitable facilities around. The plant was built to produce about two hundred grams of EPOGEN® a year. But it was so successful that by 1999, the facility was making as many grams in just one lot. "We have manufactured billions of dollars' worth of EPOGEN® in Building 6 through the years, and we made Ortho's Procrit® product there, too," recalls Bob Andren, then the plant manager. "It was Amgen's first large-scale production facility, and we tried to anticipate what the FDA would be looking for so that we could get its approval for manufacturing."

For many, the building held a lot of sentimental value. By the time it produced its last batch of EPOGEN® in 2003—it closed due to age, upgrade costs, and other business considerations—eight couples had met there and married. "As one of the last staff members in Building 6, it was my job to lock the door and turn off the lights," says Joe Cochran. "It was hard to do. I had some of the best memories of my career in that building. Working there was something we were all truly proud of." △

Above: Mark Witcher (middle) meets with Gordon Binder and former president Jimmy Carter. Carter came to Amgen in July 1991 to express his gratitude for the company's donation of 398,000 vials of EPOGEN® to China through Global 2000, a branch of the Carter Center dedicated to improving health and agricultural services in developing nations.

"Building 6 is the gold standard from a manufacturing perspective. We had a lot of challenges, but we went almost five years straight with 100 percent success. People in that plant were extremely dedicated and we were constantly working to meet the demand. There was a level of commitment and accountability that as a plant manager I struggle to recreate today."

— Caroline Jewett, operations, hired in 1987

Opposite: A close-up of EPOGEN® fermenters in Building 6 during the early 1990s

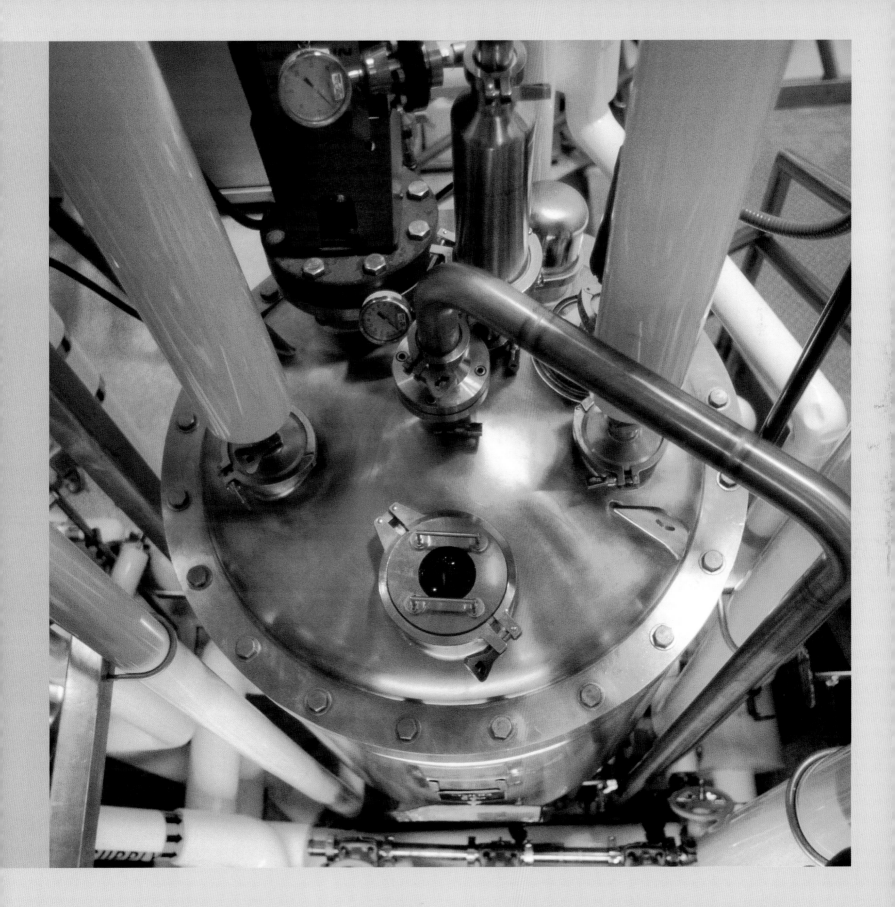

epo Is Coming!

Dated material enclosed of interest to business and science writers on the third major human hormone produced by genetic engineering.

Above: Press materials from May 1984 detailed Fu-Kuen Lin's successful cloning of the erythropoietin gene and Amgen's new deal with Kirin.

Below: In 1989 *Fortune* magazine named EPOGEN® one of its products of the year.

The first day, we shipped $20 million worth of product. So it paid off."

Bob Andren, who designed and oversaw the facility's construction and operations—and then ran the plant—concurs: "That plant has made $8 billion in EPOGEN® revenue. In fact, it far outperformed anything we could have imagined. For our first lot of EPOGEN®, just nineteen grams came out of the purification area. By 1996, the plant was making twenty-five times that amount. There was tremendous pressure on everyone, but we had a lot of confidence in ourselves."

EPOGEN® was an instant hit with everyone—patients, physicians, nurses, pharmacists, investors, and the media. *Fortune* named it "Product of the Year," *Business Week* called it one of 1989's best products, and *Science* magazine lauded EPOGEN® as the "most productive scientific molecule."

By the summer of 1990, 65 percent of eligible patients were receiving EPOGEN®, some fifty-five thousand dialysis patients with chronic kidney disease. On April 20, 1990, Kirin Brewery of Japan, Amgen's partner in Kirin-Amgen, received approval from the Japanese Ministry of Health to market its erythropoietin product to dialysis patients in Japan. Meanwhile, Johnson & Johnson, under its license with Amgen, was selling its erythropoietin product Procrit® in the United States and abroad.

In 1990, total revenues bounced up 102 percent—from $147.6 million to $298.7 million—and Amgen stock blasted to a high of

$149 after a two-for-one split, giving the company a market cap of $6.4 billion, one third larger than drug giant Warner-Lambert. On August 25, Amgen was added to the NASDAQ 100 Index.

During this time, Amgen began a public education effort that included extensive educational programs for dialysis patients and support programs for nephrologists, dialysis nurses, administrators, and pharmacists. The company that had as recently as 1983 struggled to stay afloat was now issuing grants and financial support to organizations such as the National Kidney Foundation and the American Academy of Nephrologists, while establishing programs to distribute both low-cost and free EPOGEN® to patients in need.

Lightning Strikes Twice

Now just a decade old, Amgen was fortunate to have one major product on the market that was bringing in hundreds of millions of dollars and impacting tens of thousands of patients. But the company was about to experience a phenomenon virtually unprecedented in the drug industry: the launch of two blockbuster products in less than two years. While EPOGEN® vials were moving like wildfire, Amgen's recombinant granulocyte-colony stimulating factor (G-CSF) was completing its final human testing, which consisted of more than forty trials, 150 sites, and one thousand patients worldwide.

On February 21, 1991, NEUPOGEN® was approved by the FDA to decrease the incidence of infection associated with chemotherapy-induced neutropenia in patients with

Below: One of five Diana Awards given to Amgen by the Healthcare Distribution Management Association, formerly the National Wholesale Druggists' Association (NWDA). Amgen received this award in 1991 for "Best New Product Introduction" for the launch of NEUPOGEN®. The NWDA also lauded Amgen in 1996, 1998, 2001, and 2003.

The Science of NEUPOGEN®

"It's been very rewarding to watch cancer patients get the chemotherapy treatment they need without having to put up with the side effects. That's thanks to NEUPOGEN®."

— Dr. Linda Bosserman, medical oncologist, San Antonio Community Hospital

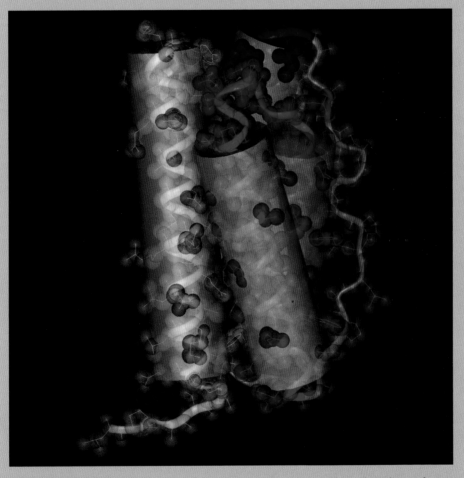

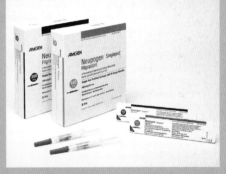

NEUPOGEN® (Filgrastim) is produced by bacteria through genetic engineering and recombinant DNA technology. The drug is similar to the naturally occurring protein granulocyte-colony stimulating factor (G-CSF), which is produced by the immune system and stimulates the formation of neutrophils, a type of white blood cell. Neutrophils are responsible for detecting and destroying harmful bacteria and some fungi. When the white blood cell count is low—often as a result of chemotherapy—the human body is much more vulnerable to infections and fevers. NEUPOGEN® can help by stimulating white blood cells in the bone marrow to multiply and form colonies. By reducing the time it takes to recover the white blood cell count, NEUPOGEN® helps decrease the incidence of febrile infection in people undergoing chemotherapy.

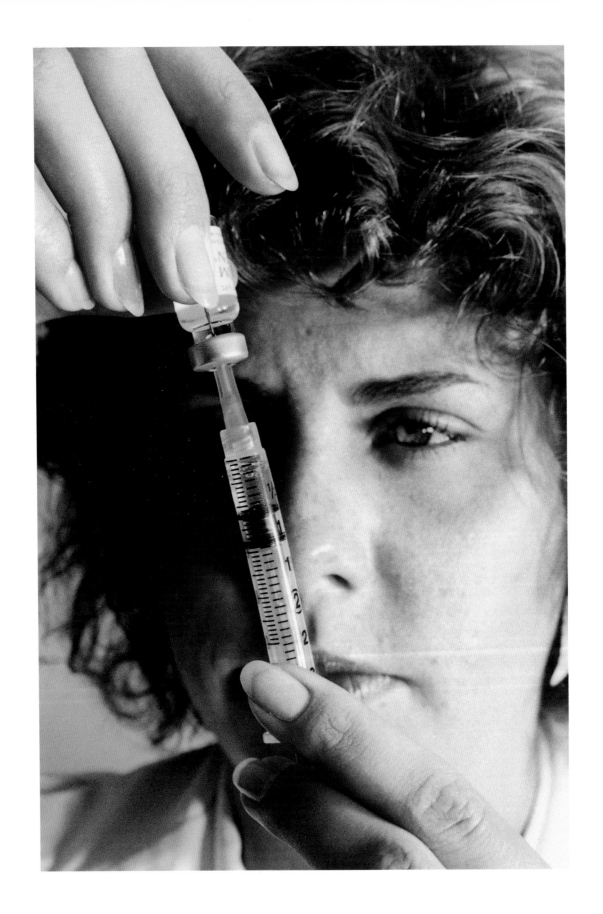

non-myeloid cancers receiving myelosuppressive chemotherapy. The drug promptly brought in $50 million in its first two days on the market, swelling to $233 million in its first year. EPOGEN® and NEUPOGEN® ranked second and fourth respectively in first-year sales for all U.S. pharmaceuticals, and *Fortune* magazine named NEUPOGEN® the "Product of the Year" in 1991, adding that the drug was "following hard on the same designation for EPOGEN®" in 1989.

Opposite: Mary Davis, medical oncology nurse manager at Saint Joseph Hospital in Chicago, prepares a syringe with NEUPOGEN®.

Above: Mike Narachi, George Morstyn, and Martha Vincent at a NEUPOGEN® Advisory Board meeting in December 1990

To help facilitate FDA approvals and handle government-related revenue issues, Peter Teeley joined Amgen in 1993 as vice president of government affairs, opening an office in Washington, D.C. A former press secretary to President George H. W. Bush and ambassador to Canada, Teeley's responsibilities included working with the U.S. Health Care Finance Administration (HCFA) to ensure that EPOGEN® had Medicare coverage and coding for billing, and lobbying for FDA reforms to speed up and streamline the drug approval process. "The issue of reimbursement is critical to Amgen physicians," explains Teeley. "Gordon and I worked closely together, talking four to five times a day."

Above: Peter Teeley, former vice president of government affairs

Amgen Ascendant

As Amgen's product sales skyrocketed and its staff increased by the thousands, Binder and his

The Day After: The First Shipment of NEUPOGEN®

In mid-February 1991, Gordon Binder sent word to Ed Garnett to get the first shipment of NEUPOGEN® out within a day of FDA approval. It was, Garnett remembers, touch and go.

"We were making our first shipment through Federal Express, $50 million worth," says Garnett, who was director of logistics before going on to lead human resources. "I was worried, though, that the plane wouldn't be big enough to hold the entire shipment, so I told my distribution guy, 'You'd better call Federal Express and make sure we're covered.' So he called and asked, 'What kind of plane do you have down at LAX?'"

Lined up at the FedEx terminal were the delivery company's normal DC-8s—large planes, but not big enough to transport Amgen's entire shipment of NEUPOGEN®. "As I suspected," Garnett relays, "the FedEx guy called back and said, 'Uh-oh, we need a 767 for that. We wouldn't be able to ship it all.'" He shakes his head. "Well, thank God we made that call, because the last thing we could do is have our product, which requires refrigeration, sitting on a tarmac somewhere."

In the end, the crew shipped the NEUPOGEN® order on time. "The teams worked all night," says Garnett, "but we did it." ⚖

Below: Over the years, Amgen staffers have started various company teams. In 1989, a few avid bowlers formed an Amgen league and printed T-shirts, calling themselves "CHO Time!"

senior management worked hard to preserve the sense of community and entrepreneurialism that distinguished the early days. During the early 1990s the company's famous "Chili Cook-Offs" began, where teams with names like "Keep Your Chaps On" and "Red Hot Silly Peppers" battled to create the tastiest, most tongue-searing chili. Fermentation Seminars, softball and Frisbee games, volunteerism, and other social events also brought a spirit of fun to a company immersed in a period of exhilarating—if exhausting—hard work.

Amgen's high-octane but people-oriented culture—nurtured by both George Rathmann and Gordon Binder—was also influenced by its Southern California location. The campus itself had become aesthetically pleasing, with sprawling lawns, shrubbery, and low, earth-toned buildings, and it featured such perks as an on-site gym and child-care center. Ed Garnett says Adele Binder, Gordon Binder's wife, strongly supported the idea for a day care center.

"She thought that as an organization, we were a very high-stress company," says Garnett. "We worked long hours. And she said, quite frankly, 'If you're going to work people that hard, have a place for the kids.'"

Gordon Binder also expanded Amgen's

BUSINESS

Amgen building child-care center

Conejo Valley company breaks ground on facility that will serve children of employees beginning in '93

By JIM PONDER
News Chronicle

THOUSAND OAKS — Four small children ushered in a big project at Amgen Inc. Monday afternoon — a 33,000-square-foot child-care center to be completed by the spring of next year.

Several hundred Amgen employees and some of their children were on hand for the groundbreaking of the child care center, the first of its kind in the Conejo Valley.

When completed next year, Amgen's $4 million center will have a 160-child capacity for ages 6 weeks to 5 years, company spokeswoman Kimberly Dorsey said. The center also will contain a gymnasium and conference rooms.

Amgen Chairman and Chief Executive Officer Gordon Binder said company officials "agonized" over the decision whether or not a facility should be built. Questions such as legal liability and fairness to employees without children had to be considered, he said.

The decision was made to go ahead and now construction is scheduled to begin immediately, Dorsey said.

Employees with children will have to pay a price comparable to other day-care facilities in the area, she said.

Any of Amgen's more than 1,500 employees who work at the 50-acre Thousand Oaks campus may use the facility. If demand should exceed its capacity, then slots in the center will be determined by lottery, Dorsey said.

Having child care at the workplace will be a benefit for Amgen employees Chris and Marian Giffin of Simi Valley. The Giffins' 4-year-old daughter Sarah attends day care in Newbury Park.

"There's a lot of upside," Chris Giffin said. "We're planning to have a second child. This is an opportunity to have the children at hand."

Giffin also said having his daughter close by will bring more peace of mind. Parents will be able to visit their children during the work day, Dorsey said.

Sarah Giffin, 4, Dylan Betancourt, 3, Carrie Nasby, 2, and Joshua Craft, 1, left to right, help to lift the first shovels of dirt Monday during a groundbreaking ceremony for a new child care center at Amgen Inc. in Thousand Oaks.
LUCIANNE GARBINI/Special to The News Chronicle

community outreach when the company launched an in-house summer sabbatical program for high school teachers, an eight-part lecture series for students, and a biotechnology lab kit for biology classes. Amgen increased its funding to university programs and studies as well, including the endowment of a professorship at the University of Chicago in 1991 and the launch of the Amgen Center for Molecular Biology at Spelman College in Atlanta, an institution dedicated to the education of African American women.

Revving Up from Small to Large

With the success of EPOGEN® and NEUPOGEN®, the company was ready to focus exclusively on human therapeutics. In 1991 Binder decided to license Amgen's chemical products and sell off its diagnostics unit. He also dissolved its animal research projects. The following year, Amgen opened a new Distribution Center in Louisville, Kentucky, and it established a new Fill and Finish facility in Puerto Rico in 1993.

Top: The *Thousand Oaks News Chronicle* noted the groundbreaking for Amgen's childcare facility.

Above: A happy youngster at the center, which opened in 1993

Opposite: (From left) Adele and Gordon Binder, Marion and Chris Giffin with daughter Sarah, Debbie Betancourt with son Dylan, Wayne and Linda Nasby with daughter Carrie, Ginger Craft with son Joshua, Susanne Hersh, and Karyn Evens

Giving Back for Good:
Amgen Staff Donates Time, Money, and Heart

Top: As a volunteer pilot for Angel Flight West, Amgen's David Salo often flies patients and their families to doctor appointments. From left: The plane's owner, Kendall Hales; a patient and his wife; and Salo

Above: Research director Frank Martin is just one of the many Amgen staffers who take their love of science to the classroom. In this 1995 photo, Martin guides students in an experiment at Walnut Elementary School in Thousand Oaks.

Amgen's products have allowed the company to give back to the Thousand Oaks community—and ultimately, to communities all over the world.

"Once we began generating revenue," recalls Joe Staines, Amgen's former tax director, "various groups at Amgen began making donations. We soon realized that we needed to coordinate those efforts." Staines formed the Amgen Foundation in 1991 and the Amgen Matching Gift Program, which matches staff members' donations to qualifying charities, in 1993. Since then, the Amgen Foundation has donated more than $37 million, including $5 million in matching donations, to such organizations as the Arthritis Foundation, the Los Angeles Philharmonic, the California Science Center, Meals on Wheels, and Habitat for Humanity.

Today, Amgen staffers continue to find ways to share their time and resources. David Salo and Bruce Martin, for example, put their piloting skills to use for Angel Flight West, a service that provides free air transportation for patients unable to access or afford travel to medical centers. "For me, it provides a whole different perspective," says Salo, corporate accounts health systems manager. "At work, I sell our drugs and focus my attention on doctors. But when I volunteer for Angel Flight, I transport patients to doctors who are helping to save their lives. Often, it's the very same doctors I call on. It's an incredibly rewarding experience."

"Pilots are always looking for any excuse to fly," adds Martin, senior manager of corporate security, who flies for Angel Flight West every few months in his Piper Cherokee 140. "So why not do something that matters?" This conviction is one that hundreds of Amgen staff members share. And through the efforts of Martin, Salo, Staines, and others like them, Amgen has been able to help not only patients, but also hundreds of organizations around the world. ⌂

"As a values-driven company, Amgen sees corporate citizenship as more than just a responsibility. It's an integral part of who we are and a natural extension of our commitment to dramatically improving people's lives."

— Kevin Sharer, CEO, hired in 1992

Amgen has a long history of encouraging staff to participate in volunteer projects. *Clockwise from top left:* An Amgen participant in the community's Oak Tree Reforestation Project in November 1995; children leaving their handprints in cement on the Amgen campus during a Make-A-Wish Foundation event; Steve Schoch and local kids at play; Amgen volunteers helping build a house for Habitat for Humanity; Mike Savin (standing) at work for the March of Dimes; and Alan Solinger volunteering at the UCLA Arthritis Clinic

The Amgen sales force was now working in all fifty states and the Commonwealth of Puerto Rico.

In 1993 Binder dramatically increased research and development spending from $63 million in 1989 to $255 million. The leading candidates for blockbuster number three were Infergen™ for hepatitis C, in human trials in the early 1990s, and stem cell factor (SCF), which began clinical trials in 1993 for high-dose chemotherapy patients. SCF was designed to be administered with NEUPOGEN® to patients whose immune systems were compromised by chemotherapy. The combination of the drugs helped mobilize immature blood cells—peripheral blood progenitor cells (PBPCs)—from the bone marrow into the bloodstream. In addition, scientist Steve Elliott was leading a group that was looking for novel erythropoietin analogues that would be bioengineered to increase the production of red blood cells and last longer with fewer shots.

Then, in 1994, Amgen completed its purchase of Colorado-based Synergen for $254 million, paying $9.25 a share for a company that two years earlier had been selling at $67 a share. Binder decided to keep the new acquisition's inflammation projects at Synergen's facility in Boulder, but moved its neurobiological research to Amgen's facility in Thousand Oaks.

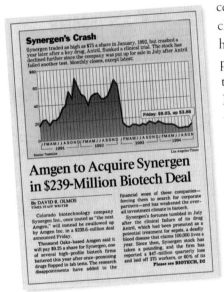

Synergen's Crash

Synergen traded as high as $75 a share in January, 1992, but crashed a year later after a key drug, Antril, flunked a clinical trial. The stock has declined further since the company was put up for sale in July after Antril failed another test. Monthly closes, except latest:

Friday: $9.03, up $3.66

Source: TradeLine — Los Angeles Times

Amgen to Acquire Synergen in $239-Million Biotech Deal

By DAVID R. OLMOS
TIMES STAFF WRITER

Colorado biotechnology company Synergen Inc., once touted as "the next Amgen," will instead be swallowed up by Amgen Inc. in a $239.6-million deal announced Friday.

Thousand Oaks-based Amgen said it will pay $9.25 a share for Synergen, one of several high-profile biotech firms battered this year after once-promising drugs flopped in lab tests. The research disappointments have added to the financial woes of these companies—forcing them to search for corporate partners—and has weakened the overall investment climate in biotech.

Synergen's fortunes tumbled in July after the clinical failure of its drug Antril, which had been promoted as a potential treatment for sepsis, a deadly blood disease that claims 100,000 lives a year. Since then, Synergen stock has taken a pounding, and the firm has reported a $47-million quarterly loss and laid off 375 workers, or 60% of its

Please see BIOTECH, D2

Above: The *Los Angeles Times* announced Amgen's purchase of Synergen in 1994. By the time of the transaction, the relative stock prices had fluctuated, changing the purchase price to $254 million.

Right: Since 1993, Amgen has relied heavily on its Fill and Finish facility in Puerto Rico.

Amgen Goes International

Above: Aart Brouwer was the first head of Amgen's European office from 1989 to 2001.

With NEUPOGEN® selling so well in the United States, Binder moved quickly to make the product available in Europe before competitors staked their claims. In 1989 the company recruited Aart Brouwer from Smith Kline & French to work with Amgen's new licensing partner, F. Hoffmann-La Roche, to market and sell NEUPOGEN® in Europe. (Amgen had already sold European rights to erythropoietin to Johnson & Johnson.) A Dutchman fluent in four languages, Brouwer was instrumental in developing and managing Amgen's European partnerships, approvals, sales, and distribution.

Brouwer chose to locate Amgen's European headquarters in Lucerne, Switzerland, near Roche. He recalls Amgen's initial growing pains: "It cost a lot of money. I had lots of discussions with Gordon because I needed money to build up the organization—and we had to pay F. Hoffman-La Roche for their services, which was something like $25 million a year."

Over the next twelve years, Brouwer opened offices in Germany, the Benelux countries, England, Spain, France, and Italy, setting the stage for Amgen to establish a direct presence in China with offices in Beijing, Shanghai, and Guangzhou—the first biotech to do so. (Amgen has since closed those offices in China.) Brouwer also played a key role in developing the distribution center in Breda, the Netherlands. "Breda," Brouwer says, "has been a great success. A model for the industry. Within twenty-four hours we can deliver to just about any hospital."

Below: A dragon boat racing team T-shirt from Amgen Greater China Ltd.

Clockwise from top left: Russell Edwards (left), Australia Country manager and regional director of Southeast Asia, and John Howard, Australian Prime Minister, at the opening of Amgen's Sydney office in March 1992; Paul Tilburgs, a network specialist in the Netherlands at Amgen Breda in 1999; the next two photos show Amgen Europe Chairman's Circle award winners celebrating their top sales successes in Mauritius in May 2004; Lisa Carroll (left), executive assistant, and Junko Suzuki, administrative coordinator, at Amgen Japan during Carroll's trip to Japan in 2001 to conduct administrative training for the support staff there; and Iqbal Husain (left) and Dr. Tomasso Bochicchio at a 2001 Mexico Aranesp® Investigators meeting in Cabo San Lucas

Above: Amgen received the European Prix Gallien award for NEUPOGEN® in 1992. This award recognizes the therapeutic product judged to have made the most significant overall contribution to patient care in terms of efficacy, safety, and innovation.

"*When we started Amgen Australia in 1991, we had about twenty-five people and sold NEUPOGEN® as our first product. It was very exciting. We were science driven, innovative, and had a wonderful product. It's just as exciting today, especially in that we're reaching so many patients. Our organization is now very integrated across functional areas. I'm proud of our value system and our diverse mix of talented people.*"

— Russell Edwards, regional director of Southeast Asia and Amgen Australia, hired in 1991

"Building that enormous logistics center in Breda was probably the most risky decision we've made in Europe," says Michael Bentley, former head of human resources in Europe. "It was a big step for such a relatively small pipeline and relatively small sales. But we knew Aranesp® was going to be a winner. It was an exciting time of growth."

Brouwer's greatest challenge, however, may have been setting up clinical trials in Europe. At first, Amgen didn't understand the necessity for running separate clinical trials in Europe; after all, the product was FDA-approved. Brouwer says, "I had to explain that the Europeans want to have their own experience with it. In every country you need a doctor or a center that has experience with the product in case something goes wrong. Things have changed over the years. You can now do things more easily. But in those days you couldn't."

Brouwer retired in 2001, but he left a far-reaching legacy. Through his initial work and the later efforts of Amgen's European staff, "we were able to build bridges to give Amgen a European face," says Brouwer. Today, Amgen has a direct presence in twenty-seven countries, plus the Commonwealth of Puerto Rico.

"Harnessing the best parts of the Amgen culture and values and applying those to a diverse group of people in many different countries is one of the most challenging parts of international expansion," says Bentley. "But the Amgen Values are global—in fact, we helped form them. We use those values as our guiding principle wherever we expand the business." ◬

Opposite: Amgen's European Logistics Center in Breda, the Netherlands, opened in 1998 and now distributes products labeled in over twenty-five languages to more than thirty countries in and around Europe. Breda runs at full capacity in two shifts.

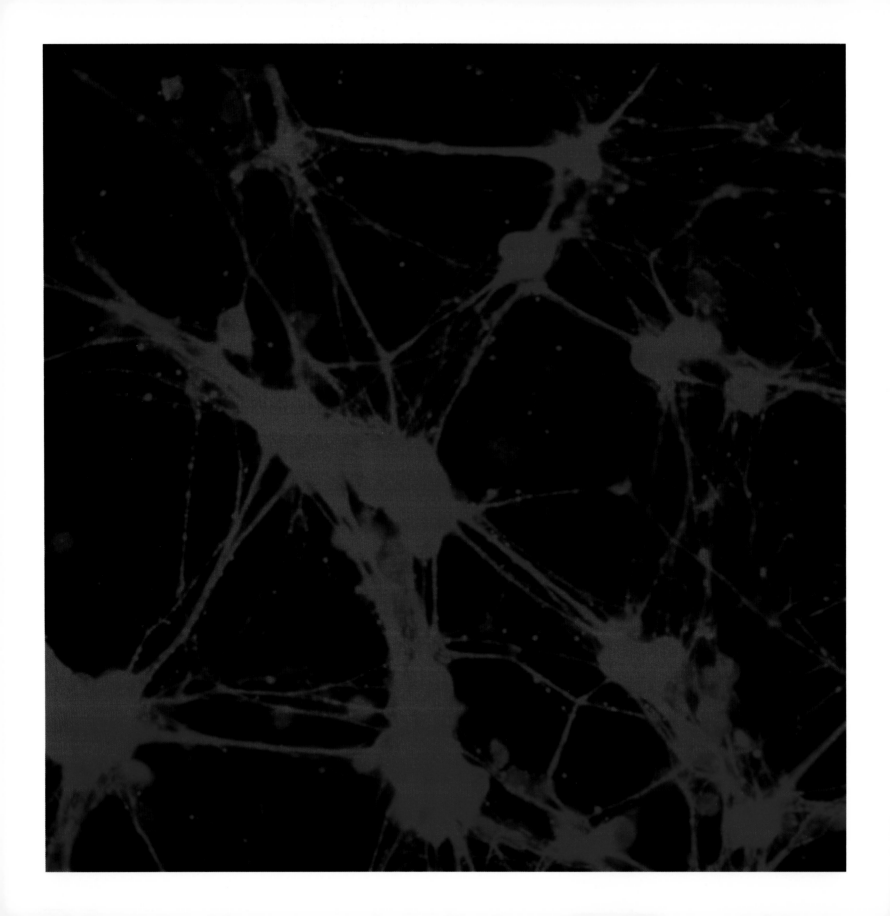

Under the agreement, Amgen acquired Synergen's product pipeline, which included glial-derived neurotrophic factor (GDNF), a potential neurobiology product for treating Parkinson's disease; nerve growth factor (NGF) to alleviate neuropathic and inflammatory pain; interleukin-1 receptor antagonist (IL-1ra) for rheumatoid arthritis; and several other potential products. Of those, the FDA approved IL-1ra—later named Kineret®—on November 14, 2001.

Other Amgen drug candidates at the time included neurotrophin-3 (NT-3) for the survival and maintenance of nerve tissue in 1990 and brain-derived neurotrophic factor (BDNF) for the degenerative muscle disease amyotrophic lateral sclerosis, or "Lou Gehrig's Disease," which entered clinical trials in 1993.

Legal Challenges

Broiling in the background were several lawsuits—part of the competition that exists among biotech and pharmaceutical companies.

In January 1989, Johnson & Johnson initiated arbitration proceedings against Amgen for a dispute involving erythropoietin. In June 1991, Amgen was ordered to pay Johnson & Johnson $164 million in reimbursement for sales of erythropoietin before Johnson & Johnson's Procrit® product received FDA approval. Amgen was disappointed by the ruling, but the company continued to pursue legal actions against Johnson & Johnson for fifteen long years. (See chapters three and four for details.)

Opposite: A culture of sympathetic neurons from a newborn rat. These neurons were grown in the presence of a novel neurotrophic factor.

Below: A Synergen collectible from 1994, the year Amgen acquired the company

NEWS CHRONICLE/Thousand Oaks, Calif./Tuesday, December 12, 1989

Amgen patent upheld by judge

By JIM PONDER
News Chronicle

BOSTON — A judge has upheld Thousand Oaks-based Amgen's patent on the process for producing a new treatment for severe anemia, but the company did not score a complete court victory.

Amgen's three-month court battle with Cambridge, Mass.-based Genetics Institute has ended for now with a 184-page decision Monday that found each company had infringed on the other's patent rights for recombinant erythropoietin technology, according to The New York Times. Amgen has used this technology to make Epogen, a treatment for anemia the company has sold since June.

The annual market potential for Epogen is more than $100 million.

Though the decision upheld Amgen's basic claim to the technology, the court ruled that the company had infringed upon several of the patent rights of Genetics Institute.

The ruling includes the judge's finding that Genetic Institute's Japanese partner, Chugai Pharmeceutical Co., had not infringed Amgen's patent, according to The New York Times. Officials at Genetics Institute said the judge seemed to make it possible for Chugai to produce the drug in Japan and import it into the United States. If so, Amgen would lose its monopoly on the drug.

"I don't know that we can keep Chugai off the market if the FDA approves" their drug, Amgen spokesman Mark Brand said this morning. "We have a ways to go before we're forced to make a determination on what we'll do."

"Amgen believes that today's decision is unlikely to affect the availability of Epogen," Amgen Senior Vice President and General Counsel Robert Weist said in a prepared statement issued Monday.

Epogen stimulates production of red blood cells, lessening the necessity of transfusions for patients suffering from anemia as the result of kidney failure.

Another legal clash had erupted in October 1987, when Amgen sued Genetics Institute and its partner Chugai Pharmaceuticals for infringement of Amgen's patent on the recombinant DNA production of human erythropoietin. Amgen also claimed that a patent held by Genetics Institute was not infringed by Amgen and was invalid. In March 1990 the U.S. District Court in Boston upheld Amgen's patent as valid, enforceable, and infringed by Genetics Institute, but found that Amgen had infringed Genetics Institute's patent.

Amgen fought back by taking its case to the U.S. Court of Appeals in Washington, D.C. In March 1991, the court affirmed the Boston court's ruling that Genetics Institute had infringed Amgen's patent, but reversed the ruling regarding Genetics Institute's patent. The remaining claims of Genetics Institute's patent were found invalid for lack of enablement—a major victory for Amgen's legal team. Genetics Institute and Chugai Pharmaceuticals tried to appeal the Appeal Court's decision to the Supreme Court, but on October 7, 1991, the Supreme Court denied a petition to review the appellate decision.

Above: The Thousand Oaks News Chronicle reported Amgen's win in the patent dispute with Genetics Institute. The December 1989 article states that although Amgen's patent was upheld, the company did not "score a complete victory." The judge found that Genetics Institute's Japanese partner, Chugai Pharmaceuticals, had not infringed Amgen's patent, thus opening the door for Chugai to produce the product in Japan and possibly import it to the U.S. Amgen eventually won this battle in appeal.

A Billion-Dollar Company

Biotech, as a young industry, was finally getting results. In 1991 *Fortune* magazine described the phenomenon: "Some fresh new players are on the brink of glory. After years of more promises than profits, the upstart companies that use gee-whiz techniques of genetic engineering are beginning to buzz the big guys like so many frenzied fruit flies."

For the first time in nearly half a century, Big Pharma companies such as Merck and Lilly were facing serious competition: "Already four biotechnology companies—Amgen, Genentech, Genzyme, and Immunex—are selling drugs in the U.S. market, and two more, Xoma and Centocor, are about to join them," reported *Fortune*. More than one hundred biotech drugs were in clinical trials, a dozen important drugs were on the market, and twenty had finished testing and were awaiting FDA approval. Some of these products, *Fortune* speculated, might hit the $1 billion mark—an astonishing projection since only three drugs had ever crossed that threshold.

By 1992 Amgen was well on its way to meeting that prediction, hitting $1 billion in product sales for EPOGEN® and NEUPOGEN® combined, and earning a net income of $358 million—a breathtaking surge from just $1.73 million in 1988. On January 2, 1992, Amgen was added to the S&P 500, and months later, the company debuted on the FORTUNE 500 list at number 427.

By 1994 the staff reached 3,396 globally, up from only 344 in 1988, when Binder was named CEO. The Thousand Oaks headquarters had grown, too—from half a building in 1980 into a sprawling campus with well over a million square feet of space by 1992. Local newspapers described the area as perpetually under construction. (In fact, bulldozers were still a common sight in 2004.) At first the city of Thousand Oaks resisted the expansion and made it difficult for Amgen to obtain permits and other legal requirements. "They didn't think we were going to make it," says Ed Garnett. "Now the city thinks they've died and gone to heaven. They're very happy we're here."

With so many promising products and upstarts, the biotech market surged again in 1991, with Amgen one of its star stocks. It increased 50 percent in the first quarter of 1991, compared to an average return of 18 percent for the S&P 500 and 31 percent for NASDAQ. But as always, the market was volatile. Soon thereafter, the biotech rally stalled during the Clinton administration's health-care reforms in 1992 and 1993, which promised sweeping new laws—and ultimately ended up failing.

Despite market fluctuations, by 1994 Amgen managed to jump to number 326 on the FORTUNE 500 list with $1.5 billion in sales and $319.7 million in net income. NEUPOGEN® brought in $829 million and EPOGEN® garnered $721 million as R&D spending jumped to $323.6 million. By the end of the year Amgen had $697 million in cash—after repurchasing 12.9 million shares of common stock totaling $593.8 million.

These numbers protected Amgen from the biotech nosedive

Below: Amgen's Building 7 is one of the first in the industry licensed to manufacture multiple biotech products under one roof. It has long been the worldwide supplier of NEUPOGEN®, Neulasta®, and cell cultures for Aranesp®. Although the construction was completed in 1992, numerous renovations have followed.

Right: This 1992 talent show trophy, the Genny, was given to Marta Fields for her rendition of the song "Never Never Land," from the Broadway musical *Peter Pan*. Everyone who participated in the talent show received a Genny. Longtime staff member Fields admits, "I have a collection of them from over the years!"

AMGEN TALENT SHOWCASE 1992

Amgen's courtyard at the center of the photo will be expanded some day. The company complex is situated on 105 acres.

Welcome to Amgenville
Thousand Oaks, Biotechnology Firm Agree Theirs Has Been a Match Made in Heaven

By MARY F. POLS
TIMES STAFF WRITER

THOUSAND OAKS—On its way to becoming the world's most successful biotechnology firm, Amgen made plenty of smart moves.

But John Fleschko, the company's director of clinical manufacturing, says the smartest move of all may have been starting the company in the suburban city of Thousand Oaks.

He moved here from New Jersey to join the company 12 years ago—long before annual revenues spiked beyond the $1-billion marker—and settled into a world of intense scientific discovery. "Everyone worked day and night," he said.

On the rare occasion when he wasn't monitoring experiments bubbling away in a fermentation tank, he hit the few local bars, discovered the joys of sushi and drove out Kanan Road to the beach in his Alfa Romeo convertible. He was young and single and smart, and California was a world away from New Jersey. He loved it.

But Thousand Oaks wasn't exactly cosmopolitan.

Conejo Valley chamber President Steve Rubenstein at new Super Crown Books.

"If you wanted to go out for dinner at night, there weren't a lot of choices," he said. Driving to Los Angeles was a hassle, but back then it was a must to find culture, entertainment and any other diversions from biological research.

A lot has changed since then for Fleschko.

Amgen's John and Theresa Fleschko, with their children in North Ranch.

Above: In 1995 the *Los Angeles Times* wrote a glowing article about Amgen's relationship with the city of Thousand Oaks, calling it "A Match Made in Heaven." Locating the company there, the paper reported, may have been "[Amgen's] smartest move of all."

that occurred in 1994, as investors grew skittish after several promising drug candidates failed and a raft of new start-ups were unable to attract further investment. On February 2, 1990, Genentech and Roche Holding Ltd. announced an agreement in which Roche would acquire a 60 percent ownership interest in Genentech, with an option to acquire the remaining shares at escalating prices over the next five years. Chiron Pharmaceuticals, too, watched as Ciba-Geigy bought almost 50 percent of its stock after several of its potential drugs proved unsuccessful. "Amgen may be the cure for biotech blues," proclaimed a headline in *USA Today.* The article went on to say, "Biotechs are divided between the haves and the have nots. Amgen is on top of the haves."

By 1994, after five years on the market, more than 320,000 dialysis patients with chronic kidney disease had benefited from EPOGEN®—including 160,000 that year alone. "The new generation of dialysis patients will never know what life was like before EPOGEN® existed—when patients were alive but lacked the energy to live a full life," Amgen wrote in its 1994 annual report.

Amgen's second wonder drug, NEUPOGEN®, was also improving the lives of thousands of patients. "Before I used

NEUPOGEN®, my white blood count would go down to zero, and I would get really sick," said Mat Solomon, then a twenty-year-old patient with severe chronic neutropenia. "I had to stay in bed most of the time…and missed a lot of school. Now, with NEUPOGEN®, I'm pretty much the average guy."

Early Amgen legal counsel Alan Mendelson says that his own brother, Larry, became ill with lung cancer and at one point was using both EPOGEN® and NEUPOGEN®—drugs that kept him healthy and able to function. "These are miracle drugs," Mendelson says. "It was Genentech and Amgen that proved that this science was not just something in the lab for university scientists to play around with—it could actually impact people's lives. Fu-Kuen Lin won't get a Nobel prize for the discovery that led to EPOGEN®, because it was commercial. But someday they should write on his gravestone, 'I saved millions of lives.'"

By 1994 Binder had led Amgen to spectacular success. Despite having to fill the shoes of the revered founding CEO, Binder was able to transform a small company with no products on the market into the most successful biotech company in history—one that was breathing down the necks of the top ten Big Pharma companies. But success can present challenges, too, as the fourteen-year-old company would soon find out.

Below: NEUPOGEN® patient Mat Solomon chats with a fellow classmate before heading back to his dorm. Solomon was diagnosed with severe chronic neutropenia in 1979 at the age of five. "With NEUPOGEN®," he attested, "I can be a normal, twenty-year-old guy."

National Medal of Technology: America's Highest Technological Honor

In 1994 Amgen became the first biotech company to receive the National Medal of Technology. The award is considered by the U.S. government to be on par with the Nobel prize. Given that year by Vice President Al Gore and Commerce Secretary Ron Brown, the award recognized Amgen for "its leadership in developing innovative and important cost-effective therapeutics based on advances in cellular and molecular biology for delivery to critically ill patients throughout the world."

Amgen's delegation included Gordon Binder and two other staff members—Laura Monk and Eric Guempel—whose names were drawn from a lottery. They later joined other honorees in an Oval Office ceremony with President Bill Clinton and Vice President Gore. "Creative, imaginative, and tenacious in the face of obstacles," said Gore, "you have brought forth a new fundamental understanding, techniques, and products that contribute so much to our nation's prosperity, health, security, and overall quality of life. You are true national heroes."

Binder, of course, was thrilled to accept the award. "On behalf of Amgen's 3,200 outstanding men and women, I am deeply honored and very proud that Amgen has been named a winner of the National Medal of Technology," he said at the time. "This award is the first for our industry in its very short but remarkable history. The ability to make a significant impact on patients' lives and health care around the world is the hallmark of Amgen and its people. The National Medal of Technology is the recognition of our vision and our pioneering spirit, which is unique to the United States." ⚗

Top: Dan Vapnek speaks to the Amgen staff at the 1994 awards celebration.

Above: Larry Souza is interviewed by the press during Amgen's National Medal of Technology celebration.

Above: The program for the 1994 National Medal of Technology

Below: The annual award recognizes outstanding technological contributions to the nation's economic, environmental, and social well-being.

Opposite: Vice president Al Gore presents the 1994 National Medal of Technology to CEO Gordon Binder. The award is the highest honor awarded by the President of the United States to America's leading innovators.

chapter three

⇐ *Opposite:* Amgen staffing manager Michele Jurbala took both Aranesp® and Neulasta® after receiving treatment for breast cancer. Jurbala attends a monthly lunch at Amgen that she established for cancer survivors.

1995–1999

Growth and Struggles

"Between the early days of Amgen's biotech breakthroughs and the maturing of the company was what I call the 'middle term.' We were learning to be big while trying to retain our entrepreneurial spirit."

— Jan Meier, operations, hired in 1992

EPOGEN®
(Epoetin alfa)
EPOGEN® is indicated for the treatment of anemia in patients with chronic renal failure on dialysis.

NEUPOGEN®
(Filgrastim)
By 1998, NEUPOGEN® is FDA approved for bone marrow transplant and acute myeloid leukemia patients.

On Friday, April 7, 1995, a tanned and trim Gordon Binder stood before almost four thousand staff members, family, and friends to celebrate a birthday—Amgen's fifteenth. The party was set up under a dark, menacing sky on the lawn behind Building 34, where vast tables of chili, hot dogs, and ribs stood ready as the "Rolling Clones," a band cobbled together by the marketing staff, prepared to play. ⌘ Almost on cue, the sun burst forth from behind the clouds as Binder shed his characteristic suit jacket. Fifteen years ago, he declared, no one would have dreamed that this throng of thousands would be standing here on a campus of thirty-nine buildings with enough food to feed a small army. At that time, Bill Bowes and Amgen's small team of investors and scientists had not even decided where to locate their new company, let alone what it would produce. With seed money of just $80,000, they hoped to eventually rival Genentech and Cetus, though that seemed a stretch. Certainly, no one believed that in 1995 Amgen would have a market cap of $9 billion and sales of $1.8 billion—almost twice the market cap and revenues of Genentech that year, and more than four times those of Chiron, the company that acquired Cetus in 1991. ⌘ But now, after the phenomenal success of EPOGEN® and NEUPOGEN®, Amgen had become a globe-girding FORTUNE 500 company with almost four thousand

Opposite: Ruth Miranda is a manufacturing specialist at Amgen Manufacturing Limited in Puerto Rico. At this Fill and Finish facility, Miranda and others fill and label drug vials and ship them to Amgen's distribution centers in Louisville or Breda, the Netherlands.

staff members and a slew of potential products in development. Sales continued to skyrocket, with the FDA poised to approve additional uses for NEUPOGEN®. And each year Amgen products were reaching hundreds of thousands of patients overseas as sales expanded in Europe, Asia, Canada, and Australia.

Inspiring patient stories about Amgen's two blockbuster drugs now ranged in the many thousands. Innumerable people who might have been debilitated by anemia associated with chronic kidney disease or infections associated with chemotherapy were resuming normal activities.

"Biotech executives often say that they want their company to be the next Amgen," *Science* magazine would declare one year later, "and with good reason: Amgen's sales of EPOGEN® and NEUPOGEN® totaled $1.8 billion in 1995."

The stock price was soaring, too, and had split several times. If you were an Amgen stockholder in 1995, you happily watched your investment increase by 101 percent that year. The stock would continue to surge during the late 1990s, defying the dizzying fluctuations of a runaway bull market that saw biotech companies being adored one moment because of a favorable clinical result and vilified the next

because of an unfavorable ruling by the FDA. Amgen was largely immune to the deep dives because, unlike other biotech companies that were burning through cash and had no income stream to generate profits, Amgen was highly profitable. "We actually generate cash," Binder reminded the *Los Angeles Times*.

In February 1995 persistent rumors of a takeover had gone public when the *Wall Street Journal* and other major media reported that Bristol-Myers Squibb was considering making a bid to acquire Amgen—news that bumped up Amgen's stock by as much as $10 a share on one frenzied day of trading. Other

Above: Gordon Binder leads celebrations at Amgen's fifteenth anniversary picnic— a huge milestone for a once-fledgling company. For a moment, staffers stopped the frenetic pace of daily operations to celebrate their company's fantastic success.

November 13, 1995
The FDA approves NEUPOGEN® for use in peripheral blood progenitor cell transplants.

August 1995
Amgen commences arbitration, claiming that Johnson & Johnson materially breached an agreement by promoting and selling Procrit® for dialysis use.

1996
Amgen reaches annual sales of more than $2 billion.

1997
The Louisville Distribution Center celebrates shipping 100 million vials of product.

October 6, 1997
The FDA approves Infergen™ for treating patients with hepatitis C.

1997
Fortune *magazine ranks Amgen No. 74 on its list of the "Top 100 Best Companies to Work for in America."*

1997
Number of staff: 5,372

1997
Amgen establishes additional distribution operations in Breda, the Netherlands.

1998
Fortune *magazine ranks Amgen No. 53 in its list of the "Top 100 Best Companies to Work for in America."*

1998
The FDA approves NEUPOGEN® for use in patients with leukemia receiving chemotherapy.

sources claimed that F. Hoffmann-LaRoche was contemplating an acquisition that would offer as much as $100 a share. At the time, Amgen was trading at approximately $72 a share, however, and analysts soon correctly concluded that the company was too expensive even for these behemoths.

As the smell of ribs wafted across the lawn, Binder surveyed his hardworking staff—many had been there from the beginning—and quickly wrapped up his speech. The throng was ready to eat, and the "Rolling Clones" were getting restless. "Just think," he quipped to the assembled crowd, "in six years Amgen will be old enough to serve alcohol at these parties."

Filling the Pipeline

Despite Amgen's blockbuster success on the balance sheet and mounting sales of its two mega-products, the company faced a persistent dilemma as it moved into the mid-1990s: how to keep the pipeline for new products full. After the twin wallop of EPOGEN® and NEUPOGEN®, Amgen had no follow-up products ready for the market—a fact that had been trumpeted by industry analysts and the media.

Not that Amgen wasn't trying. The company spent $452 million in R&D in 1995—up from $324 million in 1994 and $255 million in 1993. The company's R&D was spinning out several promising candidates, though no one knew if they would work. "The stock was going up because of the growth of EPOGEN®," recalls Kevin Sharer, Amgen's president at the time. "But the things we needed to position for the future weren't yet there."

In the lead to fill the pipeline was Interferon alfacon-1, for the treatment of patients with chronic hepatitis C infections, which was finishing its final trials in preparation for FDA approval in 1997. Another promising product was megakaryocyte growth and development factor, or MGDF, designed to reduce the severity of platelet loss during chemotherapy. Amgen scientists developed the drug after discovering a hormone that stimulates the production of blood platelets, which

Above: In 1993, the Valley Business section of the *Los Angeles Times* asked the question every biotech watcher was wondering: Could Amgen follow the incredible success of EPOGEN® and NEUPOGEN® with a third blockbuster?

Below: A 1991 Amgen R&D booklet

Amgen's Fifteenth Birthday

Amgen's fifteenth birthday included a performance by the "Rolling Clones," games for the kids, and a time capsule to be unveiled ten years later. Another highlight was a "top ten" list created by human resources head Ed Garnett, delivered in the spirit of David Letterman. Almost four thousand people joined in the celebration, giving number nine on the list the biggest laugh.

Top Ten Tribulations of a New Amgen Staff Member

#10: Explaining to your family what biotechnology is.

#9: Looking for nightlife in Thousand Oaks.

#8: Introducing your spouse to someone really important…and forgetting his or her name.

#7: Parking near your building after 9:00 a.m. Parking within the Amgen complex after 9:00 a.m. Parking within the same zip code after 9:00 a.m.

#6: Having to move out of your office one week after moving in.

#5: Getting directly from your building to another building without the Amgen Center map.

#4: Getting directly from your building to another building *with* the Amgen Center map.

#3: Finding a restroom near your office…. Finding *any* restroom *anywhere*.

#2: Hearing your first takeover rumor…. Hearing your seventeenth takeover rumor.

#1: Learning that dressing up at Amgen means wearing a new pair of jeans and that new Amgen T-shirt you've been saving for a special occasion. ⚠

help blood to clot. Analysts predicted that if the drug proved safe and effective, it would generate $250 million by the year 2000. In April 1995 Amgen began human trials of MGDF to great fanfare.

In 1995 Amgen licensed the research for what the media had dubbed the "anti-obesity" leptin gene. This gene, discovered by scientists at the Rockefeller University in New York City, made an anti-fat protein that appeared to regulate body weight by controlling food intake and energy expenditure. When researchers injected the protein into overweight mice, their appetites decreased, and they lost 40 percent of their weight in just one month. Amgen bought the research for $20 million, agreeing to pay $70 million more if a successful drug emerged. With 71 percent of Americans classified as overweight in 1995 and diabetes on the rise as a byproduct, the market for leptin was estimated to be, well, enormous.

Below: Nature magazine chronicles the discovery of the leptin gene by Rockefeller University researchers in 1994.

Newspapers around the world carried the story on their front page with a picture of two mice used in the research—a fat mouse and a normal-sized mouse on the protein. The publicity triggered a huge response. More than two thousand people called Amgen to volunteer for human clinical trials.

Meanwhile, trials for STEMGEN® (Ancestim) continued to treat patients undergoing stem cell transplants. When combined with NEUPOGEN®, STEMGEN® increased the

Opposite: Dressed as fat to skinny mice for Halloween, (from left) Lynne Buchsbaum, Jeanne Schramm, Chris Gutierrez, Deb LaBass, and Sherry St. Andrew of Amgen's law department celebrate leptin's early animal trial results.

number of peripheral blood progenitor cells (PBPC) in patients about to undergo myeloablative chemotherapy followed by a procedure called PBPC transplant. Both drugs were given before chemotherapy to stimulate the production of PBPCs, and then removed from the patient and stored. After chemotherapy—which destroys cancer cells as well as PBPCs—the cells were collected and then re-injected into the patient to promote bone marrow recovery. STEMGEN® was approved for use in combination with NEUPOGEN® in the setting of autologous PBPC transplantation in patients at risk of poor PBPC mobilization. It continues to be sold in Australia and Canada.

Amgen also initiated Phase I trials for osteoprotegerin (OPG), an investigational drug for healthy post-menopausal women that was designed to reduce osteoporosis as it develops with aging. OPG was created using data from Amgen's human genome database of genetic information, along with a technique used to over-express genes in mice—a method by which geneticists insert a gene and document the result. In this case, over-expressing a gene led to the development of osteopetrosis, which then led Amgen scientists to discover the protein that became OPG.

Then, in December 1995, Amgen licensed from NPS Pharmaceuticals a small-molecule medication for the treatment of secondary hyperparathyroidism in patients with chronic kidney disease on dialysis. The drug represented a significant advance for kidney disease and the consequent bone disease, and strengthened Amgen's capabilities in small molecule development. The deal was valued at $43 million

and included the purchase of 12.5 percent of NPS's stock. The FDA approved the drug nine years later, in 2004, with Amgen selling it under the name Sensipar®.

Brain-derived neurotrophic factor, or BDNF, was another drug in clinical trials in the mid-1990s. Tested in collaboration with Regeneron Pharmaceuticals Inc., BDNF was created to slow the decline of the breathing function in patients with ALS, or Lou Gehrig's Disease. Phase III trials were conducted in 1997, but the drug did not demonstrate clinical efficacy.

In Europe, Amgen was conducting Phase II clinical trials for the anti-inflammatory IL-1 receptor antagonist (IL-1ra)—a naturally occurring human molecule—and for the tumor necrosis factor binding protein (TNFbp), a drug under investigation that showed promise for the treatment of rheumatoid arthritis and multiple sclerosis. Amgen inherited both molecules from its 1994 Synergen acquisition.

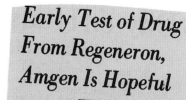

Early Test of Drug From Regeneron, Amgen Is Hopeful

By ELYSE TANOUYE
Staff Reporter of THE WALL STREET JOURNAL

Regeneron Pharmaceuticals Inc. and Amgen Inc. said early testing of their drug to treat Lou Gehrig's disease indicates that it slows the loss of breathing capacity caused by the disease.

The drug, called brain-derived neurotrophic factor (BDNF), was recently tested in 283 patients in the U.S. and Canada for up to six months. Preliminary results show that patients who took the drug experienced about half the rate of deterioration of breathing capacity than those who took a placebo, according to the companies. Loss of breathing capacity is a major cause of death from amyotrophic lateral sclerosis (ALS), or Lou Gehrig's disease.

Opposite: Amgen staffers load a Federal Express truck with the April 19, 1997, FDA filing for STEMGEN®.

Below: Amgen scientists, looking for an effective treatment for osteoporosis, continue the work they began on osteoprotegerin (OPG) in hopes of helping patients better manage this disease.

Above: In June 1995, the *Wall Street Journal* reported promising early results of brain-derived neutrotrophic factor (BDNF). Unfortunately, later trials were unsuccessful, and Amgen discontinued the program.

Left: In the mid-1980s, researcher Steve Elliott created this simple wire model to depict the 3D structure of erythropoietin. Adding two sugar chains, shown with the green flags, created Aranesp®. The drug stays in the body longer than EPOGEN®, allowing patients the same benefits with less frequent dosing.

New Colorado Plant Opens

Top: Longmont mayor Leona Stoecker speaks at the groundbreaking for Amgen's new EPOGEN® manufacturing plant in Longmont, Colorado. The facility, which also produces Aranesp®, allowed Amgen to triple production of EPOGEN®.

Above: (From left) Marty Simonetti and Dennis Fenton of Amgen, Longmont mayor Leona Stoecker, Chris Treharne of the Longmont Area Economic Development Council, and Michael Bevilacqua of Amgen break ground for the Longmont manufacturing plant.

Transforming a small, bench-scale experiment into a large-scale manufacturing process is no easy feat, but Amgen has always managed the transition extraordinarily well.

On October 1, 1999, after three years of construction, Gordon Binder cut the ribbon on Amgen's new 450,000-square-foot manufacturing site in Longmont, Colorado—the company's first bulk manufacturing facility outside California, and at the time, the world's largest biotechnology plant. The Longmont plant was designed to do all of Amgen's Epoetin alfa manufacturing, including what had been done in Building 6 in Thousand Oaks. Faced with increasing demand, Amgen decided in 1995 to build a new plant to increase capacity for Epoetin alfa. With more than three times the production of Building 6, the plant increased Amgen's workforce to 6,409 worldwide.

Longmont continues to play a key role in Amgen's success. On July 31, 2002, the plant was approved by the European Commission to manufacture Aranesp®. "This is not just a Longmont Manufacturing victory," explains Jan Meier, then-director and plant manager for the Longmont Manufacturing facility. "It took many other staff, from those in Colorado to those in Thousand Oaks and even those in Cambridge, U.K., to make this happen. There were more than three hundred people supporting this effort."

Amgen's nearby LakeCentre facility is just as important in manufacturing drugs to meet patients' needs. This location manufactures Kineret® and pipeline product candidates in late-stage clinical development, including palifermin for treating oral mucositis, and AMG 162 for treating bone loss that stems from osteoporosis and other ailments. ⚠

Opposite: In Longmont, Colorado, manufacturing associate Jeff Cornish examines a bottle containing cell cultures in the warm room of Amgen's new manufacturing facility.

"These past few years have been significant, with breaking ground in Colorado, getting the Rhode Island plant up and running, and continuing to expand in Puerto Rico. The number of potential products has increased significantly and we continue to look for opportunities and collaborations in more places than we ever have in the past. We're delivering on our promise to dramatically improve people's lives."

— Dave Bengston, operations, hired in 1983

SMART SCIENCE

Unlike its rivals, biotech leader Amgen emphasizes lab research—not market research.

Business people are surrounded by a cacophony of voices, and one key to innovative strategy is to listen to new ones. That's what CEO Gordon Binder did at Amgen, whose 68% average annual return over the past decade leads the FORTUNE 1,000. Drug companies succeed or fail based on a handful of blockbuster drugs; Amgen, for example, has only two drugs on the market—one helps dialysis patients; the other is an immune-system booster that helps people fight infections—but each brings in a billion dollars per year. With economics like that and with many projects crying out for investment, you have to pick which voices to hear.

Conventional wisdom says listen to the market. Says Binder: "Most pharmaceuticals companies, and quite a few biotech ones as well, are basically market-driven. They see that large numbers of people have a particular disease and decide to gather some scientists to do something about it."

Amgen heard things differently. Rather than start with the disease and work back to the science, Amgen assumed that the opposite strategy is superior—that companies should

CEO BINDER: *"Most pharmaceuticals companies are basically market driven."*

take brilliant science and find a unique use for it. The company's immune booster, for instance, helps keep the side effects of chemotherapy from killing cancer patients.

Starting with the science helps in other ways too. Each year the feds pour untold millions into universities and hospitals for medical research. "That kind of money will produce a lot of interesting things," says Binder.

To get a piece of it—and to bring in still more new voices—Amgen has collaborative arrangements with about 200 colleges and universities. It looks like one of those will pay off big. Last year at Rockefeller University, a professor discovered that a gene—now licensed by Amgen—may yield new treatments for obesity. Talk about potential blockbusters—more than 20% of adults in the U.S. are clinically obese; along with others who think they're chubby, they spend upward of $30 billion a year to shed pounds. Just a small percentage of that could plump up Amgen's bottom line even more.

— R.B.L.

Above: This 1997 *Fortune* article commended Amgen's emphasis on research.

Opposite: Research associate Anne Navratil (left) and research scientist SungAe Suhr Park of pharmaceutics at work in Building 8. During the development of protein-based therapeutics, hundreds of variations are tested to ensure that the one selected maintains the native structure of the active product.

IL-1ra, later named Kineret®, worked so well in clinical trials that Amgen submitted it for FDA approval in December 1999.

Meanwhile, Amgen researcher Steve Elliott and his team continued to work on the novel erythropoiesis stimulating protein, or NESP, later named Aranesp®. The idea was to create an erythropoietin product that was longer-lasting than EPOGEN®. Clinical trials began in 1996, and immediately Aranesp® helped patients sustain their production of red blood cells approximately three times longer than EPOGEN®. Amgen applied for FDA approval of Aranesp® in December 1999, the first time the company had submitted two FDA filings simultaneously.

Also during this time, Amgen researcher Olaf Kinstler was experimenting with a longer-lasting form of NEUPOGEN®. Kinstler hoped his new drug would reduce the number of trips to the doctor for injections that patients would need to maintain the right levels of infection-fighting white blood cells in their bodies.

Amgen was pouring millions into these potential products, but there were no guarantees that any of them would work. So the researchers at the Thousand Oaks campus continued to look for additional promising molecules and processes. Then, not long after Amgen celebrated its fifteenth birthday, Gordon Binder issued a crucial memo, reiterating that the primary strategy of the company would be the development of novel human therapeutics, rather than branching out into other products. "We have gone through a dry spell in our pipeline which followed the launch of EPOGEN® and NEUPOGEN®," Binder wrote. "After considerable discussion, Amgen has reached a broad consensus to continue to follow our science-driven, breakthrough-product strategy, and protect, sustain, and grow each product."

Today, Binder explains that the company had considered using its revenues and cash to diversify into other areas such as over-the-counter medications in a bid to become another Johnson & Johnson or Bayer, but decided against it. Amgen, Binder elaborated in the memo, would remain science-driven,

Below: A "Super NEUPOGEN®" T-shirt marked the drug's fifth anniversary in 1996.

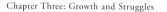

not market-driven—which meant further collaborations with university researchers and a large amount of cash to be spent on basic research. Meanwhile, EPOGEN® and NEUPOGEN® had grown to spectacular success, enabling Amgen to create subsidiaries in twenty-seven countries by 2004, including France, Germany, Italy, Spain, the United Kingdom, the Benelux countries, Australia, and Japan. By 1995, more than 1.5 million patients around the world had benefited from these blockbuster drugs. Then in 1999 the FDA approved EPOGEN® for the treatment of anemia in children with chronic renal failure who were undergoing dialysis. This regulatory green light came as the tenth anniversary of the initial approval of EPOGEN® approached.

"EPOGEN® is one of the most significant medical advancements in the last twenty years," said Kathy Jabs, M.D., medical director of

dialysis and renal transplantation at the Children's Hospital in Philadelphia and co-principal investigator of the pediatric clinical trial. "Anemia associated with dialysis is often more severe in children than in adults. Prior to EPOGEN®, the majority of children depended on repeated blood transfusions. So this is a welcome change."

In Europe, operations were expanding out of the headquarters in Lucerne to all European Union countries, including the establishment in the late 1990s of a distribution center in Breda, the Netherlands. Former head Keith Leonard worked with Aart Brouwer—who'd led Europe before him—to set up the Breda center. Breda was designed to distribute NEUPOGEN®, which Amgen had agreed to co-market and sell in Europe several years before with the assistance of F. Hoffman-LaRoche. The partnership had been established in the fall of 1988, even before NEUPOGEN® had FDA approval.

"As contractually agreed, we took back our rights from Roche and began selling NEUPOGEN® on our own on January 11, 1998," recalls Leonard, who headed up the tiny but enthusiastic staff. "We rolled out in eleven countries over a four-month period. It was hard work, but we didn't miss a single date." Later, in 1999, Breda began gearing up to distribute Aranesp®.

Legal Twists and Turns

Since 1989 Amgen had been embroiled in the trench warfare of major legal cases, primarily with Johnson & Johnson. This war had heated up again in 1997, when Johnson & Johnson filed a suit claiming that Aranesp®, Amgen's second-generation erythropoietin, was covered under its 1985 licensing agreement with Amgen, which allowed

"When we received approval of Aranesp®, we realized that we were entering a new era for Amgen Europe. We'd been addressing an unknown market in a therapeutic area completely new to us. Since then, we've achieved market leadership in nephrology and in oncology, and a terrific number of patients have benefited from it."

Johnson & Johnson to sell erythropoietin to certain markets in Europe and North America. Amgen responded that Aranesp® was distinct enough chemically to be a new product, and therefore was not covered by the 1985 licensing deal.

In December 1998, after wrangling with Johnson & Johnson lawyers in arbitration, Amgen won the eighteen-month battle over the rights to Aranesp®. This decision allowed Amgen to retain exclusive marketing rights to the drug in North America, Europe, and South America. After approval in 2001, Amgen could also provide Aranesp® to patients suffering from anemia associated with chronic kidney disease and chemotherapy-induced anemia—a major coup considering that under the 1985 agreement, the company could not sell EPOGEN® to treat conditions other than anemia associated with end-stage renal disease.

When the arbitration victory was announced in 1998, Meirav Chovav, then a biotechnology analyst with Salomon Smith Barney, told the *Los Angeles Times*, "This is huge." Aranesp®, she said, "could be a third billion-dollar drug for Amgen." That day, Amgen's stock spiked to $109, settling down at $100—a 14 percent gain.

"This was a big decision," Kevin Sharer says. "This win ensured our independence. It gave us another blockbuster product, and allowed us to better serve patients and compete head-to-head with Johnson & Johnson in more markets."

Sticking to Values

Amgen, a close-knit company that had started with just a few dozen staff members, was

Professional Rivals: Amgen and Johnson & Johnson

In September 1985, Amgen signed a licensing deal giving Johnson & Johnson's Ortho Pharmaceutical affili-

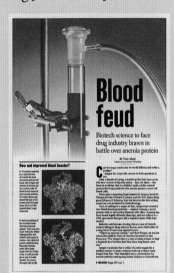

ate the exclusive right to promote and sell Epoetin alfa for non-dialysis use in the United States and for all indications worldwide except in Japan and China. Amgen retained the exclusive right to promote and sell its brand of Epoetin alfa, EPOGEN®, for dialysis use in the United States. (Johnson & Johnson calls its Epoetin alfa product Procrit® in the United States and Eprex® elsewhere.)

The legal disputes ranged from whether Johnson & Johnson was breaching its contract by dipping into Amgen's exclusive market (the court said it was) to whether Aranesp® should rightfully be licensed out for Johnson & Johnson to sell under their previous agreement for EPOGEN® (the court said it shouldn't). Arbitration began in 1989, with major victories and losses on both sides—but most resolutions favored Amgen. 🜂

Top: A July 2001 article in the *San Francisco Chronicle* was among hundreds to cover the legal battles between Amgen and Johnson & Johnson over Aranesp®. The dispute was decided in Amgen's favor.

growing rapidly. "Some years we had 30 to 40 percent growth," says Binder. "We barely survived it. The new staff came so fast, they didn't have time to learn the Amgen way." Once, Binder learned that a new group of sales and marketing people recruited from Big Pharma companies had been holding meetings to prepare for the monthly marketing meeting which focused primarily on guessing what he wanted to hear. "I told them, 'That's not Amgen. We'll have one meeting, and you'll tell me what I need to know, not what you think I want to hear.'"

The Amgen Values were formalized in 1996 and relaunched in 2003 to preserve the verve, entrepreneurialism, and high ethical standards that marked the early years. Each month, Binder gave Amgen Values presentations to new staff and their spouses. "Our values are what set us apart," explained Sharer in a speech to Amgen staff during the relaunch. "They are our compass. We are guided by them and measured against them. But our values are only real as long as each of us lives them. I'm counting on each of you to walk the talk, live our values, and keep what is special about Amgen alive." The Amgen Values are:

• Be Science-Based
• Compete Intensely and Win
• Create Value for Patients, Staff, and Stockholders
• Be Ethical
• Trust and Respect Each Other
• Ensure Quality

Above: Gordon Binder at one of many speaking engagements

Opposite: Staffers helped develop the principles that guide the way Amgen conducts business. The early mission statement (far left) has evolved into the current mission, aspiration, values, and leadership attributes that rolled out in 2003.

• Work in Teams
• Collaborate, Communicate, and Be Accountable

Of those, only the last value was revised in 2003. It originally said: "Collaborate, Communicate, and Build Consensus." While staff members appreciated the importance of gathering diverse opinions and conflicting views, they realized that reaching unanimous agreement before making a decision was not always possible and could slow things down too much. Competing to win, they agreed, means making decisions quickly and being accountable for them. So they revised the values to say, "Collaborate, Communicate, and Be Accountable."

The Amgen Aspiration was also created during this era. Initially, Amgen had aspired to be one of the top ten biotechnology companies. Kevin Sharer, then the company's president, had a healthy debate about Amgen's Aspiration statement. After much discussion with staff, the Aspiration was elevated to read: "We aspire to be the best human therapeutics company. We will live the Amgen Values and use science and innovation to dramatically improve people's lives."

Meanwhile, the parties, Chili Cook-Offs, Frisbee, volunteerism, and softball games continued, and new clubs—ranging from an Amgen karate team to a group of sports car enthusiasts—were formed.

Below: Amgen softball began almost as soon as the company itself. The men's team, pictured in a 1997 game, was called Amgents and the women's team was called DNAmites.

Spicing Up the Company Culture

Above: Tommy Beard, former vice president of sales, samples an entry at the first Chili Cook-Off in 1991. Beard and other executives judged the entries.

On May 3, 1991, clinical support specialist Lois "Lo" Binkley, senior marketing manager Jeff Bass, and a few other lovers of incendiary victuals started an informal Chili Cook-Off at one of the Fermentation Seminars then held on the lawn near Building 9. "For the first one," recalls Bass, "a bunch of us got together on one of those Friday afternoons, set up booths, and handed out chili. The next year it got a little more organized, and then the next year human resources took it over."

Former human resources vice president Ed Garnett remarks that his team, "Road Kill World-Class Chili," always won a prize. "We'd meet at someone's house two weeks before and go shopping," he says. Each year, there were several prizes—for the best chili, best decorations, and best theme. "I was always the emcee," says Garnett, "and our team always won something." He smiles. "People would say it's fixed. I'd say, 'Get over it!'" The Chili Cook-Off still continues on the Thousand Oaks campus, taking place each May, and has expanded to other Amgen sites.

In Washington, staffers gather each September for the Seattle Chili Cook-Off and the Bothell Chili Cook-Off. And each summer Amgen's Rhode Island team takes this longstanding Amgen tradition and gives it some New England flavor with its annual Chowda Cook-Off. This cook-off features teams of competitors vying for the title of best chowder: clam, seafood, Manhattan, or corn. With decorated booths and themed costumes, the campus is transformed into "Clamgen" for the weeks leading up to the event. More than eight hundred staff members and their families enjoy the chowder, a barbecue picnic, and fun and games at the Rhode Island manufacturing site. ◮

Competition for the Chili and Chowda Cook-Offs grows more fierce every year. Winning entries in 2004 included the "Happy to Be Alive Cow Diner" team for best costumes, "Martha Sings the Blues" for best decorations, "LeadBelly Chili" for best name, "Willy Wonka's Chili Factory" for best theme, and for tastiest chili, the "Blues Bayou" team. Other notable participants from the cook-offs have included *(clockwise from top left):* Jeff Bass of marketing was part of the 1993 "Road Kill World-Class Chili" team; the 1997 Hale Bopp Comet Booth, created for a space-themed contest; the backsides of "Heartburn," the marketing communications team; Rhode Island's "North Park Pirates," who snagged first for best seafood chowder as well as second for best overall; a raucous 2003 group dressed for "Rocky Horror Chili"; and, finally, a group at "The Great Amgen Chili Rush" in 1999, the 150th anniversary of the gold rush.

Above: An active game of soccer was one of many team-building exercises at a national sales meeting held in Thailand in the mid-1990s.

Above: Amgen's old fitness center on the Thousand Oaks campus. In a contest to rename the gym when it relocated to Building 38 in 2002, 40 of 190 entries suggested the winning "Amgym."

The prevailing style, both then and now, was a typically California blend of casualness, fun, and intensity.

As the company expanded, staff members tried to export the California culture abroad. "We tried in the beginning to make the culture the same everywhere," Ed Garnett says with a chuckle, "and quickly realized we're not going to change the Swiss. And we're certainly not going to change the Japanese. I spent a lot of time on the road trying to understand other cultures, and then realized that while our values can be the same, the way we apply the values has to be different. That was a big issue for us, because we believed we would be able to take the Hawaiian shirt, Bermuda shorts image international."

Working at Amgen

Amgen's tenacity in sticking to its founding values paid off. "We were more like a family than most companies," says Binder, who oversaw the building of a childcare center, a gym, and other amenities touted by staff and headhunters to prospective staff. In 1995, *Working Mother* magazine recognized Amgen as one of the best companies in America for working parents. And from the mid-1990s to its twenty-fifth anniversary in 2005, Amgen was frequently on the list of *Fortune* magazine's "Best Companies to Work For," ranking seventy-fourth in 1997, fifty-third in 1998, twenty-seventh in 1999, and thirty-third in 2003.

The company's emphasis on people, and the area's beaches, sun, and plethora of housing options helped draw high-caliber staff to the relative isolation of Thousand Oaks, where the nearest major science and research centers were miles away in Los Angeles, Pasadena, and Santa Barbara. "We have hired some of the most talented people in the industry as part of the Amgen family," Binder says. He notes that during this period, only one in fifty people who applied for positions were actually offered jobs. "And 70 percent of those offered jobs accepted," says Binder. "An amazing number."

The company worked to make Thousand Oaks more attractive, too, investing heavily in the city's infrastructure. "We fixed the corners up, and we improved and built all these roads," says Garnett. "All the traffic signals, and all that stuff around the campus. The city loves us for that." And in 2000 the company contributed $25 million to the Amgen Foundation, most of it to

Opposite: Shirley Koger on stage at Amgen's One World Together diversity festival, an event she helped organize.

Below: In 1995 *Working Mother* magazine listed Amgen in its "100 Best Companies for Working Mothers." Amgen's onsite childcare center is central to the family-friendly company culture.

BABES AND BUSINESS: Employees are more productive when they're happy; and they're happy when their small children are close by with on-site day care. . . . So goes the philosophy at Amgen of Thousand Oaks, which won a spot on Working Mothers magazine's list of 100 best companies **(D9A)**. The program gives new mom Michele Berlin peace of mind to concentrate on work. "It's hard to leave Kyle," she said. "But having the facility here helps ease any concern I might have."

Below: Gordon Binder's racing boots, part of his racecar driver attire for the 1998 "Drive for 75" campaign. The campaign's goal to raise Amgen's stock value to $75 was reached within days of Binder's presentation.

support charitable activities in communities where the company maintains plants, labs, and offices.

One outcome of Amgen's success was that much of the staff found the value of their stock options soaring. A $100 investment in Amgen stock made on December 29, 1989, was worth $5,888 by the end of 1999, significantly outperforming the S&P 500. The sudden wealth changed the lives of thousands of staff members, though those who just wanted to spend their money soon left. "People who loved the work stayed with the company," Binder says. "There wasn't much noticeable change."

Yet because Amgen distributed an unusually high number of options to its staff compared to other biotech and drug companies, the management felt added pressure. If the stock went down, it wasn't just the shareholders who would complain, but the staff. "We needed to serve patients, stockholders, *and* staff," says Binder. "We couldn't serve any of these well unless we served all three well. Still, the idea that the company should serve staff is not universal."

Products and Politics

During its first few years, Amgen could afford to ignore politics, especially in distant Washington, D.C. Later, when foreign competitors lobbied Congress against the Orphan Drug Law, Amgen learned to play defense in Washington. By 1993 it

Issue 19 June 1998

NASDAQ

The International Magazine of The Nasdaq Stock Market℠

Biotech delivers in abundance

The R&D pays off: Gordon Binder on Amgen's new product stream

became clear that Amgen should open a Washington office with full-time staffers. That same year Peter Teeley, former press secretary to President George H. W. Bush and former ambassador to Canada, came aboard to run Amgen's new office. Having a Beltway insider such as Teeley in place became critical in September 1997, when HCFA abruptly administered a reimbursement change for EPOGEN®.

Previously, HCFA, which at the time administered Medicare, had stipulated that eligibility for a dialysis center or clinic to be reimbursed for the cost of EPOGEN® must be based on the patient's medical necessity.

Above: In a June 1998 interview with *Nasdaq* magazine, Gordon Binder shared his views on biotechnology ethics and on why Amgen had become one of the few fully integrated biotechnology companies.

Opposite: Amgen started its internship program in 1993 to foster a love for science in students through hands-on learning.

The Amgen Awards for Science Teaching Excellence

Top: About two hundred people attended the Amgen Awards for Science Teaching Excellence in 2002, with Bill Nye the "Science Guy" as Master of Ceremonies. To highlight the science theme, Nye led the audience in a short, hands-on experiment.

Above: (From left) Bill Nye and award winners Richard Buck, Juanita Ryan, Craig Fox, Carol Fujita, and Rachel Tenenbaum with Amgen's Roger Perlmutter

Since 1992 Amgen has recognized excellence in science teaching. Each year, to help elevate the nation's level of science literacy, the company gives the Amgen Award for Science Teaching Excellence in states and communities in which it has staff and facilities: California; Colorado; Louisville, Kentucky; Boston and Cambridge, Massachusetts; Rhode Island; Seattle, Washington; and Juncos, Puerto Rico.

The monetary awards honor public or private school science teachers, grades K–12, who demonstrate outstanding science teaching and have a great impact on the lives of their students. Nominations are solicited every January, and a panel of independent judges selects the winners. Judges base their decisions on evidence of the teachers' creativity and effectiveness in the classroom, application and development of science education, motivational talents, mastery of the subject matter, and instructional skill.

"Most young children love science, but something happens between when they're small and when they're this age," says tenth-grade biology teacher Suzanne Black of Inglemoor High School in Kenmore, Washington. Black won an Amgen Award for Science Teaching Excellence in 2004. Several of her students have gone on to pursue science and medical careers. "I spend a lot of time convincing them that science is not scary, fact-laden, and filled with jargon," Black says. "Science, especially biotechnology, is built on the magic of discovery—the same kind of discovery my students enjoyed as children, watching butterflies fly." ⚐

Opposite: Program founder Daryl Hill awards a check to Sam Kane of Colina Intermediate School of Thousand Oaks at the third annual Amgen Awards for Science Teaching Excellence.

"If I want my students to become lifelong learners, then I must be one. To know I can help children believe in themselves gives me a sense of fulfillment."

— Darleen Horton, 2004 Science Teaching Excellence award winner, Chenoweth Elementary School, Louisville, Kentucky

Above: California's former first lady Gayle Wilson spoke at the 1994 award ceremony. After earning a degree in biology at Stanford University, she later served on the board of trustees for Caltech and for the Center for Excellence in Education.

But the new rules based eligibility on the levels of a patient's hematocrit or oxygenated blood cells. If the patient's levels were below 36 percent, HCFA would pay for the EPOGEN®; if they were higher, HCFA would deny payment. In the face of the new reimbursement rules, some dialysis providers began to reduce patient hematocrits by administering smaller EPOGEN® doses, adversely affecting EPOGEN® revenues— and, more important, patient health.

Above: Amgen's Washington, D.C., office head Peter Teeley (left), Senator Barbara Boxer of California, and CEO Gordon Binder, circa 1998. Teeley and Binder devoted time to educating government leaders on the importance of biotechnology research and drug access for patients.

According to the National Kidney Foundation, these new eligibility guidelines were not in the patients' best interest. Unfortunately, such rules were seldom overturned; they came during a time in which managed care and cost reductions were sweeping the nation. Still, Binder—then the chairman of the board for the Biotechnology Industry Organization, the industry's lobbying group—decided to fight back. Along with the National Kidney Foundation, Amgen spearheaded new Dialysis Outcome Quality Initiative guidelines that recommended keeping patients' red blood cell counts at higher levels. "We took a risky line in working closely with the government to show them how important this drug is to patients," he says. "We did the science and showed the government all of our results."

In March 1998 good science and patient health care won as the reimbursement policy was changed to allow for higher hematocrit levels. Amgen also won a smaller

battle that allowed clinics to be reimbursed for patients who self-administered their EPOGEN®. "This turned out to be a big victory for patients and the company," recalls Sharer, "because the government changed its decision. And that was all Gordon. Many people didn't think he could do it."

Binder and Teeley led an industry initiative to reform the FDA, helping to update what Binder says were World War I-era laws and streamlining the review process for new drugs and medical devices. The measure won in a voice vote in the House of Representatives, and in a vote of ninety-eight to two in the Senate. In 1997 Binder and Teeley attended the White House ceremony where President Bill Clinton signed the FDA Modernization Act.

Their other major victory, several years back, was defending the Orphan Drug Law, which allowed a company to have exclusive

Below: Gordon Binder was active in updating the FDA. *The Moorpark Star* featured President Bill Clinton signing the FDA Modernization Act in November 1997.

FDA: President Clinton signs FDA Modernization Act after 3-year wait

Continued from A1

because it renews and strengthens a popular expiring program that has already sped up reviews of new drugs dramatically. Under the so-called user fee act, drug companies pay fees in return for more staff at the FDA and faster reviews.

A hard-fought compromise, the FDA Modernization Act of 1997 took three years to hammer out. A major player in its development was Binder, chairman and CEO of Amgen Inc., the biotechnology giant in Newbury Park.

BINDER

"This was a long and difficult process, but Gordon took the lead way back in December 1994 when he headed a biotechnology task force to determine how the FDA could be brought into the last twentieth of the 20th century," said Carl Feldbaum, president of the trade group Biotechnology Industry Organization in Washington, D.C.

Feldbaum said that, at the beginning, Binder established two principles the industry would follow in helping to develop the legislation. The first was that the country and the industry needed a strong and independent FDA. Second, the FDA's standards of safety and efficacy would not be changed.

"Then Gordon, leading this effort, convened a group of other CEOs and came up with a number of proposals, many of which were signed into law Friday by President Clinton," Feldbaum said.

Many of the act's provisions have been put into effect administratively through Vice President Al Gore's "reinventing government" programs.

"We know that for many patients, experimental treatments represent their best — perhaps their only — chance for recovery," Clinton said. "That's why this bill writes into law current FDA policies that allow doctors and patients to use new drugs before they are formally approved.

"Already thousands of AIDS, cancer, and Alzheimer's patients have found new hope — even new life — with these experimental therapies."

Amgen spokesman David Kaye said the new law's major impact would be on products already on the market.

It will allow drug companies to educate physicians about the additional uses of drugs by distributing articles published in medical journals before the FDA approves the additional use. Previously, any additional use of a drug had to have FDA approval before literature on it could be given to doctors.

Also, the new law doesn't do much for shortening the amount of time required for clinical trials, Kaye said. But it does speed up the FDA review of the data from those trials.

CELEBRATION: After three years of working out its details, President Clinton signs the FDA Modernization Act. Looking on are, from left, Rep. Anna Eshoo, Sen. Jim Jeffords, Vice President Al Gore, Sen. Edward Kennedy and Rep. Joe Barton.

The Associated Press

Clinton allies applauded the new law.

Sen. Edward M. Kennedy, D-Mass., said the challenge now is to implement the legislation rapidly and effectively so the full benefits of the changes will be available to patients and industry as soon as possible.

But Dr. Sydney M. Wolfe, director of Public Citizen's Health Research Group, called the new law the worst attack on the Food and Drug Administration's ability to protect consumers and patients in 91 years.

"Americans will be exposed to

defective drugs and medical devices that Europeans with their weaker laws have been exposed to for a long time," Wolfe said.

He contended that political contributions greased the bill's progress through Congress and added: "This bill is good for corporate profits and bad for public health — period."

Feldbaum turned aside Wolfe's criticisms. "This bill passed the Senate and House by unanimous votes," he said. "Every letter and apostrophe was examined for its potential consequence to human health."

rights to a drug for seven years if it served a population of fewer than two hundred thousand patients—creating an incentive for biotechs to develop drugs for diseases that impact small numbers of patients. Several foreign companies and their U.S. subsidiaries tried to gut the legislation, "so we made our case and then-president Bush vetoed legislation that would have adversely changed the Orphan Drug Law," says Binder.

In Sacramento, Binder worked successfully to make the tax structure for drug companies and other businesses more in line with other states that favored in-state businesses over out-of-state companies. And in 1999 he became the chair of Pharmaceutical Research and Manufacturers of America (PhRMA).

Working Toward the Next Big Thing

As the biotech bubble rapidly expanded in the late 1990s, the NASDAQ biotech index doubled and investment in new offerings soared, despite a spate of high-profile clinical failures for many biotech companies. In 1996, for the first time in Amgen's history, annual product sales exceeded $2 billion. Three years later Amgen's annual product sales would skyrocket to $3 billion, its net income hitting $1 billion for the first time.

On October 6, 1997, after six long years of the company's waiting for another approval, the FDA approved Amgen's third product, Infergen™, for treating patients with chronic hepatitis C infections. The authorization was faxed to Amgen's regulatory affairs team at 2:00 p.m. that day, triggering a marathon logistics operation to get the first shipments from the Puerto Rico

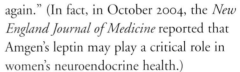

Below: Amgen traditionally celebrates product approvals with a champagne toast. Infergen™ was approved by the FDA on October 6, 1997. The first shipment was available to patients within thirty hours. Infergen™ was later licensed to Intermune Inc. for treatment of chronic hepatitis C virus.

Fill and Finish facility, to the Louisville Distribution Center, to drug wholesalers, and finally, to patients. The first batch was headed to wholesalers by 8:55 the following evening.

Unfortunately, Infergen™ sales turned out to be far below expectations, garnering only $26 million in 1999. Other drug candidates fared even worse. In 1998 Amgen dropped MGDF when some patients developed antibodies that neutralized the effects of the drug. Leptin was also a disappointment: while it helped trim pounds off overweight mice, it didn't have the same effect on overweight humans. "In the end, the drug didn't work as we had hoped," says former Amgen researcher Pam Hunt, who headed up the leptin efforts. Hunt retired as vice president of R&D in 2002. "But you never know about these things," she added. "Maybe in the next decade it will come off the shelf again." (In fact, in October 2004, the *New England Journal of Medicine* reported that Amgen's leptin may play a critical role in women's neuroendocrine health.)

On top of that, although scientists were still keen on pursuing GDNF, the product was experiencing some glitches. And although Kineret® was approved, its sales numbers were insignificant. Aranesp® was the only one among the major drugs in the pipeline in 1995 that would go on to be successful.

Sharer emphasizes that this ratio is not bad—and that luck is a big factor. "If the ball had just bounced the right way," he says, "things could have been different."

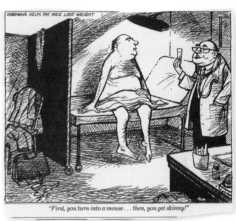

"First, you turn into a mouse . . . then, you get skinny!"

Above: A 1995 cartoon refers to the disappointing leptin trials. After Amgen licensed leptin from Rockefeller University in 1995, more than two thousand people called to volunteer for trials. Amgen's initial results with mice were promising, but human trials were unsuccessful.

Binder agrees. "It would have been great to have had big success in the 1990s. Typically, though, it takes eight or nine years for a drug company to ramp up and produce new products. I used to tell shareholders and others that Amgen's large-scale funding of R&D started around 1993 to 1994, so to expect major products in 1998 or 1999 was highly optimistic."

Even so, Amgen was working toward that goal. Between 1990 and 1995, R&D spending increased from $72 million to $452 million. By 2000, the year Binder stepped down, R&D was at $845 million. In 1999 Amgen also invested in its own internal human genomics program and in outside genomics companies that were tapping into human genome project data. These projects were all the rage, as many thought companies such as Celera would mine the genome and pluck out genes that could be transformed into new drugs. But just one of Amgen's internal genomic projects would eventually show promise: OPG.

"We invested in these companies, like everyone else," says Sharer. "Like the rest of the world, we hoped that the sequencing of the genome would lead to new discoveries. This was a tough period. But that just happens. It wasn't that we weren't trying hard."

And as Binder notes, the nine-year rule has, indeed, played out.

Above: Bill Boyle worked with Josef Penninger and Young-Yun Kong to discover OPGL, a gene that triggers the body's cells to cannibalize its own bone, leading to severe osteoporosis. The research was the first to clearly identify the molecular cause of the bone deterioration characteristic of many inflammatory diseases, and pave the way for future research into the prevention of arthritis and osteoporosis.

"For the past few years," he explains, "Amgen reaped the rewards of the R&D surge of the mid-1990s, with several new drugs coming out."

A New Kind of "Synergy": Amgen Acquires Synergen

In 1994, Amgen acquired Synergen—a Colorado-based biotech that seemed on the brink of going out of business—for $254 million. The takeover remains a sensitive issue for many staff members. Synergen provided Amgen with several important molecules and a state-of-the-art manufacturing facility, but even Sharer admits that the integration should have gone more smoothly. In 1997, due to business conditions, Amgen closed its inflammation unit in Boulder and, although some researchers relocated to Thousand Oaks, nearly one hundred people were laid off. "That was the darkest day of my twelve years at Amgen," says Sharer, "when we closed down that inflammation lab in Colorado."

But another drug acquired in the purchase, IL-1ra—later named Kineret®—looked promising. Synergen scientists had cloned this naturally occurring anti-inflammatory molecule in 1989. In 1994, after it had

Opposite: (From left) Ulrich Feige, Dave Litzinger, and Hiko Kohno review lab results outside Building 14's cold room. Among the team's many projects was the effort to reengineer leptin to enhance its solubility.

Below: These juggling balls embossed with Kineret®, Aranesp®, and Neulasta® logos were created to acknowledge staff members who divided their time among all three products—a task especially daunting when working on regulatory filings.

failed to treat the life-threatening systemic inflammatory disease known as sepsis, Amgen researchers began to explore whether it could be used in rheumatoid arthritis patients.

In February 1995 the team led by Dottie McCabe, then head of clinical operations in Boulder, convinced Amgen management not to pull the plug on IL-1ra until the results of the Phase II study were out. "The more information we got, whether through data or anecdotally, talking to physicians in clinical trials, the better it looked," explains McCabe. Kineret® was approved for use in reducing the signs and symptoms of rheumatoid arthritis by the FDA in 2001. Sales, however, have remained slow.

A Twist on Two Favorites: Creating Aranesp® and Neulasta®

Despite all the challenges of the period, there were two products in the works that held great promise: Neulasta®, a longer-acting version of NEUPOGEN®, and Aranesp®, a longer-acting analog of EPOGEN®. Aranesp® had been in the works for years and had involved many staff members. "It began as pure research," explains research fellow Steve Elliott. "Our goal was to better understand how Epoetin alfa worked."

While Elliott's team was investigating Epoetin alfa, another team led by Joan Egrie, Tom Strickland, and Jeff Browne was studying its carbohydrate component to determine its structure and function. "Back then, we didn't fully understand the significance of the carbohydrate other than it had to be there for Epoetin alfa to be fully functional in the body," Elliott recalls. "Initially, we were studying how we could reengineer the protein itself, and what would happen if we changed it. We then wondered what the outcome would be if we reengineered Epoetin alfa to produce a molecule that had more carbohydrate than naturally existed."

Not everyone was on board with this new research. Many scientists—who thought Epoetin alfa was already the best it could be—were skeptical of the team's efforts. But the team remained more determined than ever. Elliott explains, "A scientist spends most of

Below: Aranesp® had been on the market for almost a year when *Scientific American* featured it in a story on how sugars play critical roles in many cellular functions and in disease. By adding two additional sugar chains to erythropoietin, Amgen scientists created Aranesp®, a molecule that offers increased staying power.

Above: Researcher Steve Elliott, whose team created Aranesp® by adding two sugar chains to erythropoietin. Aranesp® stays in the body longer than its precursor, EPOGEN®.

The Science of Aranesp®

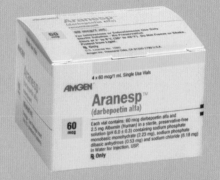

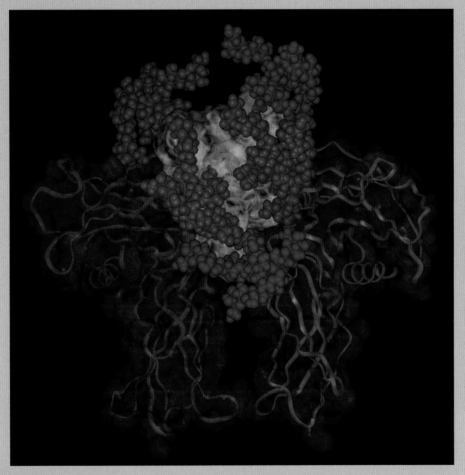

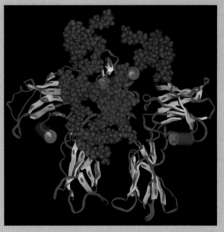

Like EPOGEN®, Aranesp® (darbepoetin alfa) is produced in Chinese hamster ovary cells using recombinant DNA technology. Aranesp® is the glycosylation analog of erythropoietin, the naturally occurring protein that is produced in the kidney and stimulates the production of red blood cells. When the kidneys are damaged, the amount of erythropoietin in the body may be diminished, resulting in anemia, a condition caused by a low level of red blood cells. This often happens in patients who have chronic kidney disease or are undergoing chemotherapy. Like EPOGEN®, Aranesp® is used to treat anemia by stimulating red blood cell production. Aranesp®, however, contains two additional sugar chains. These extra chains increase the molecular weight of the protein—causing it to stay in the body longer, thus reducing the frequency of injections needed for patients.

Mutn	WT		R1A-P	R1A-N	F12-R	D11-R	D11-G	R binding [2]	UTI CFU	(16FU) 968A	SFO 7mRA	968A 468N
					<0.06	24,23				17	33	
						22,20		[7.4] [22]			139	
pDEC273 6/22/92 EPL					<0.06		36			20	73	
pDEC278 6/3/92 PEPL			18.8		20.6 37,31,32	24,24,24					19,33	
pDEC311 6/2/92 arg		18,19.5			31,25,25 9.1,10.4,8.4				250,275	31	
pDEC315 6/2/92 glu thr		30			20,22,23,18 14,13.6,13				32	33	
pDEC1 7/6/92 WT		16.4				0.67		20 [145][13.2]			
pDEC283 8/7/92 STV FLR		<0.14	25		92,332 26.5	26,29		7.4	9.5 (-43)		
pDEC240 8/7/92		17			29,95	39,43			130		
pDEC341 8/7/92 SN PL			102		34,137,61	66,73					
pDEC309 8/7/92 lys		37			55,55	16.5,18.3				42	
pDEC318 8/7/92 leu thr		36,40	04.5		28.5,32.1	13.7,17.7			40,54	<2	
pDEC341 8/7/92 leu ala thr leu		22			59.5,45.8	36,39.4,31.2		[20] <1		23	
pDEC293 8/2/92 pro ala		48			<0.06	0.53,1.30,67		<0.06 <0.5	34,24		
pDEC283 3/2/92 STV FLR					<0.06	21.2,23.2,19.7		[<0.1]			
pDEC321 8/2/92 NTVNT AHPWP	27		<0.2		<0.06	<0.06			360		
MCC1 8/4/92			<0.14			1.5,23					
pDEC322 9/8/92 NTVNT	16				23,21	20,18					
pDEC285 10/8/92 TFGI SN	21				26,29.4	12.5,11.5			39.5		
pDEC288 10/8/92 T GI LSNT	21				18,19	15,14.5			32		
pDEC313 10/8/92 LSNT	14.3				21,21.5	12.4			5		
pDEC320 10/8/92 NLSNTV	17.7				29,29	14.9,16			13		
pDEC185 10/26/92 ileu	29				37,30,23	13.7,13.4					
pDEC323 10/26/92 thr ala arg arg	12.8		29			28,24	24.7,25.5			11,15.7	97
pDEC324 10/26/92 gln thr ala arg arg arg	11.9				32,29						
pDEC325 10/26/92 gln thr arg arg											

his or her time learning and understanding things. You need a special kind of personality to be in the business because most of what you do fails. In fact, if you do ten experiments—some of which take years to finish—nine of them are going to fail. Often it's the intellectual stimulation that keeps you going. And every once in a while, your hypothesis is right."

After several years of hard work on Aranesp®, the team's research efforts finally came together. "It took years to create these new molecules with more carbohydrate," says Elliott, "but it was worth it. As we suspected, these molecules were more active."

When Joan Egrie and Jeff Browne presented the findings to senior leaders, Sharer and Binder were strong supporters—and Aranesp® moved forward into clinical trials. In December 1999 Amgen's regulatory team submitted the U.S. and European applications for the treatment of anemia associated with chronic renal failure. Both were approved in 2001. In 2002 Aranesp® received FDA approval for the treatment of chemotherapy-induced anemia in patients with nonmyeloid malignancies.

Meanwhile, scientists were also taking another look at NEUPOGEN® and how to give it to patients in a more convenient and longer-lasting form. Amgen researchers had always known there was potential for another product.

The Amgen Cancer & Chemotherapy Educational Support System™

It's not unusual to meet an Amgen staffer who is also a patient. Throughout the late 1990s, Amgen marketing manager Paula Bass depended on NEUPOGEN® in her battle against breast cancer. Her fight motivated her and her colleagues to create the Amgen Cancer & Chemotherapy Educational Support System™ (A.C.C.E.S.S.). With this program, patients could contact Amgen toll-free for information that was specific to their needs.

"When I was on chemotherapy, I realized just how important information is," explains Bass, who was featured in Amgen's first television commercial. "Information helped me take control and fight my disease. It helped me be an active participant in my treatment decisions."

Regulatory Filings Require Heroic Efforts

The Simi Hostages, who holed up in a hotel for ninety-three days in 1987 to complete paperwork for the FDA approval of EPOGEN®, have become folkloric figures at Amgen. Several years later, other heroic efforts followed in the submission of NEUPOGEN®. But nothing could have prepared Amgen's regulatory team for what happened in 1999. After winning the Johnson & Johnson arbitration in December 1998 and completing successful clinical trials of Aranesp® for instances of anemia in chronic renal failure and Kineret® for rheumatoid arthritis, Amgen decided the time was ripe to file the products with the FDA—simultaneously. The staff also filed for Aranesp® in Europe, applying for approved use in a total of eighteen countries.

Cheryl Anderson, then the associate manager for the regulatory affairs renal group, led the charge for the dual Aranesp® applications, coming up with one common document that would satisfy both the FDA and the European reviewers. "We had just won this major arbitration decision with Johnson & Johnson, confirming that Aranesp® was ours, so we saw it as the future of the company," Anderson says. "We wanted to file it as quickly as we could. It was all hands on deck."

Several Cambridge Aranesp® team members temporarily relocated from the United Kingdom to work with the Aranesp® team in Thousand Oaks. With new document management technology, the Thousand Oaks team was able to conduct round-the-clock activity on the application with the remaining team in Cambridge, taking advantage of the eight-hour time difference: as one team reviewed and revised documents, the other would sleep at night.

The teams were under a tight deadline, working to file both Aranesp® for the United States and Europe, and Kineret® for the United States. "We were under constant pressure because we wanted the licenses for both products filed before Christmas," says Ralph Smalling, head of regulatory affairs at the time. "I was absolutely going nuts, reviewing both Aranesp® and Kineret® documents and trying to keep the molecules straight."

The Aranesp® and Kineret® teams moved to separate suites in the basement of Building 24. "We used to raid each other's kitchen depending on which team had the better food that day," says one anonymous team member. During the final weeks of December 1999, Amgen printers had processed 501,195 pages, and the 100-member team had attended 467 meetings, consumed 10,453 sodas and 3,485 Frappuccinos, and snacked on 10,240 Gummi bears, 48 pounds of malt balls, and 5,430 licorice vines.

The original Aranesp® submission totaled 62,354 pages, with the electronic statistical data adding the equivalent of another 384,000 pages. The Kineret® application totaled 39,000 pages, with equally massive electronic statistical data.

Multiple copies of the regulatory submissions for both Aranesp® and Kineret® arrived at FDA headquarters in Rockville, Maryland, on December 28, 1999.

Smalling gives Cheryl Anderson much of the credit for pushing through the simultaneous U.S. and Europe filings and for creating a common technical document that could be used for both. "Getting out both the U.S. and Europe Aranesp® submissions was an enormous effort," explains Anderson. "Everything had to be double-checked and cross-referenced. We burned a lot of midnight oil and weekends." It was well worth the effort. Aranesp® was approved September 18, 2001, and Kineret® got the FDA nod two months later on November 14. ⚗

Top: (From left) Steve Elliott, Ralph Smalling, and George Morstyn celebrate the Aranesp® and Kineret® FDA filings. *Above:* Yvette Rae and John Oakes of Amgen's legal department celebrate the approval of Aranesp®. *Left:* It's T-shirt time again: a shrink-wrapped shirt announced the FDA's approval of Aranesp® on September 18, 2001.

We got the o.k.

New From Amgen

Introducing ARANESP™

From Lab Coats to Cowboy Boots: Kirby Alton Comes Full Circle

Kirby Alton doesn't want to be remembered for taking the rectal temperatures of calves—but his job during Amgen's experiment with interferon in Idaho still makes

those laugh who remember the great cattle round-up.

Trained as a molecular biologist in Dan Vapnek's lab at the University of Georgia, Alton also worked as a graduate student in the lab of Genentech founder, Herb Boyer, at the forefront of the recombinant DNA revolution. When he finished his Ph.D., Alton had an offer from Genentech, but at Vapnek's request, he interviewed with Amgen in 1981 instead. He went on to become Amgen's head of development from 1985 until his retirement in 1999.

Alton guided all of the products during the first twenty years through trials and regulatory approval. "George could have hired some other person who knew development," says Alton, "but he said he would take his chances on me."

Now the retired Alton, who was raised on a tobacco and peanut farm in Georgia, has gone back to his roots as a rancher in Montana. There, he works on his ranch as the "project leader" for 650 heads of Angus cows—but now, he lets others take their temperature. △

Above: Kirby Alton (left) and Gordon Binder at a 2001 Amgen celebration, which honored George Morstyn before he retired

Early on, it was discovered that when attached to other molecules, polyethylene glycol (PEG), a water-soluble polymer, slows down the excretion. Then, research scientist Olaf Kinstler found "an elegant way" to attach just one PEG, instead of the usual many PEGs, to protein molecules. At a weekly Friday-morning seminar in Building 8, he unveiled his discovery.

"It is every chemist's dream to have his product be developed and used in the clinic," says Kinstler, who immigrated to the United States from Latvia in 1988 with just two suitcases. "From the lab bench to the clinic, things usually fail for one reason or another. I was extremely lucky."

Like Aranesp®, Neulasta® showed great promise: Designed to keep the NEUPOGEN® molecule in the body longer, the product now allows for less-frequent dosing, enabling patients to receive it just once during each chemotherapy cycle. Neulasta® also gives patients protection against chemotherapy-related infections.

The research was slow, but by 2000 Amgen had applied for FDA approval for the new drug. And in January 2002, Neulasta® received the green light from the FDA.

Kevin Sharer Takes the Reins

The second half of the 1990s saw the retirement of some key Amgen leaders including

Below: (From left) Susan Serdar, Doug Hunt, Farnoosh Zamani, Kendyl Hall, and Debbie Koch of Amgen's regulatory team. The team submitted the Neulasta® filing electronically with just one binder of paperwork—a far cry from the reams required in the pre-electronic days.

Below: Raymond Baddour, an early investor in Amgen and member of the original board of directors, in 2004

Above: President and COO Kevin Sharer ended the decade primed to step in as Amgen's new CEO—the third since the company's founding. Sharer officially assumed the role in May 2000.

Dan Vapnek, Kirby Alton, Larry Souza, and, from the board of directors, Raymond Baddour. In early 2000 Gordon Binder also decided to retire, and the board chose his successor, Kevin Sharer, to take over as CEO on May 11, 2000. For years Sharer and Binder had split responsibilities, with Binder presiding over R&D, finance, and government affairs, and Sharer running sales, marketing, and manufacturing. It had worked well because, as Sharer explains, "I always knew who was the CEO, but Gordon was able to give me enough independence to make a difference. While our styles were different, our goals and values were the same. We were a good team."

Sharer was ready to become CEO when Binder handed over the company to him in late spring of 2000. "To be president for seven years is a long time," he observes. "I wasn't going to wait forever."

The board knew that Sharer was approaching a fork in the road. "As Kevin became more and more familiar with the company," says Steve Lazarus, who retired from the board in 2004, "we knew we were going to face the necessity to have a transition. Because you don't keep a guy like Kevin in the number two position forever. He was very marketable. And we knew some recruiter would come along and just pull him out for a telecommunications or a big manufacturing industry job. That was

probably the most delicate problem the board ever worked on. But ultimately it worked out extremely well."

"I left at just the right time," Binder agrees. "Like an athlete, there comes a time for the CEO to leave. We were about to launch preparations for several new products, and Kevin was ready to take command."

By any standard, Binder had an incredible run. During his watch the company took in total revenues of more than $17 billion—with a net income of over $4.5 billion—and spent $3.5 billion on R&D. When Binder stepped down, Amgen was the fourteenth-largest drug company in the world, having outstripped its early biotech rivals years earlier.

"We did it right," says Binder. "Following George Rathmann's lead, I stayed as chairman for about six months for the transition. And then I left. And I think that's good. I don't think having the old CEO around looking over the shoulder of the new one is beneficial."

"Gordon loved the company," says Sharer, "and he loved the job. Under the surface, I'm sure he wanted to stay. I probably will, too, when my time comes."

Below: In announcing Kevin Sharer's succession to Gordon Binder, the *Wall Street Journal* suggested that the freedom allowed to Sharer as second-in-command was one reason Amgen was able to retain his talent when other companies were recruiting him.

A Lesson on Keeping a CEO Heir Apparent From Jumping Ship

Kevin Sharer Was Amgen's No. 2 For Seven Years Before Getting Nod for Top Slot

By JOANN S. LUBLIN AND RHONDA L. RUNDLE
Staff Reporters of THE WALL STREET JOURNAL

Last year, Amgen Inc. President and Chief Operating Officer Kevin Sharer pondered giving up his quest to become the company's chief executive. He thought about going to another company that would give him a specific timetable for becoming CEO—which Amgen's board wouldn't do.

But last week, Mr. Sharer's seven years of waiting ended when Amgen named him CEO. He will succeed 64-year-old Gordon M. Binder next May. Mr. Sharer had coveted the promotion since October 1992, when he left the telecommunications world to become the second-highest officer of the Thousand Oaks, Calif., biotechnology giant. During his long wait, doubts set in and other temptations emerged.

"There were lots of days when I wondered when it would happen," recalls Mr. Sharer, a beefy executive known for his impatient pace. Any No. 2 "who isn't anxious to get the CEO job probably shouldn't," he says with a laugh. At times, his impatience led him to consider high-level jobs with telecom, pharmaceutical and venture-capital concerns.

YOUR CAREER MATTERS

Anointed Ones
Seconds-in-command and their pursuit of the corner office:

NAME	COMPANY	NAMED #2	DATE EXPECTS TO BECOME OR BECAME CEO
David Cote	TRW Corp.	Nov. 1999	By July 1, 2001¹
Kenneth I. Chenault	American Express Co.	Feb. 1997	April 2001
Edward J. Ludwig	Becton Dickinson Co.	March 1999	Jan. 1, 2000
Craig R. Koch	Hertz Corp.	Aug. 1993	Jan. 1, 2000
Lloyd Ward	Maytag Corp.	Feb. 1996	August 1999
James R. Tobin	Biogen Corp.	Jan. 1994	Feb. 1997²

¹If he doesn't become CEO by then, he will walk away with a $10 million severance payment.
²He resigned in December 1998.
Source: WSJ reports

Amgen's success at retaining Mr. Sharer as a potential heir offers a blueprint for businesses everywhere. Even as the corner office remained elusive, Mr. Sharer, 51, got broad operational freedom, hefty pay boosts and steady encouragement from influential board members. "To keep somebody like Kevin, there had to be some of those tiny strands that the Lilliputians tied up Gulliver with," observes Steve Lazarus, a longtime Amgen director and venture capitalist.

In coming from another industry, Mr. Sharer faced a steeper learning curve than an insider. But executive recruiters can't cite another instance where an industry novice waited so long to advance from president.

Seconds-in-command often bolt to become a top dog faster elsewhere. In what was seen as an effort to prevent the possible exodus of American Express Co. President Kenneth I. Chenault, a hotly pursued executive, Harvey Golub announced last April that Mr. Chenault will succeed him at the helm in 2001.

Other No. 2 officials demand a guaranteed consolation prize for not moving up soon. David Cote, TRW Corp.'s new president, will walk away with a $10 million severance payment if he doesn't gain the No. 1 spot by July 1, 2001. In November 1996, AT&T Corp. recruited John R. Walter as president

and its chairman's expected heir. He quit nine months later after learning he wouldn't get the highest post—and collected $26 million in severance and forgone pay.

Mr. Sharer's drive to quickly snare the corner office made friends doubt he would stick with Amgen long. A U.S. Naval Academy graduate trained as an aeronautical engineer, he held various management posts at General Electric Co. following a stint with consultants McKinsey & Co. He quit GE in 1989—on the same day that the concern offered him a corporate officer's title plus one of the three top spots in its huge aircraft-engines unit.

Instead, Mr. Sharer became a division president at MCI Communications Corp., a predecessor of MCI WorldCom Inc. "I had a chance to compete for the top job," he says. But he left MCI when "it became clear I was never going to be a candidate for the No. 1 or No. 2 job," he continues.

Mr. Sharer told GE colleague James McNerney he was taking Amgen's No. 2 job largely because "I have a good shot to run this company," his ex-colleague remembers. Still, "no promises were made" about Mr. Sharer's eventual advancement, notes venture capitalist Franklin P. "Pitch" Johnson, another Amgen board member.

Mr. Binder, the CEO, nevertheless split his duties, putting his new No. 2 in charge of manufacturing, logistics, and sales. "We weren't competing for the same space," Mr. Sharer says. Mr. Binder also kept him informed about everything going on inside and outside the company. Armed with the same information, the two often had similar thoughts about strategic direction.

Please Turn to Page B16, Column 1

Dare to Dream: An EPOGEN® Success Story

Top: EPOGEN® patient Bryon Vouga is shown with his wife, Heather, after finishing the month-long cross-country bicycle trek that he began in June 1999. Vouga suffered kidney failure at age sixteen and underwent kidney dialysis for three- and-a-half hours three times a week. Vouga is the first person with kidney failure in history to accomplish such a feat. *Above:* A triumphant Vouga prepares to dip his front tire in the Atlantic Ocean to signify the end of his cross-country bike trip.

On June 25, 1999, Bryon Vouga, a thirty-year-old high school teacher and EPOGEN® patient, began a 2,700-mile bicycle trek across the United States. Vouga, who suffers from chronic kidney disease, called his effort "Dare to Dream."

"I want to put a human face on this disease," he said at the time. "I'm using my cross-country trip to prove to myself and to others that we don't have to be victims of kidney disease, dialysis treatment, or anemia. Even though not every patient will be able to bicycle across America, I want people to know that each of us can dare to dream our dreams."

Vouga started taking injections of EPOGEN® in 1989 after undergoing two failed kidney transplants. "Before I started taking the drug, I was tired all the time," he said. "The medication helped almost right away. I began training and I could bike ride for twenty or thirty miles."

A crew and forty Amgen staff members joined him for the first twenty of the Dare to Dream miles. Throughout his journey, Vouga underwent fifteen dialysis sessions required as treatment for his chronic kidney failure. He was welcomed in Phoenix by the Hopi-Pima Indians, who did a ceremonial dance; had an emotional meeting with young dialysis patients at Texas Children's Hospital in Houston; and was given a proclamation from then-governor George W. Bush at the state capital in Austin. Locals showed their support, too, by creating welcome banners and cheering as he biked mile after mile across deserts, bridges, and major highways. Reporters in some cities even rode with him to get interviews. Vouga completed the ride one month later, on July 26—ten years after the introduction of EPOGEN® to the market. △

Opposite: Bryon Vouga is interviewed in Jacksonville, Florida, after finishing his 2,700-mile journey.

"The mantra 'Every patient, every time' was never more evident than with the heroic efforts of Building 6 staffers, who for ten years produced the United States' supply of EPOGEN®. The plant was designed to produce a few hundred grams. With leaders like Dennis Fenton, Bob Andren, and Dave Bengston, science leaders like Tom Strickland, and a cast of hundreds, Building 6 generated thousands of grams to keep up with demand. It was extraordinary."

— Wayne Pearl, operations, hired in 1985

⇐ *Opposite:* LeAnne Elliott was diagnosed with psoriatic arthritis at age seventeen. It became so debilitating by twenty-three that she changed jobs. Elliott experienced significant results in the Enbrel® clinical trial in 1999. Now, her pain and swelling are gone.

2000–2005

A Worldwide Leader

"Amgen is the dominant force in biotech, with a world-class management team to take the company forward. As long as the scientists continue to discover new product candidates, and Amgen is able to in-license great discoveries from other companies, the future is unlimited."

— **George Vandeman, former general counsel, hired in 1995**

EPOGEN®	**NEUPOGEN®**	**Aranesp®**	**Kineret®**	**Neulasta®**	**Enbrel®**	**Sensipar®**
(Epoetin alfa) EPOGEN® benefits severely anemic patients on dialysis who, in the past, could only be treated by blood transfusions.	*(Filgrastim)* NEUPOGEN® is indicated for use in peripheral blood progenitor cell transplants.	*(darbepoetin alfa)* Aranesp® is approved in 2001 for anemia in chronic renal failure patients and in 2002 for chemotherapy patients.	*(anakinra)* Approved in 2001, Kineret® is the first treatment for rheumatoid arthritis that blocks interleukin-1.	*(pegfilgrastim)* The FDA approves Neulasta® in 2002 to reduce infections in certain cancer patients on chemotherapy.	*(etanercept)* First approved for rheumatoid arthritis, Enbrel® is approved for four other indications by 2004.	*(cinacalcet HCl)* Sensipar® is approved in 2004 to treat secondary hyperparathyroidism in dialysis patients with chronic kidney disease.

n the summer of 1999, twenty-two-year-old Tejal Jambusaria drove to her first interview at Amgen world headquarters on Amgen Center Drive, winding through a myriad of buildings that stretched across the sun-drenched valley. Far removed from its modest beginnings in 1980, Amgen had now grown beyond Thousand Oaks. Products were being manufactured in Colorado and California, filled and finished in Puerto Rico, and shipped around the globe from Louisville and Breda. Salespeople were pitching Amgen's products in multiple languages, getting much-needed medicine into the hands of hundreds of thousands of patients from Portland to Paris. △ Nearly two decades earlier, not far from where Jambusaria drove, the twenty-two-year-old Tim Osslund had gone in search of a new biotech company located in an industrial park north of town. He finally located it inside a squat, concrete building, where CEO George Rathmann sat behind a desk in the sweltering heat. △ A young Dennis Fenton—now executive vice president of operations—had taken this journey, too. In 1981, he interviewed with Rathmann after flying in from Connecticut, where he worked at Pfizer. Rathmann told Fenton that Amgen would one day be the size of Pfizer. "I thought Rathmann was dreaming," says Fenton, though he signed on anyway. △ Jambusaria's arrival eighteen years later could not have been more different. The enormous

Opposite: Gerjan Koopman (front) and Nikki Chapman of the international customer services division at the Breda Logistics Center in the Netherlands. Koopman's job was to ensure that all wholesalers and pharmacists in the Netherlands received their NEUPOGEN® orders on time, while Chapman did the same for the rest of Europe. Today, Koopman is a nephrology administrative coordinator in Breda.

campus was now filled with low-slung buildings carved in steel and glass and dotted among acres of lawns, gullies, and shade trees that shimmered green in the rising heat of the day.

Having emigrated at age thirteen with her parents from Gujarat in western India, Jambusaria grew up near Amgen, attending Canoga Park High School, where Amgen scientists often taught classes. "I liked science, and I wanted to work at Amgen some day," she says. After graduating in 1994, Jambusaria earned a biochemistry degree at the University of California, Santa Barbara in 1998. She left a job in Los Angeles when she heard that Amgen was hiring temps for a new program. "My friends thought I was crazy to leave a permanent job for a temp job," she says. "But I wanted to work at Amgen."

Eventually, Jambusaria was given a permanent job. Now twenty-seven years old, she works out of a small office in Building 25, which she shares with four other scientists. Outside her window she can see the landscape that held such promise for Bruce Wallace in 1980—the bright California sun, trees, and rolling hills. Working as a quality associate, she helps oversee the accuracy and maintenance of equipment ranging from balances and pH meters to the software of complex gene

sequencers and arrays. "This is where I imagined myself to be back when I was in high school," she says with a smile, "and it's amazing to be here now."

Above: Quality associate Tejal Jambusaria at work in the lab in 2004, checking to ensure that all the equipment is well maintained and up-to-date

Sharer Shakes Things Up

Kevin Sharer, who became Amgen's third CEO in 2000, likes to dress in jeans and casual shirts and tends to smile and laugh easily. He has a management style that is at once personal and to the point, but also slightly distant. A former naval officer, he is direct, sometimes disarmingly so. "Kevin took us out to dinner once," says George Morrow, executive vice president of global commercial operations, "and he told us that if anyone got too political, they'd be fired."

May 11, 2000
Kevin W. Sharer is elected CEO.

2000
Number of staff: 7,326

2000
Amgen acquires Kinetix Pharmaceuticals.

January 19, 2001
Judgment is given in Amgen's favor in the patent litigation against TKT and Aventis relating to erythropoietin.

2001
The FDA approves Aranesp® to treat anemia associated with chronic renal failure.

2001
The FDA approves Kineret® to treat the signs and symptoms of moderately to severely active rheumatoid arthritis in patients who have unsuccessfully tried one or more disease-modifying medicines.

December 5, 2001
Amgen and NASA team up to study Amgen's osteoporosis treatment, OPG, on the space shuttle Endeavour.

2002
The FDA approves Enbrel® to treat symptoms of psoriatic arthritis, Neulasta® to decrease infection in patients with non-myeloid cancers receiving myelosuppressive chemotherapy, and Aranesp® to treat chemotherapy-induced anemia in patients with non-myeloid malignancies.

July 15, 2002
Amgen acquires Immunex.

Sharer expects his team to fire right back, to put forth arguments persuasively and with confidence. It's his way of testing people.

Sharer learned his management style from the legendary CEO of General Electric, Jack Welch. "Welch always said: 'Deal with reality. Know your people. Demand high results. Be hard-headed and soft-hearted,'" he says.

He likens running a biotech to operating a casino. But even a seasoned gambler might blanch at the quadruple wagers Sharer made in the first few months after taking over Amgen as CEO. In a whirlwind, he revamped top management, reorganized and reinvigorated

Below: CEO Kevin Sharer in front of a portrait of the ill-fated General George Custer—a painting that reminds him never to underestimate the competition. This photo appeared in a May 2004 article in *USA Today.*

R&D, sent four products through the FDA approval process after a ten-year dry spell, initiated an aggressive sales strategy against competitors, and engineered the largest biotech merger in history.

"The fact that we decided simultaneously with these product launches to buy Immunex was certainly a risky decision that others may not have pursued," he observes. He pauses and smiles. "Yeah, maybe it was borderline crazy."

A New Team in Town

Right away, Sharer grabbed hold of the management structure of the company and rattled it hard. In a matter of months, he transformed Amgen from a loosely run organization that still behaved like a start-up into a more disciplined company run by powerful lieutenants recruited from the senior ranks of Big Pharma and other large companies—people who knew how to manage a global enterprise and could go head-to-head with major competitors. First on his list were Roger M. Perlmutter, M.D., Ph.D., and George Morrow. Sharer announced both hires on January 9, 2001.

Perlmutter became Amgen's executive vice president of research and development.

"When Kevin took over as CEO, he forced us to examine whether we would really be able to compete in the marketplace, not just in the courtroom. Before, we didn't have to compete as hard. We still treat our staff incredibly well, but now we're all about business. Can we take on Big Pharma in the marketplace? We've proven we can."

— Ilana Meskin, human resources, hired in 1991

2002
Number of staff: 10,118

October 18, 2002
An arbitrator finds that Johnson & Johnson breached its license agreement with Amgen by promoting Procrit® into Amgen's reserved dialysis market. Amgen is awarded $151 million in damages.

December 23, 2002
The FDA approves Amgen's Rhode Island manufacturing facility for Enbrel®.

2003
Amgen earns the No. 3 spot in Science magazine's "Top Biotechnology and Pharmaceutical Employers" list.

2003
Number of staff: 12,886

2003
The FDA approves Enbrel® for reducing the signs and symptoms of ankylosing spondylitis and other expanded indications.

2004
Amgen is ranked No. 64 among the world's largest economic entities, including nations.

2004
The FDA approves Enbrel® for the treatment of chronic moderate to severe plaque psoriasis and Sensipar® for the treatment of secondary hyperparathyroidism in chronic kidney disease patients on dialysis and in parathyroid cancer patients.

June 24, 2004
Amgen submits FDA application for palifermin.

August 13, 2004
Amgen acquires Tularik.

October 28, 2004
Mimpara® (cinacalcet HCl) receives regulatory approval in the European Union.

April 8, 2005
Amgen turns twenty-five.

2005
The Dora Menchaca patient care center wing opens at UCLA.

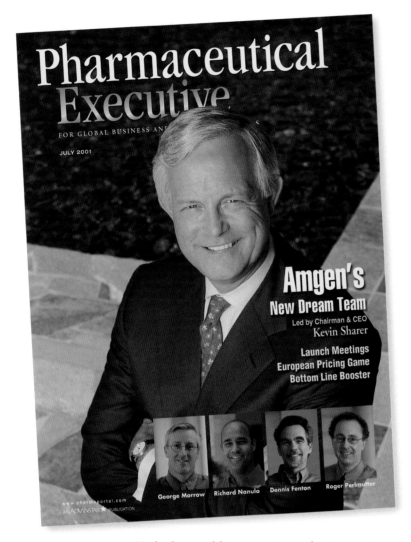

Pharmaceutical Executive

FOR GLOBAL BUSINESS AN[...]

JULY 2001

Amgen's New Dream Team
Led by Chairman & CEO
Kevin Sharer

Launch Meetings
European Pricing Game
Bottom Line Booster

George Morrow   Richard Nanula   Dennis Fenton   Roger Perlmutter

www.pharmaportal.com
AN ADVANSTAR PUBLICATION

Above: Kevin Sharer and Amgen's executive management team were featured in the July 2001 *Pharmaceutical Executive* magazine—the top trade journal in the industry. Sharer and the team discussed Amgen's strengths and long-term outlook.

He had started his career in academia, serving as chairman of the Department of Immunology at the University of Washington, where he was an investigator for the Howard Hughes Medical Institute. He then went on to head up research at the Merck Research Laboratories—known at the time as the Harvard of research labs. "When I first visited Amgen," Perlmutter says, "I knew within a half hour that this was a great opportunity. It was the chance to become part of a financially powerful organization that was still young enough to dream of actually changing the practice of medicine."

Sharer assigned Morrow to be executive vice president of worldwide sales and marketing. In 2003 his role was expanded to executive vice president of global commercial operations. Before joining Amgen, Morrow was president and CEO at GlaxoWellcome Inc. in North Carolina, where he was responsible for $6.5 billion in U.S. revenues. When Sharer approached him, Morrow was absorbed with the merger between GlaxoWellcome and SmithKline-Beecham. "Initially, I didn't really want to leave," he says. "With just two monopoly products, no one was that interested in Amgen, except to buy the company. But Kevin was very articulate in laying out his vision."

Over the next year and a half, Sharer continued assembling his roundtable of trusted advisors. He brought on Brian McNamee as senior vice president of human resources, Richard Nanula as executive vice president and chief financial officer, Beth Seidenberg, M.D., as senior vice president of development and chief medical officer, Joe Miletich, M.D., Ph.D., as senior vice president of research and pre-clinical development, Hassan Dayem, Ph.D., as senior vice president and chief information officer, and Fabrizio Bonanni, Dr. Chem., who arrived at Amgen in 1999 as head of quality and compliance and later became Amgen's senior vice president of manufacturing.

Dennis Fenton and Steve Odre, the former head of the legal team, were the only long-time staff members who remained in Sharer's top tier. Odre joined Amgen in 1986 and successfully oversaw much of the company's litigation until

"Amgen has been remarkable in its ability to manage growth while still maintaining its values. When you bring on thousands of staff, it requires good management and a strong culture to integrate them effectively. Leaders continue to focus on making Amgen a good place for staff to work."

— Judith Pelham, president and CEO, Trinity Health, Amgen board of directors, joined in 1995

Above: George Morrow, executive vice president of global commercial operations, addresses his staff in a November 2003 meeting.

he retired in 2004. David Scott, formerly general counsel at Medtronic, replaced Odre as Amgen's general counsel. Seidenberg resigned at the end of 2004 and was replaced by Willard Dere, M.D., who had been vice president and head of general medicine.

Fenton joined the company as a researcher in January 1982. When he became executive vice president of operations, he brought his experience in running various parts of Amgen to the fore, working with Sharer to transform the company while retaining its core entrepreneurial spirit.

With the new team in place, staff saw a very different style of leadership begin to emerge. Sharer explains, "I have what you would call a prime ministerial view of this job. My feeling is that each of my folks has a very powerful position in his or her own right. And if I were ever to lose the support of my 'council of ministers,' I should also lose my job.

"I'm sort of like George Martin," Sharer adds, referring to the legendary producer for the Beatles. "I'm in the studio with my team. I surround myself with people I like and trust. It's an informal but intense environment."

Above: His understanding of the many key steps between developing an idea and delivering a product to the sales force gives Roger Perlmutter, executive vice president of research and development, the tools to help his team focus and move forward appropriate product candidates.

Aligning the Troops

After a decade of thriving on two monopoly products, Amgen was now entering a high-stakes competitive environment and continuing to expand at a rapid pace. In order to sustain such growth, Sharer knew the company had to do more than just change the way it conducted business—it had to be transformed.

In 2001 Sharer and his team kicked off the Alignment Initiative, an all-encompassing effort to transform Amgen from a two-product company into an all-out competitive powerhouse. The initiative involved five hundred staff members and centered on four critical business components:

- Blockbuster-building commercialization
- Beating the competition
- Relentless focus on results, efficiency, and effectiveness
- Balance of empowerment with discipline and accountability

As various teams reviewed their own processes, members identified 150 areas that could use significant overhaul. The leadership acted on many of these suggestions, but one change was most significant: the formation of Product Strategy Teams (PSTs) to replace Amgen's long-established Product Development Teams, many of which had grown to sixty members or more.

Today, Amgen has almost fifty PSTs, consisting of five cross-functional experts from

Below: (From left) Executive team members Joe Miletich, Kevin Sharer, Steve Odre, Fabrizio Bonanni, George Morrow, Brian McNamee, Richard Nanula, Dennis Fenton, and Hassan Dayem met up with riders in an Amgen-sponsored 520-mile California Coast Classic bike tour in September 2003 to raise funds for the Arthritis Foundation. Not pictured: Beth Seidenberg.

Above: Mike Savin, vice president of sales and marketing operations, was a leader of the 2001 Alignment Initiative, an undertaking that resulted in a more rapid transition from successful research to effective products.

Below: Naturally, a project T-shirt commemorated the effort.

operations, development, marketing, regulatory, and project management. Each PST is devoted to specific research projects.

"PSTs are clearly here to stay," says Monte Levinson, associate director of R&D strategic operations. "Initially, our goal was to foster the partnership between development and marketing. That's been a success. And we wanted clearer decision-making. That's been a success. These smaller teams are much better able to ensure that the products R&D is developing can actually be sold by sales and marketing."

Sharer's shake-up touched every part of the company—and most agree that it was sorely needed. When Sharer took over, executives still made decisions based on casual chats in the hall or walks across the campus; researchers sometimes forged ahead on projects that had no

link to proven patient need; and salespeople lacked strict output guidelines and were rewarded as a regional group instead of for their individual successes.

Under the new leadership, the company became much more ambitious and much less willing to carry people. Sales team members were soon compensated based on their own performance records. They were also required to make a certain number of calls a week and to pass competency tests on product and disease knowledge to ensure they could engage physicians in high-quality conversations.

These changes initially rankled some staffers used to the old ways. But soon even the longest-tenured staff members began to admit that Amgen needed the new rigor to keep from drifting. Tom Boone, who joined Amgen in 1981 as a researcher and is now senior director of protein science, explains, "Kevin brought in new, high-caliber people who really want to do well. For a while here before the changes, the morale was very low. But now, people have much more of the old gung-ho spirit. It's similar to the way it was twenty years ago, but on a much bigger scale."

"Kevin's starting to look pretty smart now," says researcher Tim Osslund. "He's challenged people who've been here for a long time to step it up. He put people's feet to the fire. Not everyone adapted. Some are heartbroken because the company has changed so much."

The Yin-Yang Approach

In the summer of 2002, Sharer fused his rigorous approach to work and play with a California-style New Age vision for the company. In an all-staff meeting, Sharer unveiled a

Opposite: Tom Nusbickel, Stewart Turner, Darby Keeney, and Rob Murphy of the Cinacalcet HCl Product Strategy Team (PST) received the Best Global Perspective award during the 2004 PST celebration. Their expertise helped bring Sensipar® to market in 2004.

yin-yang chart to explain what parts of the company he wanted to preserve and what he wanted to change. Written on the white "yin" side of the symbol were the words "Transform to Prevail," "Relentless Focus on Results," and "Blockbuster-Building Commercialization." On the "yang" side he listed "Preserve the Core," "Improve People's Lives," and "Be Science-Based."

"Kevin created an internal crisis in the company," says Ilana Meskin, senior director of human resources, who joined Amgen in 1991. "Before Kevin took over, we considered words like 'mandatory standards,' 'policy,' and 'governance' bad because we were afraid to lose our entrepreneurial spirit. But now we see that to compete, we have to achieve a new level of efficiency, scale up in the right way, and become more disciplined.

"Some of the longtime staff saw the writing on the wall and said, 'This isn't the Amgen I know,'" Meskin continues. "Those of us who stuck it out experienced moments of grief. On the other hand, now we're looking for systemic ways to grow up as a company— to hold on to the things we cherish but to be clear about what doesn't make sense anymore."

Along with instituting sweeping change, Sharer set grand goals, proclaiming that each year revenues would grow by 30 percent and profits by 25 percent. Analysts, however, were

skeptical. World events such as the September 11, 2001, terrorism, a worldwide recession, and, later, war in Afghanistan and Iraq would continue to buffet an already turbulent market, and Amgen's sales had risen an anemic 10 percent in 2001.

"Even established companies such as Merck and Bristol-Myers are having trouble bringing drugs to market," wrote Arlene Weintraub in *BusinessWeek* in March 2002. "Everything has to go right for Sharer to reach that target. He has to devote considerable energy and resources to marketing while developing a lineup of lucrative drugs that treat a broad range of diseases."

Three New Products, Entry into Oncology

When Sharer assumed the top job in 2000, EPOGEN® was still the company's workhorse, providing medication to two hundred thousand patients a year and generating $2.3 billion in revenues. Meanwhile, Amgen's other dynamic therapeutic, NEUPOGEN®, had been approved for use in ninety-eight countries, dispensed to 3.5 million cancer patients, and earned $1.4 billion in sales.

But other products were in the works, and for the first time in years, things looked more promising than ever. In late 2001 and early 2002, Amgen received three product approvals and an expanded indication for one of them within just four months.

Above: A Forbes magazine article from September 2001 examined Amgen's incredible transition from a two-drug company into a large, successful corporation.

Left: The Alignment Initiative adopted the "yin-yang" symbol to show how new initiatives can coexist with traditional company ideals.

Transform to Prevail

Relentless Focus on Results

Blockbuster-Building Commercialization

Preserve the Core

Improve People's Lives

Be Science-Based

Dora Menchaca: Losing a Friend

On September 10, 2001, Amgen's Dora Menchaca, an associate director of clinical research, was in Washington, D.C., to brief the FDA on the progress of PLENAXIS™, a candidate Amgen was pursuing to treat prostate cancer. That night, she told Amgen oncologist Scott Fields, who had accompanied her to Washington, that she was flying back to California on standby the next morning—September 11, 2001.

That flight was American Airlines flight 77, which was hijacked in midair and crashed by terrorists into the Pentagon. Before taking off, Menchaca had left a voice mail message for her husband, saying she was looking forward to coming home and spending the afternoon planting roses with their five-year-old son, Jaryd.

Menchaca, who coordinated clinical studies for oncology drugs, was known as an outgoing leader. "She had a strong science background," says Dr. Fields, "but she was also very personable."

To commemorate her life, the Amgen Foundation donated $3 million to build an adult oncology wing at UCLA, where Menchaca received her Ph.D. The Dora Menchaca patient-care center wing is scheduled to open in mid-2005.

Amgen also dedicated an Area of Reflection on the Thousand Oaks campus, where a tree and rose garden were planted in Menchaca's memory and a sculpture was created in her likeness. A stone bench there bears the words "Scientist. Mother. Wife. Colleague. Mentor. Friend. Much admired. Greatly missed."

"For those of us who knew her," said former Amgen staffer Robert Heard at the dedication, "we should reflect on and recall those precious moments spent in the company of her lively and energetic spirit. It is therefore my privilege to hereby dedicate the Area of Reflection as a permanent memorial to the life of Dora Menchaca. We will never forget." △

Above: Dora Menchaca, associate director of clinical research, was aboard American Airlines flight 77, which was hijacked and crashed by terrorists into the Pentagon on September 11, 2001. Menchaca is remembered lovingly by colleagues, friends, and family.

The Science of Kineret®

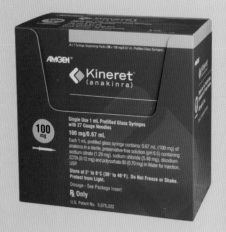

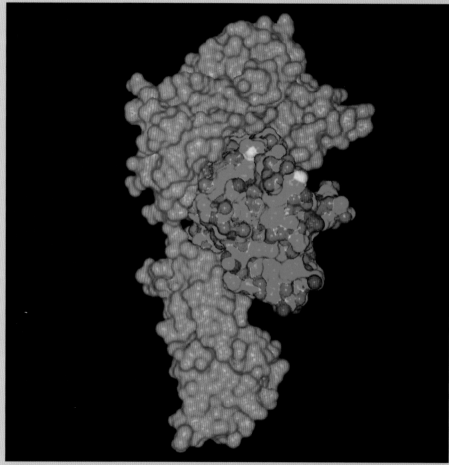

Kineret® (anakinra) blocks the biologic activity of human interleukin-1 (IL-1), a protein produced by inflammation and immune responses. IL-1 is found in increased amounts within joints that are inflamed in rheumatoid arthritis patients. When stimulated, IL-1 attaches to receptors on tissues and to white blood cells, causing joint inflammation and promoting the release of enzymes that can destroy the cartilage and bone. Indicated to reduce signs and symptoms in moderately to severely active rheumatoid arthritis in adults, Kineret® is a man-made interleukin-1 receptor antagonist. It can prevent IL-1 from attaching to the receptor by attaching to the receptor in its place, thus helping to stop the inflammatory and enzyme-releasing effects of IL-1. Kineret® can slow the progression of structural damage for rheumatoid arthritis patients.

On September 18, 2001, the FDA approved Aranesp® in the United States for the treatment of anemia in chronic renal failure. Amgen promptly launched Aranesp® in oncology to compete head-to-head with Johnson & Johnson's Procrit®, a move that Johnson & Johnson had hoped to halt in an earlier, unsuccessful arbitration.

Two months later, on November 14, 2001, the FDA approved Kineret® for the reduction in signs and symptoms of moderate-to-severe rheumatoid arthritis. It was the only therapy to mitigate inflammation by specifically blocking IL-1, a pivotal cytokine.

"One of the most emotional experiences I've had at Amgen involved Kineret®," recalls Bob Baltera, who worked on the project. "One patient thanked me, describing how she'd gone from being bedridden and unable to move to taking Kineret® and being able to care for her family again. She was twenty-eight years old. We hit a lot of obstacles trying to get Kineret® approved, both internally and externally. But this patient made it all worthwhile."

The FDA then approved Neulasta® in 2002 for reducing the incidence of infection from chemotherapy-induced neutropenia in cancer patients with non-myeloid malignancies. Neulasta®, a longer-acting form of NEUPOGEN®, is able to offer once-per-chemotherapy-cycle injections. The *Wall Street Journal* said at the time Neulasta®

Below: The Kineret® viewfinder, an imaginative promotional item, supported the product's theme, "Take a closer look at Kineret®," at the Kineret® trade show at the American College of Rheumatology in 2002.

Above: The development of Kineret® took off in the mid-1980s in Boulder, Colorado, where David Dripps (left) and Mike Brewer, Amgen's two remaining original Kineret® researchers, continue to search for great drug candidates. Their team purified, cloned, expressed, and characterized IL-1ra, and identified the mechanism that makes IL-1ra effective in slowing inflammation rates.

was introduced that it "may have had the best launch of any drug in biotechnology history."

Later that year, on July 22, the FDA approved Aranesp® for the treatment of chemotherapy-induced anemia. This further fueled the competition with Johnson & Johnson, since Procrit® held a corner on the oncology market.

By 2003 Aranesp® had made strong market gains against Procrit® in the United States and Johnson & Johnson's Eprex® and other rivals in Europe—but staffers know the work isn't over. "It's critical that we outsell and out-execute the competition—we cannot let the market stabilize," explains Joe Turgeon, vice president of sales for Amgen's oncology business unit. "Our biggest challenge is to truly beat the competition with Aranesp® and to continue the strong growth of Neulasta®. Our goal is nothing short of market leadership."

R&D Raises the Bar

While these products debuted on the market, Roger Perlmutter was organizing a far more diverse R&D pipeline, building capability in

Neulasta® Sprints to Market

Before the FDA approved Neulasta® on January 31, 2002, NEUPOGEN® was the only prescription drug available to fight infection due to febrile neutropenia, a serious and common complication of chemotherapy. NEUPOGEN® was a success, but Amgen knew there was potential for another product. Thousands of patients were being hospitalized for neutropenia each year, largely because less than 10 percent of those patients had received proactive protection. The extensive dosing NEUPOGEN® required often caused healthcare professionals to use the product only after the infection had appeared.

As a result, Amgen scientists began researching methods to keep the NEUPOGEN® molecule in the body longer. Early on, it was discovered that when attached to other molecules, polyethylene glycol (PEG) slows down the excretion. From this discovery, Neulasta® was born. Neulasta® allows patients to endure fewer injections to maintain the right amount of infection-fighting neutrophils. Like its predecessor, Neulasta® has helped millions of people, generating $463.5 million in U.S. sales its first year. △

Above: According to Olaf Kinstler, creating a marketable drug is every scientist's dream. Kinstler's dream came true with Neulasta®.

large molecules, proteins, monoclonal antibodies, peptides, and small molecules. His goal: to reshape and re-energize Amgen's scientific engine. Quickly, he implemented a more rigorous review of projects and opportunities, dropping one hundred research programs—about half the total—to focus on those with the most promise.

Working with George Morrow, he also improved the organization's strategic focus, breaking down the wall between marketing and R&D; clarified lines of authority; and ushered in his own management team. Perlmutter joined forces with Miletich, Seidenberg, and Paul Reider, whom he recruited as head of chemistry research. (Reider devised the intricate formula for Crixivan®, a pill for treating HIV.) These crucial hires led to the recruitment of other top scientists who would populate the cluster of Amgen labs in Thousand Oaks and other company research facilities around the world. "Roger Perlmutter is the scientific leader," says Sharer. "I don't make any of the scientific decisions; I only monitor the performance. Mine is a dashboard view, watching the dials and gauges. As CEO, I back him up by being willing to financially and contractually bet on things that are quite risky, but might work."

Perlmutter's R&D team also began to more aggressively pursue drug candidates from small companies.

HISTORICAL AMGEMS

Q: Who once had a license plate that read "GCSF"?

A: Martha Vincent of clinical development

Below: To celebrate Amgen's first $1 billion in Neulasta® sales in 2003, Amgen staffers received piggy banks tagged "Thanks a billion."

The Science of Neulasta®

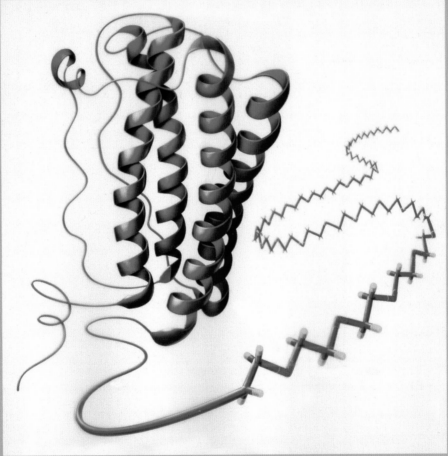

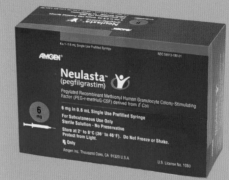

Neulasta® (pegfilgrastim) is a longer-acting version of its predecessor, NEUPOGEN®. Neulasta®, like NEUPOGEN®, is similar to the naturally occurring protein granulocyte-colony stimulating factor (G-CSF), which stimulates the formation of neutrophils, a type of white blood cell. When the white blood cell count is lowered by chemotherapy, Neulasta® can help by stimulating white blood cells in the bone marrow to multiply and form colonies. Neulasta® differs from NEUPOGEN® in that it has an attached molecule of poly-ethylene glycol (PEG), a waxy chemical. The PEG expands the molecule and allows for Neulasta® to remain in the body longer. As a result, fewer injections are required, making it, for many patients, a more convenient treatment choice than NEUPOGEN®.

Amgen in Space

On December 5, 2001, the space shuttle *Endeavour* blasted into orbit, carrying two dozen mice. Half the mice had been treated the day before with osteoprotegerin (OPG), a key inhibitor of bone loss that was discovered by Amgen scientists. Sean Morony, who helped coordinate the experimental procedures prior to the launch and after the landing, explains, "We collaborated on site with more than two dozen researchers and technicians from seven different institutes."

The experiment mimicked the effects of the rapid bone loss that astronauts experience due to microgravity, which deprives bones of the normal weight-bearing forces that are required to maintain a healthy skeleton. OPG works by inhibiting RANK ligand, a key protein responsible for the bone loss that occurs with osteoporosis. When the *Endeavour* returned 12 days later, mice treated with OPG had significantly greater bone density compared to their placebo-treated shuttle mates. According to principal scientist Paul Kostenuik, the OPG-treated mice actually had greater bone density than would be found in untreated mice that had remained on earth.

These initial mice studies have contributed to Amgen's continued research on OPG and other inhibitors of RANK ligand, including AMG 162, which currently is in clinical development for the treatment and prevention of osteoporosis and other forms of bone loss. "RANKL antagonists could be ideal for space travel because a single treatment might be able to prevent bone loss for months at a time," Kostenuik says. △

Top: NASA guest badges identifed spectators at the liftoff. *Above:* The "mission patch" worn by the *Endeavour* crew of STS-108 *Right:* The American flag, given to Amgen by NASA, commemorates the five-million-mile voyage and reads: "Amgen's OPG defeats NASA's microgravity."

Opposite: The space shuttle *Endeavour* awaits takeoff on its launch pad at Cape Canaveral, Florida.

Above: A NASA security clearance badge allowed Amgen's Sean Morony access to Cape Canaveral Air Force Base and Kennedy Space Center.

Perlmutter's team launched getting-to-know-you meetings in San Francisco, San Diego, and other biotech hotbeds, using Amgen's sizable quantity of cash as leverage. One purchase occurred with Swedish company Biovitrum, which was trying to license out a candidate for diabetes treatment. Though Biovitrum wanted to entertain only offers from larger companies such as Merck, a determined Perlmutter flew to Stockholm to meet with Biovitrum director Nicholas Simon, and Sharer cut short a vacation to meet with CEO Mats Pettersson. In a competitive bid on September 9, 2003, Amgen announced the licensing deal, paying $86.5 million up front—too much according to some analysts.

Yet Amgen considered it to be a worthwhile gamble. "It will cost Amgen about $150 million to see if the program is viable," says CFO Richard Nanula, "a small investment if it becomes a blockbuster." The jury is still out. To date, the program remains promising and is in clinical trials.

Sharer Goes Shopping

On December 14, 2000, Sharer closed a deal for $172.2 million with Kinetix Pharmaceuticals Inc. Based in Medford, Massachusetts, its staff was small at forty people, but had expertise in the areas of inflammation and oncology,

Above: Another milestone, another T-shirt

Opposite: Philip Tagari, director of chemistry research and discovery, and molecular pharmacology scientist Chi-Hwei Lin examine a medium that may help detect chemical entities that stimulate cultured liver cells to produce erythropoietin.

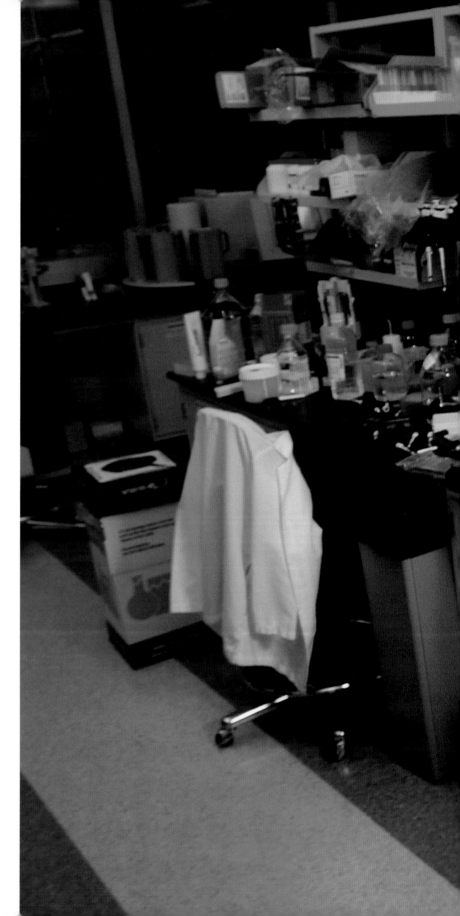

The Science of Enbrel®

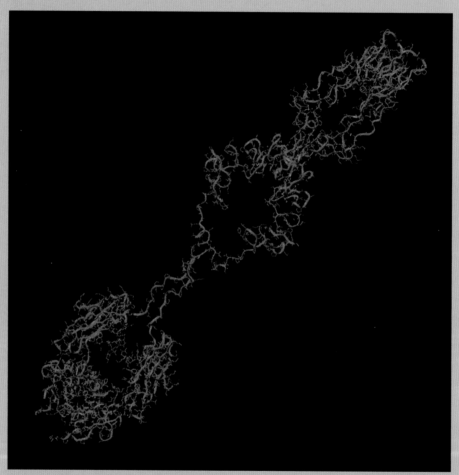

"*It is gratifying as a physician to see patients on Enbrel® experiencing long-term improvement of painful joints and unsightly skin lesions. Enbrel® has allowed them to resume normal activities of daily living and participate confidently in family, social, and work life.*"

— Dr. Philip Mease,
lead study investigator,
chief of rheumatology
clinical research,
Swedish Hospital
Medical Center,
Seattle

Enbrel® (etanercept) is manufactured to bind to tumor necrosis factor alpha (TNF alpha), one of the body's chemical messengers that regulates the inflammatory process. During a normal immune response, TNF alpha causes cells in the body to release chemicals that can contribute to inflammation. When the body produces excess TNF alpha, its immune system cannot control inflammation in the joints or of the skin. Enbrel® works to bind and deactivate some TNF alpha molecules before they can trigger inflammation. By interrupting the chain of events leading to inflammation, Enbrel® can work with the immune system to help reduce symptoms like pain, tenderness, and swelling in people with rheumatoid arthritis, ankylosing spondylitis, and psoriatic arthritis as well as help clear the skin of patients with psoriasis and psoriatic arthritis. Enbrel® also can inhibit the progression of joint destruction in people with rheumatoid and psoriatic arthritis.

Above: Craig Smith (left), Ray Goodwin, and Pat Beckmann (not pictured), helped create Enbrel®, which has delivered relief to thousands of people who suffer from rheumatoid arthritis and psoriasis.

having developed several promising compounds. The Kinetix deal provided additional strength in chemistry and gave Amgen a research facility on the East Coast. Amgen's oral-drug development programs also gave Perlmutter's operation the research capability to pursue small molecule drugs rather than the recombinant drugs the company had developed in the past.

This merger was just one of several industry acquisitions at the time, as large companies such as Johnson & Johnson and Millennium Pharmaceuticals began to swallow up smaller, faltering companies with promising products. But Kinetix and the company's 1994 acquisition of Synergen were just warmups for Sharer's biggest wager of all. On December 16, 2001, in a move that stunned the industry for its size and audacity, Amgen announced plans to buy the Seattle-based Immunex, a leader in the area of inflammation with $1 billion in revenues, $858 million in cash, and a $14 billion market cap. The company was best known for its blockbuster

drug Enbrel®, led by scientists Ray Goodwin, Craig Smith, and Pat Beckmann who "helped discover some of the most important new drug targets in decades," according to *Forbes* magazine. A leading treatment for rheumatoid and psoriatic arthritis since it was approved by the FDA in 1998, Enbrel® was also showing great promise for treating psoriasis.

Once a high flier, Immunex had stumbled after its highly touted asthma drug NUVANCE® had failed in human trials. Also, the company couldn't manufacture enough Enbrel® to keep up with demand. At the time of the acquisition, forty thousand sufferers of rheumatoid arthritis were on a waiting list for the drug. Strapped for cash, Immunex had licensed the manufacturing of Enbrel® to a company in Germany while it struggled to bring its Rhode Island plant on line.

But though its stock had nosedived, no one expected the company to be bought out. Most analysts assumed that Immunex would be protected from a takeover because drug giant Wyeth held a large stake in the company. But Wyeth had been hit hard recently by the negative press and multiple lawsuits associated with its diet drug fen-phen, which had been implicated in several deaths. The company needed cash to cover the fen-phen settlements, which were running into billions of dollars.

"It became known to me that Wyeth was going to monetize their Immunex investment," says Sharer. "They were about ready to go with another company." Quickly, he took the opportunity to his team.

Above: The Amgen Rhode Island manufacturing facility supplies Enbrel® for commercial use. Its creed: "We make Enbrel® so that no patient goes without."

"We're a science-based company, and we have great marketing minds here. But we're all about the patient. When we discuss various solutions to a challenge, we're always thinking, What's the right thing for the patient?"

— Joe Turgeon, sales, hired in 1989

Immunex at a Glance

On September 9, 1997, Immunex heard some great news: Phase III clinical trials of Enbrel® showed promising results for rheumatoid arthritis patients.

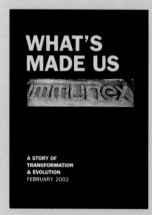

The creators of Enbrel®, scientists Ray Goodwin, Craig Smith, and Pat Beckmann, had started working on the project years after other companies. Smith recalls, "Every day we expected to read in the paper that another company had cloned a TNF receptor. We started so late in the game—the cards were stacked against us." Immunex won the race because the scientists used an innovative method called direct expression cloning. Goodwin says, "We made expression libraries to try to clone these genes as opposed to other people who were trying to do the same thing by purifying the protein."

As with any drug, the patient success stories make all the work worthwhile. Gloria Baswell, who participated in Enbrel® clinical trials, testifies, "I know what hell is like and I know how good it feels to come out of it. I feel like I've gotten my life back."

Goodwin says, "It's both satisfying and humbling when you can see that your work has led to a product that benefits people." ▵

Above: A 2002 booklet on the story of Immunex

"This was not something that everyone jumped on from day one," says Fabrizio Bonanni. "We had a new team, and we were diving into competition with Johnson & Johnson. I had to take a deep breath and ask myself, Can we absorb Immunex? But in the end, everyone supported the decision. My own reasoning was that we shouldn't be dependent on two products. We needed Enbrel®."

Sharer agrees: "We concluded that Enbrel® was an important drug with a big future. It was more than a product—it was a footprint in the new, large therapeutic area called inflammation. We paid a lot of money for that company, but it was a competitive bidding situation, and we could clearly see where Amgen could add value."

The deal was finalized on July 15, 2002. The acquisition allowed Amgen to leapfrog into the top tier of the fifteen largest drug companies, giving the company revenues of at least $5.5 billion at the end of 2002, with a combined market value of about $80 billion.

Amgen worked hard to make the integration work, having learned what not to do from the firings and disorganization accompanying the Synergen acquisition. "We assigned one person, Scott Foraker, to take charge of the integration," says Sharer. "He reported directly to me and to a small group." Amgen also made an effort to assimilate the staff and labs, and to keep up morale, especially in Immunex's Seattle research facilities.

Opposite: Immunex survivors of the Enbrel® FDA filing process lost sleep but not their sense of humor.

Below: In May 2002 the *Thousand Oaks Star* highlighted Amgen's impending purchase of Immunex. Before the merger, a backlog of patients was waiting for Enbrel®. Amgen got the Rhode Island plant up and running quickly and began meeting that pent-up demand right away.

The newly combined company's first priority—and challenge—was to get the Rhode Island plant up and running. Sharer assigned Bonanni to make it happen. "I focused on this 100 percent of the time," says Bonanni. "The plant had been built ten years earlier but had never been used. Some of the people had been there the whole time and had never made a product. They were disillusioned. We had to win their hearts and minds, and we did."

The team secured FDA approval in a matter of months, and was able to manufacture enough Enbrel® for every patient that needed it. "That was one of the great success stories in Amgen history, getting the drug out to these people who were suffering while they waited," says Dennis Fenton.

Was the acquisition a winner? Some think it's too early to decide. Yet Enbrel® leaped in sales to $1.3 billion in 2003, its first full year after the merger, and held or gained in market share despite entering a highly competitive market. By then, the FDA had approved the drug for four indications in the United States: rheumatoid arthritis, juvenile rheumatoid arthritis, psoriatic arthritis, and ankylosing spondylitis. The following year, Enbrel® was approved for use in the treatment of moderate-to-severe plaque psoriasis—especially good news for Amgen's Tejal Jambusaria and the millions of others who suffer from this chronic and potentially disabling skin disease.

"I've had psoriasis since I was eleven years old and have always had to deal with messy topical ointments," says

Above: To celebrate the merger with Immunex, Amgen placed this advertisement in the *Wall Street Journal* as well as in Seattle, Los Angeles, Colorado, and Rhode Island newspapers. The ad's headline reads: "What would a 32-year-old cancer patient hope to see from the merger of two premier biotech companies? Grandchildren."

Jambusaria. "With Enbrel®, my psoriasis got much clearer within just a few weeks. I've heard EPOGEN® stories and I've heard Enbrel® stories, but I had to experience it for myself to realize that I'm not just working to make a living—I'm working to make a difference."

That's the kind of thing Sharer and his team like to hear. "The competitive performance of Enbrel® says more about Amgen's reorganization than any single thing I can point to. All our bets paid off," he says, reminiscing about the risks of his first few years as CEO.

Global Expansion

Meanwhile, Amgen's European operations continued to grow and increase in market share. Until 2001, Amgen Europe—with the help of F. Hoffmann-LaRoche through 1998—had been selling only NEUPOGEN®. Now the overseas staff was about to plunge into selling its second drug, Aranesp®, which went on the market in the therapeutic area of nephrology in 2001 and for supportive care in oncology in September 2002. (Aranesp® is manufactured in Longmont, Colorado, and distributed to European countries out of Amgen's Breda Center in the Netherlands.)

With the introduction of Aranesp®, European sales rose dramatically, despite the presence of two strong competitors—Eprex®, Johnson & Johnson's Epoetin alfa product in Europe, and Roche's NeoRecormon®.

HISTORICAL AMGEMS

Q: In 1998 a book coauthored by an Amgen staff member made the bestseller list in Japan. What was the book and who wrote it?

A: The Golden DNA Helix, *coauthored by Fuminori Yoshida, founder and former president of Amgen KK Japan*

Below: Beanie Babies inspired by Aranesp® colors are among promotional items Amgen's sales and marketing teams give out at trade shows and other venues.

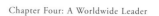

Opposite: (From left) Cambridge's then-mayor Anthony Galluccio, Kevin Sharer, Senator Edward Kennedy, and David Armistead, former vice president and site head, at Amgen's new Cambridge Research Center in Cambridge, Massachusetts, in October 2001

Sales and Marketing: Competing Intensely to Win

It's hard to imagine now that anyone could confuse household products with life-improving drugs, but Bill Ashton remembers—and he still laughs about it.

"We'd show up, the receptionists would look at our cards, and then they'd tell the physicians that someone from Amway was there to see them," says Ashton, who joined Amgen in 1989 as Pittsburgh's first territory manager and went on to become Amgen's vice president of commercial affairs in Washington, D.C. "For a while, getting our name out there was our biggest challenge." Now, nephrologists, oncologists, and inflammation specialists around the world not only know Amgen's name, they've witnessed firsthand the impact that Amgen products have made on the lives of patients.

Amgen's success stems not only from the leading science behind the drugs, but also from the new level of market competition the company's sales and marketing teams have encountered. While Amgen's first two products, EPOGEN® and NEUPOGEN®, had for years been virtually competition-free, subsequent products like Aranesp®, Neulasta®, Kineret®, and more recently Enbrel® and Sensipar® face head-to-head competition against Big Pharma powerhouses. Yet through a quantum leap in aggressiveness, discipline, and good old-fashioned sales skills—part of the foundation of the Alignment Initiative—Amgen is emerging as the market leader around the globe.

"We are *the* partner for chronic kidney disease patient care thanks to our products, educational programs, and the excellence of our sales and marketing teams," says Helen Torley, who heads up the nephrology business unit. "Our staff maintains an extremely high degree of detailed scientific knowledge so that we

Top: Amy Baker, rheumatology professional sales representative, introduces fifty-milligram pre-filled Enbrel® syringe kits to Dr. Warren Rizzo at his rheumatology office in Phoenix.

Above: Health system manager PK Rajagopal conducts in-service training on Aranesp® and Neulasta® for nurse practitioner Carolyn McCarthy-Golden and her colleagues at the New York University Clinical Cancer Center.

Below: Ginny Soto, professional sales representative for the oncology business unit, shares research on Neulasta® with medical oncologist Dr. Leonard Kalman of Oncology Hematology Group of South Florida.

can assist physicians and their offices in understanding the value of our products. Having come from leading a sales team in Big Pharma, I can attest that only an exceptional representative from Big Pharma can make it at Amgen."

Having excellent products certainly works in the teams' favor, as Laura Hamill can confirm. "Arthritis and psoriasis take fully functioning people and stop them in their tracks with very bad flu-like aches and pains," says Hamill, the leader of Amgen's inflammation unit. "We're lucky to have a product like Enbrel®. Not only are we beating the competition with it, we're helping patients beat their diseases."

Amgen Europe is emerging as a front-runner in the competition as well. While the group began partnering with F. Hoffman-LaRoche to co-market NEUPOGEN® in 1989, today it's leading the market on its own with Neulasta® as well as Aranesp® for nephrology and oncology. "In 2002, we began an extraordinary period with these new product launches—hiring new people, strengthening our team spirit, thinking big, and bringing our sales force up against our competitors," says Dominique Monnet, vice president of marketing and business operations for Amgen Europe. "Now we're ahead of our competitors with more than 40 percent of the market. And we keep raising the bar."

While sales and marketing have indeed raised the bar on competitiveness, ultimate success comes down to salesmanship, says Jim Daly, head of Amgen's oncology business unit. "We must have the unmatched ability to communicate clear, credible, and persuasive reasons why Amgen products represent the best treatment options for cancer patients," says Daly, "and we must do it with passion and professionalism." ⚗

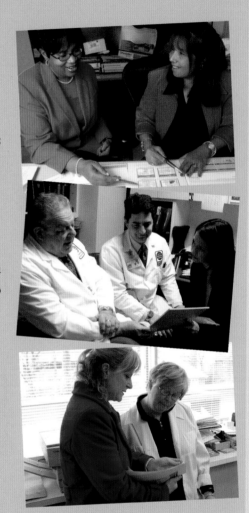

Top: Nephrology dialysis specialist Patricia Haynes with Sun Health administrator Anita Garcia in Joliet, Illinois. *Middle:* Dermatology senior professional sales representative Dawn Perry (right) with doctors at New York University Medical Center. *Above:* Amgen Canada biopharmaceutical specialist representative Nicole Danis-Ziebarth visits with nurse Jenny Brown at an Ottawa clinic.

By 2004, internal estimates showed Aranesp® was ahead of both competitors in nephrology and oncology.

By the end of September 2004, the company's international staff, mostly based in Europe but also in Asia, Canada, and Australia, had grown to more than fourteen hundred people, with international sales generating $1.2 billion. In early 2004, with the extension of the European Union into Eastern Europe, Amgen launched commercial operations in ten new countries: Poland, Hungary, the Czech Republic, Slovakia, Slovenia, Lithuania, Estonia, Latvia, Malta, and Cyprus.

In Asia, sales have been slower. Intellectual property rights for new products are not well protected in some Asian nations. "And the crown jewels are all owned by Kirin," explains George Morrow, referring to longstanding licensing deals with the Japanese brewer and drug company for EPOGEN® and NEUPOGEN®. In addition, China is still a developing country. "They have other health concerns to worry about before trying to address the symptoms of rheumatoid arthritis," Morrow says.

Yet it's the challenge of the ever-changing biotechnology industry that keeps Amgen staffers on their toes. "I tell people that there is no 'old' Amgen or 'new' Amgen," says Jim Daly, vice president of sales and marketing for oncology. "There's just one Amgen. We come to work to make the company better."

The Bubble Bursts

In the late 1990s the biotech and high-tech world went crazy. Stocks doubled, then tripled as

Right: At the Enbrel® manufacturing facility in Rhode Island: Amgen's CEO Kevin Sharer (standing, center) joins staffers (from left) Roop Kumar, Kimball Hall, Jay Marshall (seated), Tony Pankau, Jerry McAndrews, and Kathleen Retterson. Prior to Amgen's purchase of Immunex and its plant, forty thousand patients were awaiting delivery of Enbrel®. Bringing the facility online and up to standards for FDA approval required heroic cross-country coordination and the efforts of Amgen staffers throughout the company.

Below: The city of Breda in the Netherlands created a local version of Monopoly with Amgen occupying the space normally home to Park Place.

Above: The FORTUNE 500 list has long been home to Amgen. In this February 2002 issue, Amgen is ranked No. 403.

investors poured money into hundreds of companies in a stock-buying frenzy unlike anything seen before. But in late 2000, the inevitable drop-off began, and in 2001 and 2002 it turned into a full-fledged crash as many high-fliers watched their stock plummet to single digits. Pessimism descended over the industry as investors once again realized the brutal reality of the drug-making business—that only a handful of biotech companies out of the hundreds launched had ever turned a profit.

"The truth about the biotech industry," Sharer reflects now, "is that there are hundreds of companies that have all been founded on some scientific medical hope.

I'm sure those hopes are reasonable hopes. But the difference between understanding some mechanism in the body that could have an important effect on disease and translating that insight into a medicine is a gigantic leap."

Amgen's stock was not immune to the market dive—many analysts and investors felt a lingering unease about Sharer's bold moves. But in comparison to the tech market losses, which fell by 47 percent in mid-2000, Amgen's drop of nearly half that amount indicated that panicked investors saw the company as a safer bet than most. By early 2003 Amgen had recovered to its year 2000 levels, outperforming most companies in the biotech and technology sectors through early 2004.

Packing the Pipeline

Despite the travails of the markets, the newly pumped-up Amgen was charging ahead by mid-2002, with its new product approvals, the Immunex acquisition, and an increase in staff from 7,682 in 2001 to 10,118 in 2002. On March 8, 2004, Amgen celebrated the approval of its first small molecule, Sensipar® (cinacalcet HCl), licensed from NPS Pharmaceuticals.

Following the Phase I failure of the first clinical candidate, the Amgen team led by Mike Downing had selected an improved calcimimetic agent, Sensipar®, from hundreds of chemical compounds. "The cinacalcet effort represented the initiation of small-molecule drug development activities at Amgen," says team chemist Gil Rishton. "The drug, which is formulated as tablets or capsules for

Below: This model shows the structure of the calcimimetic compound AMG 073, or Amgen's Sensipar®. The black balls represent carbons, the white ones hydrogens, the green ones fluorines. The blue one is nitrogen.

Sensipar®, Amgen's First Oral Therapy

Introduced in spring 2004, the light-green Sensipar® tablets—Amgen's first small-molecule product and first drug in tablet form—offer hope to chronic kidney disease patients on dialysis who suffer from secondary hyperparathyroidism and parathyroid carcinoma patients suffering from elevated calcium levels.

Secondary hyperparathyroidism is a serious metabolic disorder characterized by an imbalance of parathyroid hormone, calcium, and phosphorus—minerals vital to good bone health. This malady occurs when the kidney function declines and the calcium and phosphorus balance in the body is upset, triggering the calcium-sensing receptor to secrete too much parathyroid hormone in an effort to restore balance. Tragically, nearly all of the more than three hundred thousand dialysis patients in the United States suffer from secondary hyperparathyroidism.

Parathyroid carcinoma causes excess secretion of parathyroid hormone, which can lead to hypercalcemia, a condition that can cause severe bone loss, bone pain, high blood pressure, muscle weakness, kidney stones, stomach problems, and mental dysfunction. Each year in the United States, approximately five hundred people develop parathyroid carcinoma.

Sensipar® acts directly on the calcium-sensing receptor, located on the parathyroid gland, helping patients achieve key target lab values for parathyroid hormone, calcium-phosphorus product, calcium, and phosphorus levels.

Amgen licensed Sensipar® from NPS Pharmaceuticals in 1996 and filed a new drug application with the FDA in September 2003. The FDA approved the drug on March 8, 2004. Amgen has also filed new drug applications in Australia, Canada, Europe, and New Zealand. △

Above: Mark Menning runs a capsule-filling machine in Building 8.

The Science of Sensipar®

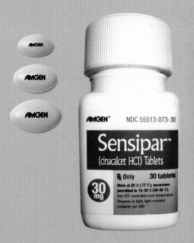

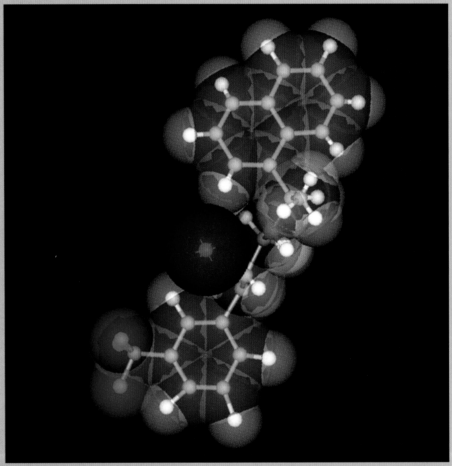

"Sensipar® represents an important therapeutic development. Physicians will now be able to safely and effectively reduce parathyroid hormone levels without increasing levels of calcium and phosphorus, making it possible to achieve recommended therapeutic goals."

— Geoffrey A. Block, lead author and director of clinical research, Denver Nephrologists

Sensipar® (cinacalcet HCl) is indicated for the treatment of secondary hyperparathy-roidism in patients with chronic kidney disease on dialysis and elevated calcium levels in patients with parathyroid carcinoma. When the kidneys are working normally, parathyroid hormone (PTH) regulates calcium and phosphorus levels by moving the right amounts in and out of the bones. In patients with kidney disease, however, the balance of calcium and phosphorus is upset, causing excess PTH to be produced. Patients with excess PTH often develop secondary hyperparathyroidism, a condition that can cause problems in the bones, heart, lungs, and blood vessels. By binding to the calcium-sensing receptor located on the parathyroid gland, Sensipar® works to lower PTH levels while simultaneously low-ering calcium and phosphorus levels.

Above: Sensipar® began as a calcimimetic project designed to find a treatment for hyperparathyroidism. The Phase I clinical trial of an earlier compound cleared too rapidly from circulation and so required high dosages and multiple administrations. After teammates Lorin Roskos and Manoj Bajpai diagnosed the problem, chemist Gil Rishton (seated) identified a superior compound that did the trick—AMG 073 (cinacalcet HCl), later named Sensipar®.

HISTORICAL AMGEMS

Q: When was Amgen's current logo unveiled and what part of the original logo was removed because it did not fit on product vials?

A: June of 1988. The plasmid was removed.

years—more than $1.7 billion in the last year alone. People have wondered, 'What are they spending that money on?' So we wanted to provide more insight into the programs that make up this R&D investment."

The bottom-line message of the seminar was that more product candidates had entered into development at Amgen during the past three years than in the previous ten years combined. With a 2003 research expense of $1.7 billion and about thirty-five thousand patients in worldwide clinical trials, Amgen's labs were brimming with possibilities. Kineret® and Enbrel® had dramatically changed the way physicians treat inflammatory diseases, especially with the FDA's 2004 approval of Enbrel® in treating moderate-to-severe plaque psoriasis. Encouraged, Amgen scientists were pursuing four other promising inflammation-fighting candidates.

In the metabolic disease and osteoporosis arena, Amgen scientists were working on 11ß-HSD1, the small-molecule program licensed from Biovitrum. This enzyme inhibitor could potentially alter the therapy for Type 2 diabetes.

oral administration, represents an entirely new business opportunity for the company. It's exceptionally rare to successfully launch a drug product that meets all of these initial criteria."

A first-in-class orally administered "calcimimetic agent," Sensipar® treats secondary hyperparathyroidism in patients on dialysis and hypercalcemia in patients with parathyroid cancer by inhibiting the secretion of excessive amounts of parathyroid hormone (PTH), which often causes a variety of medical complications including loss of bone density.

Also in March 2004, Amgen held its first "R&D Day" in New York, inviting analysts to hear about twenty-four of the forty major programs in its pipeline. "Amgen has historically been very quiet about its pipeline," explains CFO Richard Nanula. "But now that our marketed products have been launched so successfully, investors are concerned about what's next. And obviously we've been investing heavily in R&D over the last several

Osteoporosis has long been a target as well, with Amgen scientists looking at AMG 162, which grew out of the OPG studies in the 1990s aimed at maintaining bone density.

Below: The AMG 162 experimental osteoporosis treatment is one of Amgen's most promising late-stage drug candidates. AMG 162 has been shown to improve bone mineral density.

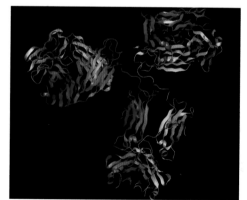

Scientists also continued to explore oncology, with nine promising product candidates in the works, including palifermin, a recombinant human keratinocyte growth factor (rHuKGF) that was

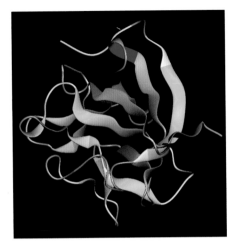

submitted to the FDA in June 2004 for the potential therapeutic indication to reduce the incidence, duration, and severity of oral mucositis in patients with hematologic malignancies. Oral mucosistis is a side effect of high-dose chemotherapy and radiotherapy characterized by severe mouth sores. Amgen also has pursued its first fully human monoclonal antibody directed against the epidermal growth factor receptor (EGFr). Amgen evaluated panitumumab as a treatment of various solid tumor cancers in partnership with Abgenix, and in 2004, initiated pivotal clinical studies on panitumumab as a third-line monotherapy in colorectal cancer patients.

At least two more product candidates were in development to join EPOGEN®, NEUPOGEN®, Aranesp®, Neulasta®, and Sensipar® in the hematology and nephrology areas, with scientists working on alfimeprase to degrade blood clots and AMG 531 to address bleeding disorders.

And finally, in neurology, scientists were busy with three major projects, including glial cell line-derived neurotrophic factor (GDNF), part of the Synergen purchase. Unfortunately, the Phase II study of GDNF for the treatment of advanced Parkinson's disease did not meet the primary study endpoint upon completion of six months of the double-blind treatment phase of the study.

Cautiously optimistic, Amgen discussed these product candidates at its first R&D Day. But apprehensive analysts forecasted that despite the surge of activity in Amgen's pipeline, there would be a slowing of revenue growth over the next few years; they didn't see another EPOGEN® or equivalent blockbuster in the near future.

Still, sales and marketing continued to expand as Amgen became more adept at direct-to-consumer marketing. From 2000 to 2004, the company launched several large-scale advertising campaigns featuring celebrity spokespersons such as Danny Glover, Rob Lowe, Deborah Norville, and Kathleen Turner to better inform patients about their disease.

By 2004, the Washington office—originally set up by Gordon Binder and Peter Teeley (who retired in 2004), and now run by David Beier, an attorney with extensive government and biotechnology industry experience—was overseeing the company's interactions with governments, both in the U.S. and globally. The global government affairs function now advocates comprehensively on reimbursement, intellectual property, tax, and other public policy issues with a substantially larger staff and greater reach.

Amgen's affiliations with universities and companies around the world continued to expand, too. On August 13, 2004, Amgen even acquired one of these companies—South San Francisco-based Tularik Inc.—for $1.5 billion. The company had been a leader in researching and developing drugs for esophageal cancer, inflammatory diseases, diabetes, and obesity. "Tularik's research engine is a rare

Above: Known within Amgen as palifermin, keratinocyte growth factor (KGF), is in the works to help patients at high risk for severe mucositis, a common side effect of high-dose chemotherapy.

Right: Actor and "By My Side" spokesperson Rob Lowe and his father. Lowe speaks nationally about his father, who, while receiving chemotherapy, acquired a lung infection that delayed treatment.

Opposite: Actor Danny Glover participates in the 2002 Los Angeles National Kidney Foundation's Kidney Walk sponsored by Anemia LifeLine, an educational initiative created by Amgen.

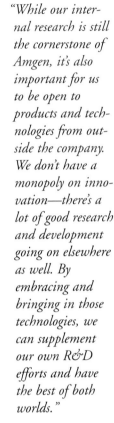

"While our internal research is still the cornerstone of Amgen, it's also important for us to be open to products and technologies from outside the company. We don't have a monopoly on innovation—there's a lot of good research and development going on elsewhere as well. By embracing and bringing in those technologies, we can supplement our own R&D efforts and have the best of both worlds."

— Scott Foraker, licensing, hired in 1994

asset and a great strategic fit," says Roger Perlmutter.

Coincidentally, Tularik founder and CEO Dave Goeddel, Ph.D., had been a graduate student in Marv Caruthers's lab at the University of Colorado, Boulder. Caruthers, a former member of Amgen's Scientific Advisory Board, had created Amgen Boulder—a small group that, among other things, supplied Fu-Kuen Lin with the probes he needed in his erythropoietin work.

Trying to Stay Human with Fourteen Thousand Staff

Some Amgen staff members had greeted Sharer's vision for the company—a fusion of the old and the new—with skepticism when it debuted in 2002. Yet by 2004, even the critics agreed that the plan was working. "The decision-making is different," says research director and longtime staff member Frank Martin. "The process is clearer now for selecting new projects and when things get decided. That's the biggest change we see aside from the general size of Amgen."

"Amgen is a little more slick than it was in the past," says Tim Osslund, "more businesslike. We also bought Immunex—and that brought really good science and ideas."

Tom Boone agrees that things have improved with the recent growth. "People like myself, Frank Martin, Dennis Fenton, and Tim Osslund help to keep a lot of the old-time values. There is a lot of talk about the Amgen Values and the Amgen culture.

Opposite: Amgen staffers celebrate milestones, awards, and just plain hard work with picnics, parties, and other events.

Below: Amgen consistently finds itself among *Fortune* magazine's "100 Best Companies to Work For," appearing for the first time in 1997 at No. 74 and rising to No. 33 by 2003, as reported in this January 2004 issue.

Global Development

For years, Amgen's global development department has been central to the company's success. For each product Amgen works to bring to market, global development sets up and oversees clinical trials—monitoring safety and regulatory matters—and conducts clinical research to determine economic feasibility. Once a product is deemed clinically effective and financially viable, the staff proceeds with product labeling and physician education, and then moves on to manage the portfolios and pipelines of Amgen's marketed drugs.

The department reaches almost every corner of Amgen, including global development operations, global biostatistics and health economics, early development, inflammation, oncology, and nephrology. Yet despite shouldering immense responsibility, staff members have learned to take time to celebrate their successes.

In 2003, the department launched its annual global celebrations, where teams from all over the world held theme parties ranging from "Animals at the Zoo" to "Rio de Janeiro Carnivals." There, staff members reflected on the various department milestones of the year. The global development department had helped Amgen sustain its aggressive growth by increasing clinical studies, publications, and FDA document submissions. The department has also achieved key filings, such as Enbrel® for use in psoriasis, and actively managed more than five hundred clinical

Top: In August 2004, Amgen KK in Japan celebrated the year's global development achievements with a summer festival. *Above and right:* Oceans apart, a carnival-themed picnic in Thousand Oaks looks a lot like a summer festival in Japan. Regardless of locale, there's no hiding the goodwill behind the colorful masks.

studies involving almost twenty thousand patients, including trials for cinacalcet HCl and palifermin.

The following year, global development continued its new tradition of celebration, this time with a Cape Cod "Escape from the Cape" theme in Washington, Canada, and Thousand Oaks; a summer barbecue venue in Amgen Europe, Cambridge, and Amgen KK Japan; and a trivia night in Amgen Australia. Again, the team members reflected on their significant achievements of 2004, including the launch of two new AMG 162 studies and the approval of Mimpara® (cinacalcet HCl) in Europe.

Speaking to her California staff, former global development head Beth Seidenberg reminded the team that the reason for all their hard work was to serve patients. This message was underscored by Michele Jurbala, an Amgen human resources staffing manager and breast cancer survivor, who relayed the ways in which Amgen therapeutics Aranesp® and Neulasta® had helped her cope with her illness.

The global development teams will continue filing, overseeing trials, and submitting approvals in the coming years. But thanks to the department's annual celebrations, the staff members are better able to carry on, encouraged in the knowledge that their work is about more than just managing products—it's about bettering lives. Ⓐ

Top: Amgen's global development staffers in Cambridge, U.K., enjoy an outdoor barbecue.

Above: Amgen Canada celebrates with a Cape Cod theme.

On the other hand, we've also been able to develop our careers, contribute in ways that we enjoy, and focus on the science. And so Amgen has actually evolved in a way that's been very positive for many of us."

The Amgen spirit has thrived, too, as teams continue to churn out T-shirts with secret compound symbols and staff members participate in games, picnics, volunteerism, and other activities. "There is an informality and an intensity that is important," says Sharer. "It's a California immigrant mentality, a 'land of dreams' mentality. We've found we can reinvent ourselves. We're on the leading edge of everything."

Today, more than half of Amgen's fourteen thousand plus staff members have been with the company for two years or less, yet they share the same sense of excitement as longtime staff. "When I talk with new sales reps, it always rekindles my spirit," says Joe Turgeon, who recalls sitting on a cardboard box between meetings when he came to interview at Amgen in 1989. "I'll often ask how long the new folks have wanted to work here, and many will say something like seven years. And I think it's because we're a science-based company. We have great marketing minds here, but we're more about the patient. I see it in everything we do."

Another landmark of the company's growth was the major expansion of the Rhode Island campus. On April 2, 2004, hundreds of Amgen staff members helped dedicate BioNext, Amgen's new 375,000-square-foot production building. The $1 billion project is made up of five buildings and will be completed in 2005. Among its many state-of-the-art features are nine twenty-thousand-liter bioreactors.

The East Coast is also home to Amgen's Cambridge, Massachusetts, research center. This 285,000-square-foot facility opened on October 19, 2001, and joined a thriving group of biotechnology research facilities in the Boston area, including those run by companies such as Biogen Inc., Genzyme Corp., and Millennium Pharmaceuticals Inc. Amgen's Cambridge research focuses on small molecule drugs, and includes research incorporated from the Kinetix acquisition.

Meanwhile, Amgen's Thousand Oaks campus continues to expand across the Conejo Valley. The William K. Bowes Jr. headquarters building (Building 38) opened in 2002; in 2004, Building 29 was renamed the George B. Rathmann Building; and the new Franklin P. Johnson Jr. Building (Building 28) opened in 2005.

Above: A T-shirt celebrating Amgen staffers who volunteer in their communities. The message: "Together We Can Make a World of Difference"

Above: Christine Smith, a quality analytical lab (QAL) associate, describes the laboratory support area of QAL at a tour during the BioNext dedication in April 2004.

Opposite: With Building 9 but a memory, construction began on Building 28 in 2003, a five-story administrative building named the Franklin P. Johnson Jr. Building after early Amgen venture capitalist "Pitch" Johnson.

Below: Building 9 was demolished in fall 2003. Thousands of Amgen staff members and more than twenty-five different functions had occupied the facility since it opened in 1989.

Seattle's Double Helix Building

In 1994, fifteen hundred "Immunoids" clad in yellow Immunex rain slickers, surrounded by patients and community members, broke ground on the Helix

Project, a new research campus in Seattle. Ten years later, in January 2004, the $625 million campus opened with parties and rave reviews from staff.

Amgen's Helix Project is the largest commercial biotechnology research lab in the northwestern United States. The facility overlooks beautiful Elliott Bay on Puget Sound, and its signature element is its double helix-designed pedestrian bridge—a nod to the ladder-like structure of DNA.

The *Seattle Times* called the building "an icon in the making for the city and its emergence in biotechnology." Designed in collaboration with scientists as an environment for the creation of breakthrough therapies, the 750,000-square-foot facility now houses researchers, process development scientists, and support personnel. More than 750 staff members from several locations throughout Seattle occupy the campus, which includes the latest technological advances in computerization and robotics to maximize efficiencies in research and process development. △

Left and above: Amgen Seattle's Helix research campus opened in January 2004. Its dramatic pedestrian bridge is visible to the more than fifty thousand drivers who pass the facility each day.

This building took the place of Building 9, which first housed Amgen staff in 1989. More than twenty-five departments have occupied this space over the years. "Building 9 housed our only cafeteria, so you'd see everyone there," says MaryAnn Foote, a medical writing director who joined Amgen in 1991. "Birds sometimes flew into the open-roofed atrium and couldn't find their way out. Often, someone would be charged with the duty of catching a bird and releasing it outside!

"The campus looked very different when I came," adds Foote. "You could stand in the parking lot of Building 9 and see forever. There were no large buildings around like there are today."

For Laura Irvin, operations administrator for worldwide operations, it was difficult to see Building 9 demolished. She also joined Amgen in 1991, and worked for several years in the building. "It's very emotional," she admits. "It's just a building, but I guess we feel that way about anything we care about."

As Amgen's campuses have multiplied—including an $800 million expansion in Puerto Rico and the new Helix facility in Seattle—so has the company's commitment to the community. Amgen continues to educate physicians, caregivers, and patients through product programs. It also remains committed to its Safety Net® program, which issues thousands of doses of free medication to the poor and uninsured. And in 2003, the Amgen Foundation granted more than $10 million in support of local and national nonprofit organizations that work to improve community resources, science literacy, and the health and well-being of patients.

Opposite: Mary Ringoff, a dialysis patient whose life has improved with EPOGEN®

Learning from the Past: Kineret®

Despite the company's lightning-fast growth—or, perhaps, because of it—Kevin Sharer insists that company leaders take time out to fully understand and commit to Amgen's values. Since early 2004, some three hundred directors and officers have attended a four-day workshop that includes real company case studies and discussions of how they would have handled various issues differently.

One of the most interesting—and painful—studies focuses on the development and launch of Kineret®. Despite the extreme dedication and hard work of so many Amgen staff members, in the months after its launch late in 2001, Kineret® failed to meet carefully constructed expectations.

By recounting missed opportunities, unaddressed issues, and insufficient attention to concerns raised by staff and outsiders, staffers have found the Kineret® saga provides rich material to draw from, exposing many lessons such as the need to adhere to the Amgen Values. Not surprisingly, the case discussions are very spirited, with participants often asking pointed questions of senior executives.

"It's extraordinary," says management consultant Richard Messina of Messina & Graham. "You can't help but be impressed by the openness and honesty on the part of company leaders who talk about what they learned from their experiences. Everyone in the room walks away with confidence that, if they see a problem, they need to raise concerns. And, if they make mistakes, it's going to be okay." △

Teamwork and a Commitment to Patients

Amgen's commitment to teamwork was amply demonstrated on February 17, 2003, in the Rhode Island plant. With the East Coast about to be socked in by a major snowstorm, most companies asked employees to stay home. But Amgen's Rhode Island facility was at a critical juncture in the manufacturing process and needed its staffers to keep the plant going.

Knowing that the crew coming off shift that Monday would probably not be able to get back to work Tuesday morning, Marci Gilchrist, Jeanene Puckett, Gayle Boulanger, and Bevin Noone—along with several members of the harvest group—decided to stay overnight nearby. They grabbed some blue scrubs to use as pajamas, and since no restaurants were open, headed to a convenience store to load up on junk food. The work was critical: cells needed to be harvested and sampled the next morning for a new batch of Enbrel®, and two other lots were in various stages of production. An interruption in this crucial step would disrupt the flow of Enbrel® to patients.

By 7:00 a.m. on Tuesday morning, these technicians were back at the plant and completed the cell harvest on schedule. "This was a great group effort," says Emily Steadman, manufacturing manager in cell culture processing. "It's amazing how these people pull together. The day shift came prepared to stay for a second shift. We had contingency plans for who would sleep when. As a result, we had a great cell harvest." △

Amgen at Twenty-five

"Who would have guessed?" asks George Rathmann, now retired and living in Palo Alto, California, where he takes regular injections of EPOGEN® for his own bout with chronic renal kidney failure. "I'm a testament to EPOGEN®," he says. "Without it, I would not have the energy to be here talking to you."

As Rathmann receives another dose of EPOGEN® at his home, hundreds of workers monitor countless red-topped vials that pass down a conveyor belt at the Fill and Finish facility in Puerto Rico. And as factories churn out drugs in Amgen plants in Colorado, California, and Rhode Island, boxes of finished products containing EPOGEN®, NEUPOGEN®, Enbrel®, Kineret®, Neulasta®, Aranesp®, and Sensipar® are filled and packed into boxes and containers in Puerto Rico, flown to Louisville and Breda, and distributed around the world. Meanwhile, hundreds of thousands of patients in dozens of countries depend on Amgen products to help improve their lives.

The operation that began in 1980 with a few investors sitting around a table now involves more than fourteen thousand staff members and a network of researchers, development experts, manufacturers, marketing and sales staff, physicians, regulators, advocacy groups, and patients. In a mere quarter-century, Amgen has become one of the U.S. stock market's most valuable one hundred companies and is listed as the world's eighth-largest pharmaceutical company in terms of market capitalization. Now, Amgen has the opportunity to grow further, serve more patients, and increase shareholder value.

"Amgen's commercial outlook is bright. You can make changes in your commercial organization and quickly see the impact in sales and market share. The question is R&D. Will the change in leadership help Amgen bring products to market in a timely fashion and inspire good growth going forward? We won't know the answer for the next five to ten years."

— David Molowa, health-care analyst, UBS Securities LLC

Below: What better gift than a miniature Louisville Slugger bat to show that the Louisville Distribution Center team will hit them out of the park every time? Created in 1993 as a one-time novelty item, the bats were so popular that Amgen visitors, guests, and vendors continue to receive them today.

Above: In March 2003, *Fortune* ranked Amgen as the fifth Most Admired Pharmaceutical, right between Eli Lilly and Wyeth. Amgen had been ranked sixth in 2001 and eighth in 2000.

At the time of the Immunex acquisition in 2002, Sharer told the world that Amgen could double its sales by 2005, from $4 to $8 billion. The company has more than hit this mark, bringing in an estimated $10 billion by the end of 2004—led by sales of EPOGEN®, NEUPOGEN®, Aranesp®, Neulasta®, and Enbrel®.

And the patients' stories keep rolling in. There is Michele Jurbala, an Amgen staffing manager who was diagnosed with stage 2 breast cancer in 2003. During chemotherapy she took Aranesp® for anemia and Neulasta® to fend off infection. Now in remission, Jurbala has formed a group of Amgen cancer survivors who meet for lunch each month. Coincidentally, she recruits physicians to work on Aranesp® and Neulasta® projects.

Then there is Jeremy Gonzales. At the age of two, he reverted to crawling. He was diagnosed with polyarticular course juvenile rheumatoid arthritis, a severe form of arthritis that can cause fever, joint pain, and inflammation. Jeremy, now age seven, rides a scooter, plays baseball, and "acts like a regular kid," according to his parents—all because of Enbrel®.

But despite such advantages, growth remains a challenge. Sharer believes that in 2004, Amgen reached the right size in order to handle current and future projects.

"We'll be very interested to see how the pipeline comes together in the next few years and how the company handles macro issues such as Medicare reimbursement," says May-Kin Ho of Goldman Sachs, who has followed Amgen since 1992. "But what Amgen really has to be careful about is growth. How big can you get before you lose efficiency?"

It's an issue Sharer clearly recognizes. "Size works against you when you're real small and real big," he explains. "When an undiversified bio-pharmaceutical company gets big enough, it can fall apart. It is much tougher to be innovative. We have to grow to stay competitive and to keep shareholders with us. But we won't know the full story until we survive going off-patent." This is scheduled to happen in the United States for EPOGEN® in 2013.

Analysts are still giving Sharer and his team high marks for the success of Enbrel® and the growth of the company. "Amgen can go toe-to-toe with most big-cap pharmaceutical companies in overall capabilities," said Christopher Raymond of Robert W. Baird & Co. in March 2003. In the summer of 2003, *Barron's* listed Amgen second after Coventry Health Care as "heading the honor roll" on a list of five hundred companies measured by investment performance. Moving up from number two hundred on the list in a single year, Amgen was described by the publication as having risen "on pure power, as the cash from a new set of drugs rolled in over the past twelve months or so, often at rates that surprised Amgen's biggest boosters."

And often at rates that surprised its own staff. Yet through all the change and growth, one thing has remained constant: Amgen still aspires to become the world's best human therapeutics company.

"How could you have a better aspiration than that?" asks Sharer. "Our destiny is in our hands."

Left: How time flies. "There is no doubt that the most exciting developments in biotech are yet to be discovered," says Phil Whitcome, who held on to this watch bearing an early Amgen logo. "As we go through the human genome, we're going to develop some amazing medicines."

After reading this book, you've seen how far we've come—at Amgen and in the biotechnology industry. But the first twenty-five years were just the beginning. In biotechnology—and at Amgen—we think the best is yet to be.

New therapies resulting from advances in biotechnology are making enormous differences in the lives of people with serious illnesses, as well as important contributions to our economy and public health. Even greater innovations are still ahead of us, as the

 sequencing of the human genome, together with increasing knowledge of fundamental biology, will lead to fresh ways of thinking about and treating disease. New scientific breakthroughs and technologies are poised to translate into better health and lives for patients around the world.

It's an exciting time to be who we are and where we are. In many ways, Amgen is uniquely positioned to help move biologically-based medicine forward. We have long been the world's largest biotechnology company—and our size does lend us strength—but our true strengths are measured in other ways than sales figures or market capitalization.

We have a unique strength in the quality of our people. We have always gone the extra mile to recruit and retain the very best talent in science and business. Over the past quarter century, more than twenty-three thousand fine people have worked at Amgen. Each of them has made a contribution to what we have accomplished, and has helped to lay the foundation for what we will accomplish tomorrow.

Another important source of strength we have is our commitment to the Amgen Values. Our values provide us with a competitive advantage, because we truly live them in everything we do. In particular, our dedication to creating value for patients and our strong base in science are vital to our success in the future, just as they have been all along. We seek to treat serious illness by following the science wherever it may lead, and we back that up with substantial investments in research and development. Not every potential product will make it—that's the nature of the business we're in. But the depth and breadth in our current pipeline, as well as our ability to attract partners for future projects, make me optimistic that our business will continue to grow as we bring important new therapies to patients.

In my thirteen years with Amgen, I've seen the company grow from a two-product company to one with seven products—five with annual sales of more than $1 billion each—and a growing pipeline of potential new therapies on the way. During that time, we've weathered our share of storms. But we also added an aspiration to be the best human therapeutics company. I believe that setting our sights upon that aspiration has helped us to chart the course.

Undoubtedly, there will be more challenges to come—navigating reimbursement and regulatory issues, building to scale as we grow, and continuing to expand our pipeline, to name a few. But Amgen is plunging into the future with the same verve, entrepreneurial spirit, commitment to innovative science, and dedication to patients as it has shown since that day a quarter century ago when it first opened its doors.

I don't know exactly what Amgen will look like twenty-five years from now—or what health care will look like. But I do know that our mission to serve patients will not change. That was our mission when we began; it remains our mission today, and it always will be.

I also know that biotechnology will play an ever greater role in improving the lives of people everywhere, and that Amgen will continue to be one of the companies in the forefront of medical innovation. Because as long as we follow the science, we will continue to lead the way.

Kevin Sharer
Chairman and CEO

This book is the result of a tremendous team effort from longtime staff members to those who've recently joined Amgen, as well as from board members, Amgen alumni, and company friends. While space prohibits us from thanking everyone who shared great stories, we've listed below a few contributors who spent many hours helping to ensure that the book is a fitting reflection of Amgen's history and its vision for the future:

Kirby Alton
Bob Andren
Raymond Baddour
Lesa Barnes
Jeff Bass
Elliot Beimel
Gordon Binder
Tom Boone
Bill Bowes
Craig Brooks
Aart Brouwer
Diana Campau
Steve Elliott
Dennis Fenton
Lorena Figueroa
Jeanne Fitzgerald
Ellen Gams

Ed Garnett
Lorraine Henwood
Matt Herlihy
Leroy Hood
Laura Irvin
Sally Jacob
Pitch Johnson
Marie Kennedy
Mary Klem
Dave Lacey
Fu-Kuen Lin
Jane Luper
Brian McNamee
Alan Mendelson
Ilana Meskin
Richard Messina

Richard Nanula
Mike Narachi
Nichole O'Connell
Steve Odre
Tim Osslund
Carol Piernot
George Rathmann
Anna Richo
Ana Rodriguez
Karen Schenk
Kevin Sharer
Jody Simon
Ralph Smalling
Barbara Tipton
Dan Vapnek
Stuart Watt
Phil Whitcome

Special thanks to Mary Thorsby, who oversaw the book from start to finish. And finally, thanks to the millions of patients around the world who have made the company's history and scientific breakthroughs all the more meaningful and worthwhile.

TEHABI BOOKS

Tehabi Books developed, designed, and produced *The Amgen Story: 25 Years of Visionary Science and Powerful Medicine* and has conceived and produced many award-winning books that are recognized for their strong literary and visual content. Tehabi works with national and international publishers, corporations, institutions, and nonprofit groups to identify, develop, and implement comprehensive publishing programs. Tehabi Books is located in San Diego, California. www.tehabi.com

President and Publisher: Chris Capen
Senior Vice President: Sam Lewis
Vice President and Creative Director: Karla Olson
Director of Corporate Publishing: Chris Brimble

Senior Art Director: Josie Delker
Designer: Kendra Triftshauser
Editor: Betsy Holt
Editorial Assistant: Emily Henning
Copy Editor: Lisa Wolff
Proofreader: Dawn Mayeda

ISBN 1-931688-20-6

First Edition
Printed by Toppan Printing Co. (HK), Ltd. in Hong Kong

10 9 8 7 6 5 4 3 2 1

The paper used in this publication meets the minimum requirements of the American National Standard for Information Sciences Permanence of Paper for Printed Library Materials, ANSI Z39.48-1992.